THE
INDIFFERENT MEAN

THE
INDIFFERENT MEAN

ADIAPHORISM IN THE ENGLISH
REFORMATION TO 1554

BERNARD J. VERKAMP

OHIO
UNIVERSITY
PRESS

1977

WAYNE
STATE UNIVERSITY
PRESS

STUDIES IN THE REFORMATION, Volume I

Copyright © 1977 by
    OHIO UNIVERSITY PRESS, ATHENS, OHIO 45701

    and WAYNE STATE UNIVERSITY PRESS, DETROIT, MICHIGAN 48202
    No part of this book may be reproduced without formal permission.

LIBRARY OF CONGRESS CATALOGING IN PUBLICATION DATA

Verkamp, Bernard J
    The indifferent mean.

    (Studies in the Reformation; v. 1)
    Bibliography: p.
    Includes index.
    1. Church of England—History. 2. Adiaphora.
3. Theology, Anglican. 4. Theology, Doctrinal—
History—16th century. I. Title. II. Series.
BX5067.V47   230'.3   77-13672
ISBN 0-8214-0387-7

Dedicated to
My Family

CONTENTS

PREFACE

THIS STUDY grew out of a paper I delivered some five years ago for a seminar on the main-currents of Anglican thought then being conducted at Saint Louis University by Professor Lawrence F. Barmann. Thanks to Professor Barmann's constant interest and encouragement, my initial inquiry developed several years later into a doctoral dissertation of approximately one thousand pages. For reading and criticizing such a mass of material I owe a great debt to the members of my Ph.D. candidacy committee, Professors Barmann, John Jay Hughes, and John William Padberg, S.J. To Professor Hughes I am also grateful for having put me in touch with Professor Robert C. Walton of Wayne State University, who, together with Professor Barmann, has given unstintingly of his time and energy over the past two years in guiding my doctoral dissertation to its present, thoroughly revised, form. By their prompt, honest, and frank criticism, Professors Barmann and Walton have both contributed greatly to whatever merit this book may enjoy. Its conclusions, however, remain, for better or worse, my own.

This book also owes much to the kind cooperation I consistently received from the librarian of Saint Louis University's Divinity School, W. Charles Heiser, S.J., and from a host of other, equally generous, librarians at Concordia and Eden Seminaries, Washington University, and the Institute of Reformation Studies in St. Louis, at the University of Illinois in Urbana, and at the University of Indiana in Bloomington. I am also indebted to my colleague, Dr. Phillip E. Pierpont, for his having read the manuscript with an eye to clarity of style, and to Mrs. Dottie Lane for her expert technical assistance.

ABBREVIATIONS

Note: Only those abbreviations are listed here which have not been clarified elsewhere in the text.

APC   *Acts of the Privy Council.* Edited by J.R. Dasent. London: 1890–1907.

Archiv   *Archiv für Reformationsgeschichte*

BDS   *M. Bucers Deutsche Schriften.* Edited by R. Stupperich. Gütersloh: 1960.

BEK   *Die Bekenntnisschriften der evangelisch-Lutherischen Kirche.* Göttingen: 1967.

CC   *Corpus Catholicorum*

CE   *The Catholic Encyclopedia*

CR   *Corpus Reformatorum*

DTC   *Dictionnaire de Theologie Catholique*

EE   *Opus Epistolarum D. Erasmi Roterodami.* Edited by P.S. Allen. Oxford: 1906–58.

EETS   Early English Text Society

EHR   *English Historical Review*

EM   J. Strype, *Ecclesiastical Memorials.* Oxford: 1822.

END   Enders, E.L., ed. *Dr. M. Luthers Briefwechsel.* Stuttgart and Leipzig: 1884–1912.

EO   *Erasmi Opera Omnia.* Edited by J. Clericus. Leiden: 1703–1706.

JTS   *Journal of Theological Studies*

LTK   *Lexikon für Theologie und Kirche*

LW   *Luther's Works.* Philadelphia and St. Louis: 1955 ff.

MB   *Melanchthon and Bucer.* Edited by Wilhelm Pauck. Philadelphia: 1969.

MW   *Melanchthons Werke in Auswahl.* Edited by R. Stupperich, H. Engelland, *et al.* Gütersloh: 1952.

NCE   *New Catholic Encyclopedia*

ODCC   *Oxford Dictionary of the Christian Church*

OL	*Original Letters Relative to the English Reformation.* Edited by H. Robinson. Cambridge: 1847.
OLS	*Omnia Latina scripta Matthiae Flacii Illyrici hactenus sparsim contra Adiaphoricas.* 1550.
OS	J. *Oekolampad und O. Myconius: Leben und ausgewählte Schriften.* Edited by K.R. Hagenbach. Elberfeld: 1859.
PEM	O. Lottin, *Psychologie et morale aux XIIe et XIIIe siècles, Problemes de morale.* Louvain: 1948.
PG	*Patrologiae cursus completus.* Ser. Graeca. Edited by J.P. Migne. Paris: 1857–1866.
PL	*Patrologiae cursus completus.* Ser. Latina. Edited by J.P. Migne. Paris: 1844–1904.
ST	Thomas Aquinas, *Summa Theologiae*
SW	*Zwinglis Sämtliche Werke.* Edited by Emil Egli and Georg Finsler. Berlin and Zurich: 1905 ff. Vols. 88–104 of *CR.*
TS	*Theological Studies*
WA	*M. Luthers Werke. Kritische Gesamtausgabe.* Weimar: 1883 ff.
WER	*The Works of the English Reformers: William Tyndale and John Frith.* Edited by T. Russell. London: 1831.
ZKTh	*Zeitschrift für Katholische Theologie*
ZO	*H. Zwinglis Opera.* Edited by M. Schulero. Turici: 1838.

INTRODUCTION

It would be convenient to think that when the English Church set out upon a course of reform in the sixteenth century its leaders and members knew exactly where they were going, agreed upon the same, and marched arm and arm into the future with unflinching certainty that God was on their side. And, to be sure, given the bravado of a "King Harry" or the headlong pursuit of the "Romish Foxe" by the likes of a William Turner or a John Bale, the era especially lends itself to such fanciful description. But, in reality, the situation was quite otherwise. There were vague and general ideas about arriving at a church which would reflect a growing sense of national identity, more closely approximate its Scriptural model, be freer, less superstitious, more responsive to a laity come of age, and so forth. But what precise meaning was to be put upon all these sentiments, and how they were to be translated into concrete action—on these and similar questions there was hardly a national consensus at the time when, in the mid-1530's, Henry VIII led the English Church out of the Roman camp.

What Henry had taken in hand were the reins of a team whose members were more than willing and ready to run, but not always in the same direction. On the team were Lollards, Protestants, and Catholics, humanists and nationalists, traditionalists, revolutionaries, and spiritualists—all with their own sense of direction. The king might easily have been made to look the fool, and the English Church left in a state of ruin. In the long run, however, and notwithstanding many an embarrassing moment along the way, that did not prove to be the case. Thanks mainly to the particular choice of a route along which it was to be pursued, the English Reformation, or at least its earliest stages, was expedited with remarkable dignity and decorum. What few rebellions there were, if aroused by religious considerations at all, would un-

doubtedly have been far more intense and widespread had the reformation followed any other route.

It has long been assumed, and rightly so, that the route taken by the
English reformers was a *via media*. But, as Roland Bainton has
pointed out, almost every group of sixteenth-century reformers possessing the slightest stability was inclined to conceive of itself as oc-
cupying a median position. Depending upon the issue at stake and the
parties over against which they were defining their own position,
Erasmians, Lutherans, Zwinglians, Anabaptists, and Schwenckfel-
dians could and did all claim in one or another sense to be in the
pursuit of a *via media*.[1] Without some further specification of the
issues at stake and the parties involved, therefore, it will mean next to
nothing to say, as many have, that the English Reformation developed
along the lines of a *via media*.

The English Reformation, however, was no less complex than the
reform movements on the Continent. It cut across not one, but a
myriad of issues. Many of these issues will go unnoticed in the study at
hand. The latter does not, therefore, represent an attempt to provide an
exhaustive or comprehensive analysis of the Anglican *via media*. It
will try to bring into sharper focus only that side of their "mean"
position which the mainline Henrician and Edwardine reformers, consequent upon their adiaphoristic appraisal of certain liturgical, ethical,
and doctrinal matters, designated "indifferent". Its immediate concern, in other words, will be to deal with only the one issue about how,
according to the early English reformers, Christians were supposed to
conduct themselves in the realm of ceremonial and like matters. It
should also be noted from the start, however, that this issue was itself
an extremely complex one, whose discussion inevitably involved the
English reformers in a debate over a variety of other issues. Their
response to questions about the relation of Scripture and Tradition,
Law and Gospel, divine and human law, and so forth, will, therefore,
also find some notice in this study, but only to the extent of its immediate bearing upon the specific question of adiaphorism under discussion.

Historians have long evidenced a general awareness of the role
played by the theory of adiaphorism in shaping that stage of the English Reformation known as the Elizabethan Settlement. Likewise, a
number of scholars like M.M. Knappen, P. Collinson, Roland Bainton,
and most notably J.S. Coolidge, have noted the relevance of adiaphorism to various phases of the ongoing Puritan-Anglican debate.[2] Nor has the role of adiaphorism in the earlier stages of the
English Reformation been entirely overlooked. The doctrinal adia-

phorism of William Tyndale and John Frith was duly, although not very sympathetically, noted by James Gairdner, M.M. Knappen, and other earlier historians of the English reformation.[3] Some twenty years ago W.G. Zeeveld called attention to the significance of adiaphorism in the thought of Thomas Cromwell's chief theoretician, Thomas Starkey.[4] More recently, W.A. Clebsch, L.B. Smith, A.G. Dickens, J.K. Yost, and others have noted its use by one or another early English reformer like John Frith, Robert Barnes, and Hugh Latimer, while J.K. McConica has pointed out, rather casually, the Erasmian influence upon the introduction of adiaphorism into England.[5] In all of these studies except Zeeveld's and Coolidge's, however, the theory of adiaphorism received little more than passing reference. And even the latter two were very limited in scope—Zeeveld's basically to Starkey's understanding of the theory, and Coolidge's to the role of adiaphorism in the Elizabethan Puritan-Conformist debate. Furthermore, Coolidge's book reached a variety of conclusions about the English version of adiaphorism with which this writer, as will be seen, finds it hard to concur. For all the value of the aforementioned studies, therefore, the exact origin, nature, and development of England's "indifferent mean" has remained anything but clear. The present study, it is to be hoped, will help to correct this situation.

Originally, it had been this writer's intention to trace the Anglican "indifferent mean" from the start of the Henrician Revolution through the Restoration by Charles II. But eventually it was decided for a number of reasons to limit the present volume to only the Henrician and Edwardine periods. In the first place, it quickly became apparent that to appreciate the English version of adiaphorism, far greater attention, time, and space than originally anticipated would have to be given to the long history of adiaphoristic thought, and the broader intellectual, religious, and political context, out of which England's "indifferent mean" emerged.

So far as this writer knows, the last published attempt at an historical account of adiaphoristic thought was made by C.C.E. Schmid, who lived from 1761–1812. In 1809 Schmid published a work entitled *Adiaphora: wissenschaftlich und historisch Untersucht.* Its title notwithstanding, however, Schmid's book contained relatively little history. Of its almost seven hundred octodecimo pages, only about one hundred and fifty concerned the history of adiaphorism, and of these about half dealt with post-Reformation adiaphorists.[6] In addition to Schmid's work, there is an unpublished doctoral dissertation on Calvin's adiaphorism by T.W. Street, which includes a brief introductory survey of the history of adiaphorism prior to Calvin's time, and, like

Schmid's work and a number of encyclopedia articles, provided this writer with some helpful leads in the investigation of pre-sixteenth-century adiaphoristic thought.[7]

That the theory of adiaphorism had been an important element in the thinking of Erasmus of Rotterdam and the mainline, sixteenth-century, Protestant, Continental reformers has also been recognized by most historians in the past. But again, apart from a few comments upon the same by Schmid, Street's discussion of Calvin's adiaphorism, and several studies of the adiaphoristic controversy during the Augsburg and Leipzig Interims by C.L. Manschreck, W. Preger, and others, little has been done previously to actually document, explain, and differentiate the adiaphoristic lines of Erasmus' and the Continental reformers' thought.[8]

A second reason for abbreviating the originally intended scope of this study arose out of the discovery that the early stages of the English Reformation had far more to yield in the way of adiaphoristic evidence than this writer initially suspected. Far from being some mere peripheral appendage to the early English reformers' thought, the theory of adiaphorism was found to lie at the very center of their thinking, profoundly affecting almost every move they made. It soon became apparent, therefore, that to present an exhaustive report of the same would require nothing less than an almost complete retelling of the development of the English reform movement during the reigns of Henry VIII and Edward VI. In the analytical approach of this volume, even such a limited project, with its preclusion of any attention to developments during the later stages of the English Reformation, proved impossible. Still, this writer would like to think that the reader will find in the following pages, if not an exhaustive, at least an accurate, skeletal outline of the "indifferent mean" as it took shape during the Henrician and Edwardine periods.

In the process, the reader will be taken over much ground and through many events with which he will probably have already been familiar. But, hopefully, he will also find therein some new light by which to enhance his understanding of these same events. For when viewed within their proper adiaphoristic context, many such events— like Henry VIII's rejection of papal rule or his claims to royal supremacy, Cromwell's legislative and policing activities, or Cranmer's liturgical projects, and so forth—will be seen to have enjoyed a much broader, and perhaps more convincing rationale than has heretofore been recognized in some scholarly or ecclesiastical circles. Other events, like Cranmer's clandestine marriage for example, to which some historians have been inclined to show only passing curiosity, will be seen to have carried profound implications about the whole thrust of the English Reformation. Still other events, or "non-events," will be seen to bear a considerably different interpretation than has sometimes been imposed upon them. Not infrequently, for example, evidence of a lack of change or of a concern for uniformity and obedience, which has sometimes been considered symptomatic of a reactionary and tyrannical spirit, will be seen within an adiaphoristic perspective to have been indicative of precisely the opposite, and very much consistent with the general thrust of the English Reformation toward a less encumbered, purer, freer, more nationalistic, specifically Anglican church.

Finally, it is especially to be hoped that by having taken into more adequate account the adiaphoristic thrust of the Henrician and Edwardine periods of reform, the relationships that obtained between the various reform or anti-reform groups of that period will have been brought into sharper and more accurate focus than has previously been the case among either those parties themselves or their historians. The Roman party will be seen to have been at odds with the reformers at a number of points in their understanding of the theory of adiaphorism, but it will also be seen that this opposition of the Roman party was to no small extent exacerbated by its rather gross misinterpretation of the reformers' adiaphoristic views. The theory of adiaphorism will also be seen to have been very much at stake in the differentiation of the Protestant reform parties themselves, and to such an extent that the identification of one or another reformer as an adiaphorist should prove to be a far more meaningful and precise label than many of the appellations commonly employed by modern historians to distinguish these groups. In fact, it will be a major concern of this study to demonstrate that unless the respective views of the mainline English reformers and their "puritan" antagonists are taken into proper account, no sense can be made of their argument over biblical authority.

NOTES

1. See R. H. Bainton, *Studies on the Reformation* (Boston, 1963), pp. 46–47; 119–21.

2. See, for example: M.M. Knappen, *Tudor Puritanism* (Chicago and London, 1939), pp. 89 ff., 187 ff.; Patrick Collinson, *The Elizabethan Puritan Movement* (Berkeley, 1967), pp. 26 ff.; R.H. Bainton, *The Travail of Religious Liberty* (Philadelphia, 1951), pp. 179–207; John S. Coolidge, *The Pauline Renaissance in England* (Oxford, 1970), especially, pp. 23–54.

3. James Gairdner, *Lollardy and the Reformation in England* (London: 1908–13) I, pp. 416–17; Knappen, *op. cit.*, p. 45.

4. W.G. Zeeveld, *Foundations of Tudor Policy* (Cambridge, Mass., 1948), especially pp. 128–56.

5. W.A. Clebsch, *England's Earliest Protestants 1520–1535* (New Haven and London, 1964), pp. 63–64, 120–21, 126, 135–36; L.B. Smith, *Tudor Prelates and Politics* (Princeton, 1953), pp. 197–98; A.G. Dickens, *The English Reformation* (New York, 1964), pp. 78–79, 180, 223, 322, 340; J.K. Yost, "Hugh Latimer's Reform Program, 1529–1536, and the Intellectual Origins of the Anglican *via media,*" *Anglican Theological Review* LIII (1971), pp. 103–14; J.K. McConica, *English Humanists and Reformation Politics under Henry VIII and Edward VI* (Oxford, 1965), pp. 4, 21, 27, 159, 160.

6. C.C.E. Schmid, *Adiaphora, wissenschaftlich und historisch untersucht* (Leipzig, 1809), pp. 546–685; 629–85. Schmid published an earlier work entitled *Controversia de Adiaphoris* (Jena, 1807).

7. T.W. Street, "John Calvin on Adiaphora, an Exposition," Unpublished Union Theological Seminary (N.Y.C.) Ph.D. Dissertation, 1954; J. Gottschick, "Adiaphora, and the Adiaphoristic Controversies," *The New Schaff-Herzog Religious Encyclopedia* I, 41–44; G. Teichtweier, "Adiaphora," *LTK* I, 145–46; E.T. Horn, "Adiaphorism," *Encyclopedia of Religion and Ethics* I, 91–93; A. Baudrillart, "Adiaphorites," *DTC*, I, 397; G.H. Joyce, "Fundamental Doctrines of Christianity," *The New Schaff-Herzog Religious Encyclopedia,* IV, 411–13; J.W. Melody, "Acts Indifferent," *CE*, I, 116–17; F. Lau, "Adiaphora," *Die Religion in Geschichte und Gegenwart,* I, 93–96.

8. See C.L. Manschreck, *Melanchthon, The Quiet Reformer* (New York and Nashville, 1958), pp. 277–292; Manschreck, "The Role of Melanchthon in the Adiaphora Controversy," *Archiv* 49(1957), pp. 165–81; Manschreck, "A Critical Examination and Appraisal of the Adiaphoristic Controversy in the Life of Philip Melanchthon," Unpublished Yale University Ph.D. Dissertation, 1948; W. Preger, *Mathias Flacius Illyricus und Seine Zeit,* II (Munich, 1861), pp. 145 ff.

CHAPTER 1

THE INTOLERABLE BURDEN

THE CHURCH IN ENGLAND at the turn of the sixteenth century was very much like the religion of Utopia imagined and described by Thomas More in 1516.[1] It was a Church steeped in ceremonies.[2] What suited More's "philosophical city,"[3] however, was not necessarily acceptable in a Christian community supposedly developing under the light of divine positive revelation. In fact, the penchant for ceremonial, which More presented as a "natural and reasonable instinct,"[4] had surfaced only at a relatively late point in the Church's initial development, and then almost always thereafter, and especially during the late middle ages and the early sixteenth century, over the protests of many Christians who were of a less rationalistic bent than More.

The Apostolic Church had apparently understood Jesus' claim that his "yoke and burden" were "easy and light" (Matt. 11:30) to mean that Christians should not be weighed down by a mass of ceremonial legislation. To be sure, some regulations, like the Apostle Paul's recommendations concerning the headdress of women (1 Cor. 11:1–16) and their silence at liturgical gatherings (1 Cor. 14:34–35), or the Council of Jerusalem's prohibition of "strangled meats" (Acts 15:20, 28–29), were issued over and above the divine commandments. But it is also true that such legislation was purposely kept to a minimum, lest Christians be subjected to an unbearable yoke (Acts 15:19, 28).[5]

By the end of the fourth century, however, synodal legislation had increased to the point where Augustine could complain that the church of his time had fallen into a condition far worse than that of the old Judaic religion. A religion that God himself had willed to be a free and modest service had been converted by some, Augustine protested, into a slave's burden. Far more attention, he concluded, should be given to the fact that Christ had left his followers a "light burden" and an "easy yoke."[6]

1

Notwithstanding Augustine's advice, the proliferation of ceremonies and laws in their regard continued.[7] This was partly due to the rise of monastic idealism. By the fifth century, the church had already condemned the encratic tendencies of the Eustatians, a group which favored making celibacy and other monastic observances requirements for Christian baptism.[8] But less extreme forms of monastic idealism survived and came to exert a considerable influence over the shape of the medieval church. Thus, to cite but one example, during the early middle ages, when the moral laxity consequent upon the barbarian invasions and the fall of the Western Roman Empire might logically have dictated a relaxation of ecclesiastical legislation, church officials of the period chose, on the whole, to press all the harder for the sort of ethical ideal embodied by the missionary monks.

Confronted, for example, with the fact of widespread promiscuity among the German and Frankish clergy, Boniface and his Roman officials seem never to have considered the possibility of allowing clerical celibacy to become again what it had once been, an entirely optional matter. The myriad synodal and papal decrees issued during these centuries either simply reiterated previous legislation requiring separation of the clergy from their wives, or attempted to strengthen the same with more stringent penalties or some other more positive measures, like vows of chastity prior to ordination, or adoption of a clerical *vita communis*.[9] Anticipating the opinion of Gregory VII, some early medieval Penitentials even went so far as to claim that any cleric having intercourse with his wife was guilty of adultery.[10] Christ's assertion that his burden and yoke were light and easy, which earlier had been used by Paphnutius to discourage the legislation of clerical celibacy, was now given a new twist to support the monastic ideal of continency.[11] Those who found that ideal beyond their capacity were shown little sympathy. Even to associate with them caused Boniface serious qualms of conscience.[12]

A similar spirit of monastic idealism could be shown to have been operative not only in the climactic legislation of clerical celibacy of the twelfth century, but also in the passage of a variety of other church laws during the middle ages on matters like the eating of foods, the wearing of distinctive clothes, and so forth. And even if monastic idealism did not always culminate in legislation as such, it nonetheless tended to spawn a multitude of special religious observances to which the Christian bent upon attaining the height of Christian perfection was inclined to feel himself bound, the simple observance of God's own laws no longer being considered sufficient toward that end.

Contributing to the proliferation of church laws and ceremonies during the middle ages was also the process of "sacralization," which had already been introduced into Christian circles by Cyprian and others in the third century.[13] Boniface occasionally issued complaints about the pagans' "superstitious discriminations of food," but he himself was instructed by the popes that the eating of wild or tame horses is "a filthy and abominable practice," and that the eating of "jackdaws, crows, starks, beavers, and hares is absolutely forbidden as food for Christians."[14] Fasting and abstinence became increasingly subject to legislation during this period, and was at least to some extent motivated by a sacral outlook, as was also the growing amount of calendrical legislation touching upon such matters as the dating of Easter, the celebration of Sunday, and the observance of other holy days.[15] Sacralization of the Mass helped to inspire new laws prohibiting priests from the exercise of their marital rights, forbidding the laity to approach the altar while the "holy mystery" was being solemnized, excluding women from the *benedictio diaconalis,* forbidding them to touch the pall or to receive communion with uncovered hands, and requiring clerics to wear non-secular garments.[16] Images, the places of assembly, the altar, chalices, and other implements used in celebration of the Eucharist now also were afforded a sacral dimension which they had not enjoyed in the early church.[17] The "significance" of these objects, as well as the celebrant's every move and gesture, was still further enhanced by the sort of allegorization which they received from Amalar and others,[18] and thereby became all the more susceptible to rubrical regulation.

In brief, the process of sacralization encouraged the differentiation of times and places, persons and things, to such an extent that many matters which otherwise might have remained entirely optional were subjected to legislation, or were at least so enhanced in the minds of Christians that their optional character was for all practical purposes forgotten.

Probably nothing, however, threatened to undermine the original levity of the Christian "burden" quite so much during the middle ages as did the passion of the medieval church for uniformity. As will be seen in a subsequent chapter, the respect for local tradition typical of the early church also carried to some extent over into the fifth and following centuries. Yet the overall thrust of the latter period was away from local authority and custom, and toward a more centrally organized and uniform church.

Stimulated by the *Cunctos populos* edict of Theodosius I in 380, which commanded all subjects of the emperor to follow that form of religion "handed by the Apostle Peter to the Romans,"[19] Roman pontiffs of the late fourth and subsequent centuries endeavored to bring the disciplinary affairs of the local churches entirely under their own control. Earlier popes had also intervened in such affairs, but the introduction by Popes Siricius (384–399) and Innocent I (401–407) of the official "decretals" represented a significant innovation in that regard.[20] Especially insistent upon the universal responsibility of the Roman See was Pope Leo the Great (440–461). His decisions, for example, that ordinations and consecrations may be held only on Sundays, that Baptism is to be administered only on Easter or Pentecost, that the clergy must be *unius uxoris viri,* that Easter must be observed on the same day throughout the world, and other decisions of a similar nature, were almost always backed up with the claim that membership in the Christian community requires not only a unity in faith but also a harmony in discipline and practice.[21] No innovation in ecclesiastical procedure, therefore, was to be tolerated. All must follow the "canons of the Fathers" and the "Apostolic and Evangelical regulations."[22]

In calling for harmony in ecclesiastical discipline, Leo had clearly had in mind also to bring the Eastern Church into closer conformity with the Church of Rome, although on certain matters, such as the dating of Easter, he showed himself willing to yield to the desires of the East, "for the sake of unity and peace."[23] Given, however, the caeseropapist tendencies of the Byzantine emperors, against which the Leonine-Gelasian theories of papal superiority had little practical effect, the diversity of customs between East and West would, as a matter of fact, increase during subsequent centuries.[24] As the gap widened, both sides took precautions lest the customs of the one would be introduced into the realm of the other. Thus, for example, while the Synod of Trullo (692) allowed priests "in the lands of the barbarians" to separate from their wives, it warned against the introduction of such a practice in the East.[25] And when Pope Vitalian appointed Theodore Archbishop of Canterbury in 668, he took the precaution of having a certain monk named Hadrian accompany Theodore to England, lest the latter, who was of Greek origin, would try to impose upon the English "any Greek customs which might be contrary to the true faith."[26]

So long as these two branches of Christendom had stayed relatively apart during subsequent centuries, at least a minimal toleration of each other's customs prevailed. This detente was almost upset in the eighth century by Charlemagne's agitation against the Council of Nicea (787), and in the ninth century when Rome sought to impose the Western customs of clerical celibacy and the Lenten Fast upon the

Bulgarians recently converted by Eastern missionaries.[27] But this latter confrontation had occurred during the Photian Schism, and with its repair, the controversy over the customs also abated for a time. Early in the eleventh century, however, East and West came into closer touch than they had been for more than six centuries,[28] and the renewed intimacy soon occasioned yet another round in the controversy over ecclesiastical practices, and the eventual schism.

Meanwhile, having sensed the futility of trying to challenge head-on the caesaropapist claims of the Byzantine emperors, Pope Gregory I had wisely chosen to concentrate upon a consolidation of the Roman position in the West.[29] His insistence upon the obedience due the bishop of Rome was as vehement as that of Leo I, and his intervention in liturgical and pastoral affairs of the local churches was unequaled by earlier popes. To be sure, Gregory himself sometimes showed a generous toleration of diversity in customs. Yet, the monks and missionaries he sent out into the remotest regions of the West often evidenced quite a different spirit.

On his arrival in England, Augustine of Canterbury lost little time in announcing that he had no intention of communing with the British and Celtic churches so long as they would not observe Easter on the same date as did the Romans. Augustine said that he would "gladly tolerate" some of the British and Celtic practices that were "contrary to the customs of the universal Church." But on the question of the dating of Easter he remained adamant. The British and Celts were no less stubborn, and the two sides separated in a mood of considerable hostility. In the controversy that raged on for several centuries after Augustine's death, the Roman party ridiculed the British and Celts for "foolishly attempting to fight against the whole world."[30]

Having been nurtured on the Anglo-Saxon monastic ideal of devotion to Rome, Boniface not surprisingly made it a central concern of his missionary activity among the Germanic tribes to bring them into conformity with the practices of the Roman Church. "I will in no wise agree to anything which is opposed to the unity of the Church Universal," Boniface swore to Pope Gregory II in 722.[31] To Pope Zachary he wrote some twenty years later that "it is our earnest desire to maintain the catholic faith and the unity of the Roman Church."[32] Shortly thereafter, he expressed to Bishop Daniel of Winchester his fear of incurring guilt by communicating with rebellious clergymen, remembering as he did that "at the time of my ordination, by the command of Pope Gregory, I swore by the body of St. Peter to refuse communion with men of that kind, unless I could convert them to the way of Church law."[33] At Boniface's instigation, a number of Frankish synods soon determined that "in all things [they] shall obey the orders of St. Peter according to the canons."[34] And consistent with these synodal resolutions, Pepin decreed in 754 that the old Gallican liturgy was to be replaced by the liturgy of Rome.[35]

As will be seen, there would remain throughout the middle ages much *de facto* diversity in the Western Church. While not a little of this diversity arose by design, much of it resulted simply from the confused state of canon law at the start of the high middle ages,[36] or from its conflict with customary law as it had developed in Germanic Europe.[37] But with the issuance of the collection of canons and decretals by Pope Gregory IX in 1234, the *Liber Sextus* of Boniface VIII in 1298, and the *Clementinae* of Clement V in 1317, an "official and universal law" of the medieval Church was eventually established.

The order and integration achieved thereby was undoubtedly impressive to some. With obvious admiration for the law and order he discovered in the fourteenth century Western Church, the Calabrian monk Barlaam exclaimed: "The whole people is ruled by laws; even the smallest matters are subject to regulation and orderly administration."[38] But such a blanket regimentation of Christian life and worship also threatened to overwhelm the Christian by the sheer number of laws and regulations it introduced. Not without reason, Thomas Aquinas had already warned in the thirteenth century that prelates should take care to "refrain from multiplying laws," lest Christians find themselves under an impossible burden.[39] Thomas added that when prelates do impose more laws than a subject is able to fulfill, the latter need not feel bound to obedience.[40] For Thomas himself, however, this remained largely a hypothetical case, for although he elsewhere cited approvingly Augustine's advice to Januarius about keeping the number of ceremonies to a minimum, he also dismissed the objection that church authorities of his time had neglected Augustine's admonishment.[41] Many late medieval theologians will be seen to have thought otherwise.

The multiplication of ceremonies and laws in their regard was, however, only a part of the problem. Even more threatening to Christian liberty than their ever increasing number was the weight and binding force that had come to be ascribed to the ceremonies and their legislation.

As already noted, the spirit of monastic idealism and the process of sacralization operative throughout the early and high middle ages had imposed upon many ceremonies, even apart from their legislation, a significance which they had not earlier enjoyed. Further enhancing the ceremonies was the then prevailing theology according to which man was thought capable in one or another sense of meriting grace and salvation by virtue of his own good works. While such a theology in itself tended to magnify the value of all externals, it also set the stage for the elevation of certain externals to the class of "sacramentals," by virtue of which, thanks to the church's supposed intercessory power, they could be said to enjoy special efficacy in the attainment of grace and salvation, although never with such efficiency as the "sacraments."[42]

This distinction between "sacraments" and "sacramentals" was brought to the fore in the twelfth and thirteenth centuries for the precise purpose of differentiating those ceremonies instituted by Christ himself from those established by the church, and for the sake of identifying which ceremonies were or were not in themselves "necessary to salvation."[43] But the mitigating effect which these and similar distinctions may have had upon the evaluation of certain ceremonies was often cancelled by what will be seen to have been the inclination of some medieval theologians to conceive of almost any and every traditional ceremony as having had its origin in the "unwritten" word of Christ and the Apostles, and by the claims church officials increasingly had come to make for the binding force of their own laws.

As Pope Victor I had tried, without success, in the second century to excommunicate the Quartodecimans for their non-adherence to Roman custom,[44] so, not infrequently during the middle ages, attempts were made to condition the so-called *jus communionis* upon conformity to Roman law.[45] More specifically, non-conformity was associated with sin. "Once having heard the decrees of the Apostolic See or rather of the universal Church," Wilfrid, the bishop of York in the seventh century, warned the Celts at the Whitby synod, "if you refuse to follow them, confirmed as they are by the Holy Scriptures, then without doubt you are committing sin."[46] In a letter to Boniface a few years before Pepin's embrace of the Roman liturgy, Pope Zachary had written that because "they do not follow the apostolic tradition, but act through vainglory," the Gauls were employing many corrupt "forms of blessings," and on that account were "bringing their own damnation."[47]

Following the lead of Zachary, and against the background of claims by the likes of Justinian and Charlemagne that their own laws were of "divine" origin,[48] other early medieval popes like Nicholas I and Adrian II would insist that papal decretals enjoyed the same force as if they had been issued by Christ himself.[49] With the *sacerdotium* and *regnum* thus vying with each other for control of Christendom, the distinction between human and divine law grew increasingly nebulous, and the burden of Christian obedience ever heavier. No less a figure than Charlemagne himself asserted toward the end of the eighth century that "the yoke imposed by Rome is almost unbearable."[50]

Having made this last remark, Charlemagne had gone on to say that for all its weight, the Roman yoke ought to be borne "with pious devotion."[51] A century later, in a letter to the English King Alfred, Archbishop Fulk of Reims would attempt to explain such "devotion" as part of the process of Christian maturation.

Just as the Apostles had not wished to burden the primitive church with a heavy yoke, neither, Fulk explained, did Gregory the Great wish to have Augustine of Canterbury "suddenly burden a rude and barbarous race with new and unknown laws." But as the English folk came of age, church authorities had no alternative but "to establish [them] more perfectly with the frequent admonition of their letters, and to strengthen them more firmly in the true faith, and to deliver to them more abundantly a way of living and a pattern of religion." Therein, acording to Fulk, lay the reason for issuance of those many papal decretals, synodal decrees, and sacred canons in subsequent centuries, the transgression or ignorance of which would be "altogether abominable."[52] By way of contrast to Fulk's views it will be seen that the reformers of the sixteenth century saw in the need for many laws an indication of weakness, not maturity.

Popes of the high middle ages hardly checked their predecessors' inclination to ascribe a divine origin to papal laws. When the reform popes of the eleventh century tried to rescue the papacy from the ill-repute into which it had fallen during the previous century and encountered opposition, they simply insisted all the more strongly upon obedience to papal rule. At Gregory's initiative, Anselm of Lucca, Deusdedit, and others undertook a revision of the canonical collections according to the principle that a "text has value only insofar as it has at least the silent approval of the pope," the main concern thereby being "the elimination of proofs in favor of a purely local discipline." Although still vague and undetermined in its content, the *corpus canonicum* was conceived by Gregory VII as "part of God's Word to his people, complementing the law of the new dispensation." Far from being a mere human invention, canon law was, in Gregory's estimation, the "inspired utterance of the several authentic organs of the Holy Spirit animating and guiding the Church." An essential ingredient of the *corpus canonicum* was, of course, the papal decrees themselves, and only if these were accepted unquestioningly, Gregory said, could one call oneself a Catholic. Later popes like Innocent III and Boniface VIII, following upon the twelfth-century development of the concept of the pope as the 'vicar of Christ,' would insist that what they decreed "was decreed by Christ himself," and that "anyone resisting the papal law, therefore, resisted the divine power itself."[53]

Given the still inchoate and sometimes contradictory state of canon law in the eleventh and twelfth centuries, the binding force of some of its prohibitions could not always be stated with absolute certitude. Gratian, for example, was very hesitant about stating exactly to what extent the ecclesiastical prohibitions against clandestine marriages and divorce were binding upon the Christian.[54] Furthermore, as will be shown in a subsequent chapter, questions were already being raised in the thirteenth and fourteenth centuries about whether human laws do or can bind in conscience at all. But on the whole, the high medieval theologians suffered few doubts about the obligation incumbent upon Christians to obey church laws. Typical of the whole period were Bernard of Clairvaux's opinion that prelates are to be obeyed as God himself is obeyed, for whatever man prescribes in God's place is to be accepted as if God himself commanded it,[55] and Thomas Aquinas' assertion that since the love of God requires that his commands be obeyed, and among his precepts is the command that superiors be obeyed, disobedience of superiors is as such a mortal sin.[56] Not surprisingly, therefore, among the things that Barlaam found to admire in the Western Church at the start of the fourteenth century was not only the broad sweep of canon law over every aspect of Christian life, but also a reverence for its canons "as the ordinances of Christ himself."[57]

Barlaam's admiration for the weighty and all-pervasive character of canon law was not, however, shared by all. Before long, many theologians could be heard complaining that the number and estimation of ceremonies in general, and their legislation in particular, had become so excessive as to have robbed many Christians of their freedom and to have spawned a blatantly superstitious confusion of values. Time and again, the sentiment would be voiced that Christians had once again been subjected to an intolerable burden.

Thanks to the prelates' "hunger for power," and the persuasion of the monks that their superiors were always to be obeyed on all such matters "as be not expressly commanded, nor forfended in God's law," John Wyclif wrote in the second half of the fourteenth century, new laws had been promulgated with such insistence and under such heavy penalties that Christians could hardly help but conclude that the same should "stand as though [they] were a part of the Gospel of Jesus Christ." Indeed, Wyclif said, men had come "to dread more the pope's lead [the seal attached to papal documents], and his commandment, than the Gospel of Christ and God's commandments." Similarly, such "undue importance" had come to be attached to the external signs of the sacraments and ceremonies in general, that many Christians "would sooner transgress the decalogue than neglect such observances." Thus, matters concerning which "Christ had declared [the Church] should be free," now so burdened her, Wyclif concluded, "that the yoke is even greater than was endured by the Church under the old dispensation."[58]

Jan Hus compared the prelates of his own day to the Scribes and Pharisees of old, who imposed many fasts, many prayers, and other hard things upon the people, while they themselves did none of them.[59] Pierre D'Ailly warned that the church was being overrun by an "evil of superfluity."[60] D'Ailly and Jean Gerson laid much of the blame for this evil at the feet of the canon lawyers, who, by way of trying to impose their own prescriptions as the precepts of divine law, had made of "the light yoke of Christ and the law of liberty an iron yoke and heavy burden, pressing upon the necks of Christians."[61] A man of Adam's stature had but one command to fulfill and failed, Gerson wrote; how then is the Christian to escape, placed as he is among innumerable commands? If Augustine could complain about the Judaic condition of the church of his time, what, Gerson concluded, would he have to say now![62] According to Wessel Gansfort, the "forest of derees and decretals" had become so dense that the Christian could scarcely find his way any longer to a study and knowledge of Sacred Scripture.[63] Even Gabriel Biel was forced to admit that the burden of Christian obedience had become heavier than the old Judaic yoke, if one took into account the plethora of ecclesiastical laws and ceremonies.[64]

The protest carried over into the sixteenth century. Comparing the present burden of Christians with the old Judaic yoke, Erasmus wrote that the latter was by far the lighter: circumcision had been eliminated, only to be replaced by baptism; the sabbath had not been abrogated, but simply transferred to Sunday; the number of fast days had become greater; the choice of foods had become less free; regulations of the style and color of dress, haircuts, and like matters had increased, as had also the laws and regulations governing matrimony. "Almost exalting the Pope's authority above Christ's," church officials, Erasmus wrote, had exaggerated the obligation of their laws to the point where many weaker Christians had become the victims of terrible qualms of conscience. And the monks had only made matters worse. "Ascribing more to their rules than to the Gospel," they latched onto immature Christians, Erasmus claimed, and filled them "with all sorts of scruples about human traditions," finally driving them "into a sort of Judaism where they learn not to love but to fear." Small wonder, then, Erasmus concluded, that "so many Christians esteem that which is indifferent and of least importance instead of that which is of highest and most essential value," or that so many placed the sum of religion in "places, garments, meats, fasts, gestures, and songs" and "judge their neighbor contrary to the Gospel's law of charity" on account of such matters.[65]

Luther repeatedly bewailed "that infinite number of commands and precepts promulgated by popes, bishops, monastaries, churches, princes, and magistrates." The *Augsburg Confession,* written by Melancthon, protested that the spirit of work-righteousness had given rise to an endless array of new human traditions such as holy days, fast days, pilgrimages, rosaries, liturgical ceremonies, cults of the saints, and so forth, much to the neglect and detriment of the Gospel and God's own commandments. Zwingli admitted that when the Apostle Peter had spoken of "unbearable burdens," he had had in mind the old Judaic yoke, but how much more, then, would Peter have objected, Zwingli concluded, had he witnessed the still heavier yoke now oppressing Christians. Echoing the same opinion, Bullinger accused the Roman Church of having set up once again, by way of its endless multiplication of ceremonies and rites, the old Judaism. According to John Calvin, the number of laws governing man's external religious affairs had become ten times greater, and their enforcement a hundred times more severe than in Augustine's time.[66]

Official English reaction to this chorus of dissent sweeping the Continent during the early decades of the sixteenth century was at first emphatically negative. While Cardinal Wolsey went about burning all the Lutheran books he could lay his hands on, the likes of Edward Lee, John Fisher, Thomas More, and the king himself set out to challenge the Wittenberg reformer with a series of their own treatises. Lutheran thought nonetheless caught on in some small English circles—most notably at first at Cambridge. Furthermore, the Lollards were still around to voice their displeasure over the ceremonies. And not all the humanists were as sympathetic to the ceremonial richness of the Roman Church as was Thomas More. John Colet, for example, while occasionally calling upon the "uninitiated multitude" to look upon "vessels, robes, and whatever else pertains to the priest . . . with great fear and reverence," undoubtedly shared Erasmus' taste for simplicity and did not hesitate to express some chagrin when to his view the multiplication of ceremonies had reached the point of obscuring the "ancient and venerable institution of the Apostles."[67] Before long, therefore, the complaint against the excessive burden of Christian obedience was also being bruited about England.

Citing both Augustine and Gerson, Thomas Bilney complained that because of the "multitude of laws" imposed upon Christians, their condition had become far more burdensome than that of the ancient Jews.[68] William Tyndale claimed that the prelates had piled one ceremony upon another until the yoke of Christian obedience had become even heavier than the one Augustine had protested against in his day.[69] To further enhance their power, the prelates, Tyndale contended, tried, with considerable success, to instill the laity and lower clergy with a great reverential fear of the ceremonies.[70] Hence, according to Tyndale, the gross superstition of the priest who will go through orders a second time for fear that he is not ordained because the bishop happened to leave one of his ceremonies undone, or of the priest who thinks that all is marred because he offered Mass, baptized, or heard confessions, "without a stole about his neck," or of the laity who "tremble" and "quake" when the child being baptized is not dipped altogether into the water.[71] Hence also, Tyndale said, the confusion of those who think it better to light a candle or to sprinkle oneself with holy water than to feed the poor, or who think it worse to miss a rubric than to whore after another man's wife, buy a benefice, or set one kingdom at war with another, or who stand ready to break the law of charity by condemning their neighbor for eating butter on Friday without a papal dispensation, or for not attending Mass "from Sunday to Sunday."[72]

John Bale wrote in 1543 that the bishops had loaded Christians down with an endless array of ceremonial matters like the canonical hours, processions, holy days, bells, beads, organs, holy water, and so forth.[73] "No Jewyshe ceremony refuse they," he concluded.[74] John Hooper, noting Seneca's criticism of the Jewish rites, wondered whether the Roman philosopher would not have been even more critical of the Christian church, given the fact that now, thanks to the bishops, "there be more ceremonies in the church of Christ than were in the church of the Jews."[75] According to William Turner, thousands in England would gladly have been delivered earlier from this "unbearable burden of seruile ceremonies"; only fear, he said, had kept them from expressing their displeasure.[76]

As will be seen, underlying the protests of Turner, Bale, and Hooper were sentiments most English reformers could not bring themselves to share. But so far as the protest against the excessive proliferation and estimation of the ceremonies was itself concerned, the moderate English reformers complained no less than their more radical countrymen. Thomas Starkey defined superstition as the false judgment whereby certain things are deemed "of necessitie to the honour of God, which in dede nothyng so doth," and claimed that it was rampant in England during the early decades of the sixteenth century.[77] Thomas Cranmer expressed the view that while the Jews of old had always shown a proclivity toward inventing "a new way unto salvation by works of their own devise," their blindness had been nothing compared to the superstition obtaining in his own time. Pilgrimages, vestments, fasts, the use of bells, bread, water, palms, candles, fire, and so forth, were all, Cranmer said, "so esteemed and abused to the great prejudice of God's glory and commandments, that they were made most high and most holy things, whereby to attain to the eternal life, or remission of sin." And what with the laws and decrees of Rome being promulgated as if they had issued from the four evangelists themselves, the confusion became so bad, Cranmer concluded, that few learned men "knew, or at least would know, and durst affirm the truth, to separate God's commandments from the commandments of men."[78] "Until these latter days," John Hilsey wrote in his *Manual of Prayers*, "the commandments of God . . . not one day [were] spoken of, for holy days and fasting days the people diligently inquired of their curates, because they have a fear of breaking of them, but of the commandments of God they nothing require, because they regard not the transgression of them."[79] Many matters which had been "but voluntary" in the primitive church, Thomas Becon observed, "grew afterward unto matters of so great weight and importance, yea unto

> such necessity, that it was made a matter of conscience, yea, it was become deadly sin to minister the holy communion without these scenical, histrionical, and hickscarner-like garments; so that now to sing Mass or to consecrate, as they use to say, without these popish robes, is counted in the church of the papists more than twice deadly sin; so far is it off that these missal vestures are now things of indifferency.[80]

Citing Augustine's complaint once again, the 1549 *Prayer Book* summed up the attitude of the English reformers by declaring that the "excess and multitude" of the ceremonies had increased so greatly that their "burden" had become altogether "intolerable."[81]

What could be done about it? During the late middle ages a variety of forces had become operative which in a very general way worked toward the mitigation of the burden of ceremonies supposedly oppressing Christians. One such force was the *devotio moderna* which had emerged from the teaching of mystics like Henry Suso, Meister Eckhart, John Tauler, John Ruysbroeck, and Gerard Groote, and had been embraced by the Brethren of the Common Life. The spirituality it encouraged went a long way toward downplaying the role of externals in religion. Its emphasis upon the interiority and simplicity of Christian life clearly influenced efforts by Nicholas of Cusa, John Pupper of Goch, Wessel Gansfort, Erasmus of Rotterdam, and others who, as will be seen, were concerned with relaxing the burden of Christian obedience.

A similar influence was exerted by the humanist movement. Papal patronage of this movement had hardly inspired optimism over the cause of reform. But as appropriated by the likes of Nicholas of Cusa, John Reuchlin, Jacques Lefèvre, John Colet, and especially Erasmus of Rotterdam, its neo-Platonic tendencies, its appeal to antiquity, its taste for simplicity, its paradoxical appreciation of diversity, and its generally non-sacral thrust, contributed significantly toward the restoration of a less cumbersome religion.

The spiritual and intellectual atmosphere engendered by the *devotio moderna* and the humanist movement also favored the advance of the doctrines of *sola Scriptura* and *sola fide,* although not all adherents of the former subscribed to a strict interpretation of the latter. But these doctrines, thanks to Wyclif, Hus, Bradwardine, John Pupper, John Ruchrat, and Wessel Gansfort, had gained a momentum of their own, even apart from the *devotio moderna* and humanist movement, and, in turn, more so even than the latter, prepared the way for a reduction in the number and weight of the ceremonial laws that had cropped up in the church down through the centuries.

In themselves, however, the *devotio moderna,* humanism, solafideism, and the doctrine of *sola Scriptura* were of a far too general character to convey the precise meaning of the protest launched by the aforementioned late medieval and early sixteenth-century theologians against the so-called "evil of superfluity." Without further qualification, the distinctions which such movements and doctrines brought into focus between divine and human law, between the contemporary and primitive church, between the universal and local church, between Scripture and Tradition, and between faith and its external dimensions could be, and indeed, as will be seen, frequently were interpreted by spiritualistic and reductionist groups in such wise as might well have left the church in a condition far more burdensome than the "superfluity" from which they would have her delivered. Sooner or later, therefore, major spokesmen for the *devotio moderna,* humanism, solafideism and the doctrine of *sola Scriptura* were forced to articulate more precisely exactly how the traditional ceremonies and laws were to be dealt with in the context of a renewed emphasis upon faith, Scripture, interiority, antiquity, and so forth. Toward that end most came eventually to espouse the theory of adiaphorism. The vast majority of early English reformers followed suit. Christians could best be relieved of their "intolerable burden," these reformers thought, by having the ceremonies appraised along adiaphoristic lines.

The theory of adiaphorism, however, had enjoyed a long history, in the course of which the term adiaphoron had itself taken on a variety of meanings. To appreciate the English reformers' adiaphoristic appraisal of the ceremonies, it will be necessary, then, to determine first in precisely what sense they used the term adiaphoron.

NOTES

1. Ceremonies abounded in the religion of More's Utopia (See *The Utopia of Sir Thomas More,* ed. M. Campbell [New York, 1947], pp. 164, 166, 167).

2. See Philip Hughes, *The Reformation in England* (New York, 1963), I, pp. 90 ff.; A.G. Dickens, *The English Reformation*, pp. 1–14; *The Rationale of Ceremonial,* ed. C.S. Cobb (London, 1910), Appendix I, pp. 53–59. Medieval theologians, it may be noted, included under the term "ceremony" "rites", "sacred things", "sacraments", and "observances" (See Thomas Aquinas, *ST* I–II, 101, 4), and it will be employed throughout this study in much the same broad sense, whether the matters to which it is applied had been subjected to legislation or not.

3. See R.W. Chambers, *Thomas More* (Ann Arbor, 1968), p. 263.

4. *Ibid.,* p. 257.

5. That Christ himself determined certain external ecclesiastical actions—e.g., baptism, breaking of the bread—to be essential is hardly debated by modern theologians. Furthermore, in regard to at least a number of these external acts, it is generally agreed that Christ himself explicitly determined their nature—e.g., baptism with water; Eucharist with bread and wine—while the nature of others was determined more directly by the Apostles—e.g.,.confirmation by laying on of hands (See E. Schillebeeckx, *Christ the Sacrament of Encounter with God,* trans. P. Barrett, et al. [London, 1963], pp. 145–150; Karl Rahner, *Kirche und Sakramente* [Freiburg, 1961], pp. 37–67). But if it is true that such determinations were indeed made by Christ and the Apostles, and that they must therefore be considered essential to the sacramental rites, it is also true that these same determinations were largely "undifferentiated and rudimentary." (Schillebeeckx, *Christ the Sacrament,* p. 149). Thus one will find in the primitive Church considerable variety and flexibility not only in the places, times, and instruments of worship (See J.P. Audet, *Structures of Christian Priesthood,* trans. Rosemary Sheed [New York, 1968], pp. 33–67; 79; 81; R. Schnackenburg, *The Moral Teaching of the New Testament,* trans. J. Holland-Smith and W.J. O'Hara [New York, 1966], pp. 179; 227–34), but also in regard to the very structure—e.g., "matter and form"—of the sacraments (See O. Cullmann, *Early Christian Worship,* trans. A.S. Todd and J.B. Torrance [Chicago, 1958], especially, pp. 26–27).

6. *Ep.* LIV, I; *Ep.* LV, 19, 35: *PL* 33, 200, 221.

7. The historical developments surveyed in the remaining pages of this chapter were, admittedly, far more complex than so brief and selective an overview will suggest. This writer's intention will be simply to illustrate by way of a few brief points why and how over the centuries, notwithstanding periodic returns to the *forma apostolica ecclesiae*, there was a general increase in the number and estimation of ceremonies. This development will be viewed almost exclusively from the perspective of the protest of the late medieval and sixteenth-century reformers. Some of its more positive dimensions therefore will be overlooked. It will be seen eventually, however, that precisely because of their adiaphoristic position, many of the mainline sixteenth-century reformers did have a keen appreciation of the role of ritual, and in any event certainly did not mean to project their own concrete solution to the problem of ritualization as an absolute standard against which to measure the whole past and future of Christian (or non-Christian) worship.

8. See the canons of the synod of Gangra (345): C.J. Hefele and C. deClerq, *Histoire des Conciles* (Paris, 1907), 1.2, pp. 1030–34. See also: A. Vööbus, *Celibacy: A Requirement for Admission to Baptism in the Early Syrian Church* (Stockholm, 1951), pp. 13–16; K. Müller, *Die Forderung der Ehelosigkeit für alle Getauften in der alten Kriche* (Tübingen, 1927), pp. 18 f.

9. See H. Bruns, *Canones Apostolorum et Conciliorum Veterum Selecti* (Torino, 1959), II, pp. 19, 204, 227, 229, 230; I, pp. 207–8; See M. Zacherl, "Die *Vita Communis* als Lebensform des Klerus in der Zeit zwischen Augustinus und Karl dem Grossen," *ZKTh* 92 (1970), pp. 385–424.

10. See M. Boehlens, *Die Klerikerehe in der Gesetzgebung der Kirche* (Paderborn, 1968), pp. 135, 90.

11. Bruns, *op. cit.*, I, 207.

12. *The Letters of Boniface,* trans. E. Emerton (New York, 1940), p. 116.

13. See Audet, *op. cit.*, p. 83.

14. *Letters of Boniface,* pp. 115, 118, 58, 161.

15. See (*NCE* 5, 847–48); W. Rordorf, *Sunday, The History of the Day of Rest and Worship in the Earliest Centuries of the Christian Church,* trans. A.A.K. Graham (Philadelphia, 1968), pp. 154–273; N.Q. King, *The Emperor Theodosius and the Establishment of Christianity* (London, 1961), pp. 108–9; W.D. Davies, *The Background of the New Testament and Its Eschatology* (Cambridge, 1956), p. 134. The Easter controversies will be referenced later.

16. See K. Adam, *Christ Our Brother,* trans. J. McCann (New York, 1962), pp. 37–38; Josef Jungmann, *The Mass of the Roman Rite,* trans. F.A. Brunner (New York, 1959), p. 28; B. Verkamp, "Cultic Purity and the Law of Celibacy," *Review for Religious,* 30 (1971), pp. 199–217; Canons 4 and 18, Synod of Tours (567): Bruns, *op. cit.,* II, pp. 187, 226; Canons 36, 37, Synod of Auxerre (578): *Ibid.,* p. 241; Canon 5, Synod of Macon (581): *Ibid.,* p. 243.

17. See P.J. Alexander, *The Patriarch Nicephorus of Constantinople* (Oxford, 1958), p. 5; Peter Brown, "A Dark-Age Crisis: Aspects of the Iconoclastic Controversy," *EHR* 346 (1973), pp. 5–9; Audet, *op. cit.,* pp. 80, 83.

18. Jungmann, *op. cit.,* pp. 67–70.

19. N.Q. King, *op. cit.,* p. 28.

20. P. Brezzi, *The Papacy,* trans. J.J. Yannone (Westminster, 1958), pp. 49, 52.

21. *Ep.* 9, 16, 4, 138: *PL* 54, 625–26, 698, 612, 1101, 614, 625.

22. See *Epistolae* 4, 6, 9, 12, 16, 66, 162. On Leo's use of the term "apostolic tradition", see Yves Congar, *Tradition and Traditions,* trans. M. Naseby and T. Rainborough (New York, 1967), p. 55.

23. *Ep.* 138: *PL* 54, 1102.

24. See the long list of differences between the Eastern and Western churches re-ported by Theodore in 668 (*Poenitentiale Theodori, Councils and Ecclesiastical Documents relating to Great Britain and Ireland,* ed. A.W. Haddon and W. Stubbs [Oxford, 1871], III, pp. 173–203; also R.W. Southern, *Western Society and the Church in the Middle Ages* [Harmondsworth, 1970], pp. 56–57).

25. Hefele-deClerq, *op. cit.,* 3.1, pp. 565–69.

26. *Bede's Ecclesiastical History of the English People,* ed. Bertram Colgrave and R.A.B. Mynors (Oxford, 1972), p. 331. F. Dvornick, it may be noted, saw the sending of Theodore as an indication of Rome's appreciation of diversity and concluded that "We can still trace the many non-Roman customs which this Greek introduced into the Anglo-Saxon Church" (F. Dvornick, "National Churches and the Church Universal," *Eastern Churches Quarterly* 5 [1942–44], p. 198). Dvornick made no mention of Hadrian's having been sent along with Theodore.

27. See Sullivan, *op. cit.,* pp. 62–63; Steven Runciman, *The Eastern Schism* (Oxford, 1956), pp. 24–25.

28. *Ibid.,* p. 34.

29. See Walter Ullmann, *A History of Political Thought: The Middle Ages* (Baltimore, 1968), pp. 49–53.

30. Bede, *Eccl. Hist.,* p. 139, 141, 199, 301.

31. *Letters of Boniface,* p. 41.

32. *Ibid.,* p. 79. Boniface added that it was his prayer that he "may be worthy to be the obedient servant of your Holiness under the canon law" (*Ibid.*).

33. *Ibid.,* p. 116.

34. *Ibid.,* p. 137.

35. Jungmann, *op. cit.,* p. 56. In Dvornik's view, it was especially the Franks who would henceforth, and even more than Rome itself, insist upon the imposition of the Roman liturgy upon the whole of the Western Church (Dvornick, *op. cit.,* pp. 197 ff.).

36. See Gabriel Le Bras, "Canon Law," *The Legacy of the Middle Ages,* ed. C.G. Crump and E.F. Jacob (Oxford, 1926), pp. 323–26. This volume hereafter cited as *LMA.*

37. J.J. Ryan, "Canon Law in the Gregorian Reform Epoch," *Law for Liberty,* ed. J.E. Biechler (Baltimore, 1967), p. 47 (This volume hereafter cited as *LFL*); E. Meynial, "Roman Law," *LMA,* pp. 366–72; 377–79; P. Vinogradoff, "Customary Law," *LMA,* pp. 287–319; W. Ullman, *op. cit.,* p. 149.

38. *Epist. D. Barlaami episc. ad amicos suos in Graeca: PG* 151, 1258.

39. *ST* II-II, 105, 1, ad 3.

40. *Ibid.*

41. *ST* I-II, 107, 4; *ST* II-II 147, 3, ad 3.

42. See, for example, Thomas Aquinas, *ST* III, 87, 3, ad 1; III, 65, 1, ad 8.

43. See *Ibid.,* I-II, 101, 4; 108, 2, ad 2; III, 64, 2, ad 1; 65, 4.

44. Eusebius, *Historiae Ecclesiasticae* V, xxiv: PG 20, 506–8.

45. At the height of the East-West confrontation, it was probably Easterners like Cerularius, Leo of Ochrida, and the Studite monk Nicetas who were most insistent upon breaking communion over a lack of uniformity in customs (See *PG* 120, 835–42; *PL* 143, 973–83). But, as another Nicetas, the Archbishop of Nicomedia, would later write, the adamancy of the East had largely been provoked by the scorn which Charlemagne and other Latins had earlier heaped upon the customs of the East (See *Spicilegium sive Collectio veterum Aliquot Scriptorum,* ed. L. D'Achery [Parish, 1723], I, p. 201). Furthermore, even so conciliatory a figure in the West as Anselm of Havelberg did not entirely escape the suspicion of having conceived of adherence to the use of unleavened

bread or other Roman customs as a test case of obedience to the Roman See (See *Ibid.*, pp. 162, 201-2; see also: Lawrence F. Barmann, "Reform Ideology in the *Dialogi* of Anselm of Havelberg;" *Church History* 30 [December, 1961], pp. 379-95).

46. Bede, *Eccl. Hist.*, p. 307.

47. *Letters of Boniface*, p. 162.

48. Justinian had declared in the sixth century that "the laws originate in our divine mouth" and are "divine precepts" (W. Ullmann, *op. cit.*, p. 35). At Alcuin's prompting, Charlemagne had come to conceive of himself as "the vicar of Christ whose decisions were those of God" (*Ibid.*, p. 69).

49. See *Ibid.*, pp. 78-80.

50. "Licet vix ferendum ab illa sancta sede imponatur jugum . . ." (Cited in Gabriel Biel, *Defensorium Obedientiae Apostolicae et Alia Documenta*, ed. Heiko Oberman *et al.* [Cambridge, 1968], p. 106).

51. ". . . tamen feramus et pia devotione toleremus" (*Ibid.*).

52. "Letter of Fulk, archbishop of Reims, to King Alfred (883-c.890), "*English Historical Documents, c. 500-1042*, ed. D. Whilelock (London, 1955), pp. 814-15.

53. Ryan, *op. cit.*, p. 44; Brezzi, *op. cit.*, p. 97; LeBras, *op. cit.*, p. 324; W. Ullmann, *op. cit.*, pp. 104, 106, 115.

54. J.T. Noonan, "Freedom, Experimentation, and Permanence in the Canon Law on Marriage," *LFL*, pp. 60-63.

55. *De Praecepto et Dispensatione* IX: *PL* 182, 871-72.

56. *ST* II-II, 105, 1; see also: II-II, 69, 1.

57. Barlaam, *op. cit.*: *PG* 151, 1261.

58. *Tracts and Treatises of John De Wycliffe*, ed. R. Vaughan (London, 1845), pp. 36, 233, 198, 38, 158, 225, 51.

59. Jan Hus, *Tractatus de Ecclesia*, ed. E.H. Thomson (Cambridge, 1956), p. 188.

60. See Johan Huizinga, *The Waning of the Middle Ages* (Garden City, 1954), p. 153. See also: Henry of Langenstein, *Ep. concilii pacis, Advocates of Reform*, ed. Matthew Spinka (Philadelphia, 1953), pp. 137-38.

61. *Liber de Vita Spirituali Animae, Opera Omnia Joannis Gersoni*, ed. E. du Pin (Antwerp, 1706), III, III, 16. For D'Ailly's views in this regard, see *Ibid.*, I, 614.

62. *Ibid.*, III, III, 17.

63. *De Sacramento Poenitentia, Opera* (Groningen, 1614), p. 809.

64. ". . . pauciora sunt onera legis christiane inquantum est tradita a christo, sed forte plura inquantum addita sunt alia per eos qui habent regere populum christianum" (3 *Sent.*, 40:2,1).

65. *Ichtuophagia*, *EO* 1, 788, 796, 793, 801-4; see also: Commentary on Matt. 11:28-30 (*EO* 6, 63-64); Commentary on Matt. 23:1-2 (*EO* 6, 117); "Letter of Easter, 1522, to the bishop of Basel" (*EO* 9, 1199); "Letter to Martin Bucer, Nov. 11, 1527" (*EE* VII, p. 232); "Letter to P. Volz" (*EE* III, p. 373); *Enchiridion* (*EO* V, 27, 36, 65); Letter to John Carondolet, Jan. 5, 1523" (*EE* V, pp. 177-81).

66. *De Libertate Christiana*, *WA* 7, 68; *Augs. Konf.* Art. XX, *BEK*, pp. 76, 78; *Acta Tiguri*, *SW* 1, p. 149; *Decades*, ed. T. Harding (Cambridge, 1850), d.3, s.7, t.2, pp. 276-77; also: *Confessio Helvetica Posterior* 27, in Philip Schaff, *The Creeds of Christendom* (New York, 1919), p. 302; J. Calvin, *Institutes of the Christian Religion*, ed. John T. McNeill, trans. Ford Lewis Battles (Philadelphia, 1960), IV, X, 13.

67. See: *The Acts and Monuments of John Foxe* (London, 1843-49), V., pp. 415-16; E.G. Rupp, *The English Protestant Tradition* (Cambridge, 1949), pp. 17 ff; Dickens, *English Reformation*, pp. 68 ff.; A.G. Dickens, *Lollards and Protestants in the Diocese of York, 1509-1558* (Oxford, 1959); J.A.F. Thomson, *The Later Lollards, 1414-1520* (Ox-

ford, 1965); John Colet, *Two Treatises on the Hierarchies of Dionysius,* trans. J.H. Lupton (London, 1869; Ridgewood, 1966), pp. 267–68, 223, 216, 228, 267.

68. Foxe, *Acts and Monuments,* IV, p. 625.

69. *An Answer to Sir Thomas More's Dialogue,* ed. H. Walter (Cambridge, 1850), p. 74.

70. *Ibid.,* p. 77.

71. *Obedience of a Christian Man,* in *Doctrinal Treatises,* ed. H. Walter (Cambridge, 1848), p. 277; *Answer to More,* p. 8.

72. *Answer to More,* pp. 76, 67; *Obedience of a Christian Man,* pp. 247–48; *Expositions and Notes,* ed. H. Walter (Cambridge, 1849), p. 113. For similar remarks by John Frith, who collaborated with Tyndale in the production of his *Answer to More,* see J. Frith, *A Mirror or a Looking Glass, WER,* III pp. 282–83.

73. J. Bale, *Yet a course at the Romysche Foxe* (Zurich, 1543), sig. I, fol. i.

74. *Ibid.,* sig. B, fol viii(v); also: C, iv; D, iv(v); L, iii(v); L, v; N, i(v).

75. J. Hooper, *A Declaration of the Ten Holy Commandments of Almighty God,* in *The Early Writings of John Hooper,* ed. S. Carr (Cambridge, 1843), p. 346.

76. W. Turner, *The Second Course of the Hunter at the Romishe Fox and Hys Advocate* (Zurich[?], 1545), sig. A, fol. viii–sig. B, fol. i. As M.M. Knappen has pointed out, the works of Bale and Turner had been inspired largely by Robert Barnes' 1535 *Vitae Romanorum pontificum,* in which Barnes had tried to contrast the simplicity of the primitive church with the cluttered condition of its medieval successor by way of providing long lists of the contributions respective popes had made to the multiplication of the ceremonies down through the centuries (Knappen, *Tudor Puritanism,* p. 64).

77. *Exhortation,* sig. E, fol. iv(v); sig. F, fol. i(v). To exemplify prevailing superstition, Starkey noted the fact that if priests were granted the liberty to marry, some would conclude "that Christian purytie were utterly then extincte," or that some would think that "Christ were utterly driven away" if the number of holy days and masses was reduced (*Exhortation,* sig. F, fol. ii).

78. T. Cranmer, *Miscellaneous Writings and Letters,* ed. J.E. Cox (Cambridge, 1846), pp. 147, 148.

79. *Three Primers Put Forth in The Reign of Henry VIII* (Oxford, 1848), p. 429.

80. *The Catechism of Thomas Becon with Other Pieces,* ed. J. Ayre (Cambridge, 1844), p. 300.

81. *The Two Liturgies, A.D. 1549 and A.D. 1552, with Other Documents set forth by Authority in the Reign of King Edward VI,* ed. J. Ketley (Cambridge, 1844), p. 156.

CHAPTER 2

INDIFFERENT AND PERMITTED

JOHN EPINUS, who served in London as ambassador from North German cities during the latter half of 1534, later complained that the theory of adiaphorism is so insidious that, among other things, it reduces eloquent people to stuttering, and makes those who are normally loquacious, utterly dumb and speechless.[1] So drastic an effect the introduction of adiaphorism into England during the sixteenth century did not have, except perhaps upon the "puritan" element itself,[2] whose distaste for the theory of adiaphorism Epinus obviously shared. The early English adiaphorists were no Shakespeares, but they were at least as articulate as has been the average English theologian of any other age.

Still, there must have been many a sixteenth-century Englishman, even apart from the "puritans," who found all the sudden talk of adiaphora a bit puzzling, if for no other reason than that the adiaphorists themselves did not all use the term adiaphoron, or its English equivalents, in the same sense.

Among the various definitions of adiaphora available to the English reformers from earlier sources was, in the first place, its original conception by the ancient Cynic and Stoic philosophers. To serve notice of their emancipation from the ordinary customs, institutions, and taboos of Greek society, the Cynics had designated these external conventions, and, for that matter, all externals, adiaphora, or literally "things that make no difference."[3] In itself, such an assertion need not have implied that the things so designated were without all intrinsic value or disvalue. But, given their doctrine of the sufficiency of virtue, that apparently is what the Cynics meant. By interiorizing "virtue" or "right reason" to the point of almost total identity with the "self," the Cynics in effect came to the conclusion that the "self," and the "self" alone, enjoyed value.[4] All that lay outside this self had neither value nor disvalue. The Cynic wise-man was absolutely "self-sufficient," as Diogenes lost little time in demonstrating.[5]

Their founder being a pupil of Crates,[6] the Stoics not surprisingly appropriated much of the Cynic view. Like the Cynics, they asserted the sufficiency of virtue[7] and spoke of virtue as an inner disposition toward "right reason"[8] or "life in accordance with nature."[9] Among the Stoics, however, this "nature" was far less restricted to the "self." Not infrequently, nature was understood as the nature of the entire universe,[10] or the "law common to all things."[11] And if they did speak of nature occasionally in the sense of man's own individual nature,[12] the latter was given a far more positive and fixed content than it had ever received in Cynic thought. In brief, "nature" for the Stoics constituted a "law" to which the "self," to be virtuous, had necessarily to submit.[13] This was to imply that values existed also outside the self. And, as a matter of fact, even while calling all external things and actions adiaphora,[14] the Stoics recognized that some external things were capable of contributing to "life according to nature," and for that reason were to be "preferred" (προηγμένα),[15] while others were to be "rejected" as "contrary to nature" (ἀποπροηγμένα).[16] Similarly, a distinction was drawn between "appropriate" and "inappropriate" external actions.[17]

When, therefore, the Stoics applied the term adiaphoron to all external things and actions, they obviously did not mean thereby (except in the case of those things and actions termed absolutely neutral), that the things and actions so designated were altogether lacking in value or disvalue. Rather they meant that the value or disvalue of such things and actions were never of such degree as to become decisive in the moral life of the wise-man. The interior disposition remained "sufficient." One thing might incline by nature to "virtue" and another to "vice," but, in the final analysis, a "preferred" thing could become evil and a "rejected" thing virtuous, depending upon the end to which it was directed by the inner disposition. Thus, one may conclude that according to the Stoics the adiaphoron was a thing or action which when considered in itself—i.e., according to its nature—could become either good or evil.

Given its immediate preoccupation with the Judaic tradition of a voluntarist conception of law,[18] early Christianity evidenced little of the concern for the intrinsic ethical quality of external things and actions implied by Cynic and Stoic adiaphorism. A revival of Cynicism during New Testament times did, however, captivate some Christians. Irenaeus stated that according to Carpocrates and his followers all things besides faith and love are indifferent, there being nothing really evil by nature. The Nicolaites also, according to Irenaeus, taught that it is a matter of indifference to practice adultery and to eat things sacrificed to idols. Irenaeus concluded that such beliefs were derived from the philosophy of Epicurus and the "indifference of the Cynics,"[19] and found therein cause enough for their rejection.

Probably the first orthodox Christian thinker to employ the term adiaphoron was Clement of Alexandria. Clement showed little taste for the indifference of the Cynics, but openly expressed his admiration for Stoic adiaphorism.[20] Origen was of a similar mind. Both gave explicit play to the term adiaphoron in much the same sense as it had been employed by the Stoics. They used the term, in other words, to suggest that many external things—like food, drink, marriage, wealth, and so forth—remain morally indifferent until brought into the realm of the human intention, even though they may be said to possess some intrinsic value or disvalue.[21] The clearest expression of this may be found in Clement's description of "intermediate things" as the "material of good and bad actions."[22]

Among other early Christian writers to employ the term adiaphoron in its Stoic sense were, most notably, John Chrysostom[23] and John Cassian.[24] Augustine also occasionally spoke of certain things being indifferent in the sense that they were able to be directed to either a good or evil end, depending upon the intention.[25] As Georg Teichweier has pointed out, many things which earlier theologians had designated "indifferent" (chastity, virginity, and marriage, for example) were now said by Augustine to be "goods."[26] But contrary to Teichweier's implications, Augustine did not mean thereby to preclude an adiaphoristic interpretation of such matters. Writing against Julian, Augustine noted that one must clearly distinguish between the "*officium*" and the "*finis*" of an action. The "*officium*" is that which is done, the "*finis*" that for which it is done. It is the latter, he said, which determines whether an action is truly good.[27] Thus, even though Augustine would refer to one or another thing or action as being "good *ex officio*," he could still conceive of the same as being "indifferent" in the sense that apart from the end to which it was directed, its true goodness remained in question. In other words, Augustine's *bonum ex officio* retained much the same meaning as the Stoics had put upon those things they classified as "preferred" adiaphora.

While they often employed the term adiaphoron in its Stoic sense, Clement of Alexandria, Origen, Augustine, and other early Christian thinkers did not apply it as broadly as had the Stoics. For while the latter designated all externals indifferent, the former, and especially

Augustine, emphasized that some actions, like debauchery, blasphemy, theft, and lying, are so intrinsically evil that they can never be converted to the side of good by the intention.[28] It was precisely in a discussion of this same last point that the Stoic conception of adiaphora would once again come to the fore of Christian thought during the high middle ages.

Bernard of Clairvaux, writing during the first half of the twelfth century, had argued that there are some things wholly good, others wholly evil, and, in between, "middle things" which, according to circumstance, place, time, and person, may be either good or evil.[29] But Bernard's contemporary, Peter Abelard, suggested that apart from the intention all human actions, considered in themselves, are indifferent.[30] There ensued a long discussion among medieval theologians, with Peter Lombard,[31] Pierre de Capoue, and others[32] insisting that there are certain actions which in themselves are so intrinsically evil as to be unable ever to become good by way of the intention, and still others, like William of Auxerre, contending that not only are there intrinsically evil actions, but also certain acts, like the love of God, which are always and necessarily good.[33] Still, by 1235 there was general agreement at least on this, that Abelard's thesis should be rejected.[34]

Thus, the philosophical realm of adiaphora was considerably narrowed from that proposed by the Stoics and Abelard. But however limited, a realm of things and actions capable of being put to either a good or evil end was still recognized and discussed by subsequent theologians. Most of the discussion centered upon the terminology by which such things and actions were to be designated. Eventually, with Thomas Aquinas, the term adiaphoron was generally limited in its philosophical application to only those acts which in themselves could be said to be "specifically" neutral—actions, in other words, like the plucking of a blade of grass or going for a country walk, whose objective tells neither for nor against what is reasonable.[35] Actions which previously had sometimes been labeled indifferent because of their openness to becoming either good or evil in the concrete, now with Thomas came to be identified generally as *bona* or *mala ex objecto* (e.g., alms-giving or stealing).[36] Like Augustine's *bona* or *mala ex officio,* such actions, however, were still seen as carrying the connotation of *id quod potest bene vel male fieri,*[37] and to that extent were equivalent to the Stoics' "preferred" and "rejected" adiaphora. In fact, even though Thomas, as noted, generally restricted the use of the term "indifferent" to such things or actions which the Stoics had designated "absolutely neutral," he also on occasion used the same term to refer to those actions or things which as a rule he classified as *bona* or *mala ex objecto.*[38]

Among the late medieval theologians who employed the term adiaphoron in its Stoic sense were most notably Jan Hus and John Pupper of Goch. Both rejected Abelard's view that apart from the intention all external actions are by nature indifferent.[39] Some acts, Hus argued, are so intrinsically good or evil that they remain such no matter what intention one may have in their regard. Such acts he called good or evil *simpliciter.* Other actions, however, were said by Hus to be neither good nor evil in themselves, because they become one or the other only by virtue of the intention, circumstance, and so forth. These Hus classified as being specifically (*de genere*) good or evil actions, thereby bringing into clear focus their adiaphoristic character. The actions which Thomas had designated "specifically" indifferent, Hus, like the Stoics themselves, referred to as being "neutral," on the grounds that by nature they dispose neither to virtue nor to vice.[40]

Wessel Gansfort and almost all the sixteenth-century Continental reformers also employed the term adiaphoron or its Latin, German, and French equivalents,[41] but, except for Zwingli[42] and Melanchthon,[43] seldom took much cognizance of the philosophical connotations. The latter did, however, figure strongly in Erasmus of Rotterdam's understanding of adiaphora.

Close attention to the Gospel message will reveal, Erasmus wrote, that "the perfection of Christ is in the disposition, not in the external modes of life." To be sure, he said, some few external actions are so intrinsically good or evil that they always remain such, notwithstanding the intention of the doer. But, "for the most part, the realm of externals consists of imperfect and indifferent things." They are indifferent because they are not "ends" in themselves. Until they are taken up into the "spirit" and afforded a reference beyond themselves, they enjoy no ultimate value.[44]

The *Enchiridion,* in which Erasmus had developed this line of thought, was very popular in England during the early decades of the sixteenth century. The English conception of adiaphora was certainly influenced by the same, as evidenced, for example, by the emphasis which will be seen to have been placed by some English adiaphorists upon the "signification" of ceremonies, or upon their hierarchical evaluation by others. But it would certainly be inaccurate to label "Erasmian" every sign of adiaphoristic thought in England during the early decades of the sixteenth century, or even to think that the rise of English adiaphorism was chiefly due to Erasmus.[45] Almost every English reformer of the Henrician and Edwardine periods employed the term adiaphoron or its philosophical English equivalents,[46] but they seldom paid much attention to the sort of philosophical connotations put upon the term by Erasmus and other earlier adiaphorists. More often than not their conception of adiaphora was of a theological sort. Far more basic to an appreciation of their version of adiaphorism than its philosophical roots and connotations, therefore, is the specifically theological line of adiaphoristic thought which had also been under long development.

While the term adiaphoron was, as has been seen, a philosophical one, the Christian thinkers who first employed it were primarily theologians, not philosophers. What ethical concerns they had centered more upon the divine positive law revealed in Scripture than upon the "right reason" or natural law with which the Stoic discussion of adiaphora had been preoccupied. Yet, it was obviously their view also that an understanding of divine positive law could be considerably enhanced by having its operations explained in philosophical terminology. And it was undoubtedly for this reason that they borrowed the term adiaphoron in the first place. When, for example, Clement of Alexandria and Origen used the term, it was almost always for the sake of elucidating what the New Testament, and especially the Apostle Paul, had meant about the Christian's freedom of choice regarding food, drinks, and similar matters.[47] Much the same could be said of Chrysostom's employment of the term.[48] Augustine used it most effectively in an attempt to explain to Jerome what attitude the Apostle Paul had actually taken toward observance of the old Judaic ceremonies,[49] and in his letters to Januarius and Casulanus, in which he advised the latter on how best to deal with those matters not covered by the biblical commands and prohibitions.[50]

Use of the term adiaphoron by high medieval theologians was often along similar lines, as evidenced, for example, by Thomas Aquinas' application of the term to those external matters which to his view enjoyed no essential connection with the "inner law of the Spirit" revealed in Scripture.[51] Given their desire to fashion a synthesis of faith and reason, these high medieval theologians at times went beyond a mere exploitation of the term adiaphoron, and used it also as a correlative to what they considered its corresponding operation of divine positive law, namely, the divine "permission."[52]

Thus, although the New Testament itself had never used the term adiaphoron, the latter, in one way or the other, was early on brought into close association with certain elements of New Testament doctrine. In the process, the term's basically philosophical connotations remained clearly in focus, and in fact, within the context of the logical priority afforded by the medieval theologians to the natural law,[53] probably had more effect upon the conception of "things permitted" than the latter did upon the definition of adiaphora. With Marsilius of Padua and especially William of Ockham, however, the medieval synthesis of faith and reason was, if not altogether broken down, at least reversed in such wise as to shift logical priority back to the divine will.[54] As a result, while some theologians would continue thereafter to define and use the term adiaphoron in its original philosophical meaning, many others, and certainly the vast majority of sixteenth-century Continental and English reformers, would not. Most of the latter retained the philosophical term adiaphoron, or its translated equivalents, but seldom paid much attention to its original philosophical content, choosing instead to define it in terms of the Scriptural doctrine with which, as has been seen, it had earlier become associated. In short, they used the term adiaphoron on the whole as simply a synonym for the New Testament notion of a "thing permitted." What the mainline Continental reformers did or did not understand by this latter notion can best be shown within the context of a brief review of their doctrine of solafideism.[55] That many English adiaphorists did not subscribe to the latter doctrine makes such a review all the more imperative, if their adiaphorism is to be shown to have been in agreement with the Continental reformers' version, as indeed it was.

By reason of his faith in Christ, the Christian, Melanchthon wrote, has been radically emancipated from all constraint of the external law. Not only the judicial and ceremonial laws, but the moral law as well has been abrogated in his regard. He becomes, in the words of Luther, "the free lord of all, subject to none." No longer does he have to prove himself worthy under the law. Although he remains a sinner, he need not despair. The accusations of the law, of the devil, of the pope, of the self, or of anyone else, can no longer overwhelm him. By faith, the righteousness of Christ is now his righteousness. His sin will no longer be held against him. He has been accepted as he is. Having recognized God, he can forget himself. His is a share in the Lordship of Christ, and he finds that now "everything is free and nothing necessary."[56]

Thus emancipated from the curse of the law, and the chains of his slavery to self thereby broken, the man of faith, Luther said, has been set free toward his neighbor and toward the world. No longer does he need to use his neighbor as party to some moralistic scheme of proving himself worthy. Nor need he any longer search out some especially "holy" vocation by which to gain self-respect and divine approval. Now, instead, his love of neighbor can be genuinely altruistic and expressed freely and confidently in the ordinary "stations" of life. Indeed, if his "lordship" is to be genuine, the Christian has no choice but to become "the perfectly dutiful servant of all."[57]

Such service will not be a "work of the law," but a "work of grace," the result of the man of faith having submitted himself to the creative lordship of Christ. The "new obedience" which it implies will be a spontaneous one, inspired and guided primarily from within—by the law of the spirit, not by the written law. Of all the Continental reformers, none pursued this last point so far as did Luther. Luther's man of faith, as Paul Althaus has noted, lives in "theonomous creativity." Possessed and moved by Christ's spirit, he no longer needs the law's "demands and warnings." He is not bound legalistically to any external law—not the Decalogue, nor even the New Testament "commandments." Indeed, to the extent that he lives in the power of the Spirit, the man of faith can write and rewrite his own law in accordance with the specific situation within which he finds himself.[58]

But Luther was no antinomian. Only the man who thinks that sin is once and for ever behind him, he said, will consider himself no longer in any need whatever of the law. But, in his view, the Christian remains at once a righteous man and a sinner. Thus, for all his talk of the abrogation of the law, Luther would also conceive of the law as continuing to play a role in the life of the Christian. Not to mention its "civil function," the law will continue to function "theologically," he said, by serving to remind the Christian of the twofold sense in which, notwithstanding his righteousness, he remains a sinner—that is, "totally," insofar as while living "in Christ," he remains *"an sich,"* in his own "empirical sinful existence," and "partially," to the extent that the "flesh," the "old man," persists in warring against the "spirit" or the "new man" now abuilding within him under the impetus of faith. Cognizant of the "good news" of Christ's saving grace, the Christian will not let such a function of the law drive him, as it did before his reception of the Gospel, into despair. It will, however, goad him into renewing ever again his original act of trust in God, and into carrying on the daily struggle against the "flesh."[59]

But there is, according to Luther, still a further function of the law in the Christian's life.[60] To the extent that the Christian remains "partially holy" and "partially sinful," his discernment of God's will is clouded.[61] In his efforts to live a life of love such as will not jeopardize the unity of Christian ethical judgment, it will be necessary, therefore, that he take into serious account the moral "norms" or "directives" to be found in divine positive law.[62] Among the latter are to be counted the Ten Commandments,[63] and even more the "new decalogues" by which Christ and his Apostles brought into sharper focus the original intention of the Decalogue, and, among other things, delineated the various "stations" in the context of which Christians are to work out their love for one another.[64] To avoid giving the impression that such directives are "legally" binding upon the Christian or necessary, in a moralistic sense, to salvation, Luther chose to refer to them not as laws, but as "commands," "precepts," "exhortations," "remedies," and so forth.[65] Furthermore, and probably for the same reason, he seems never to have used the expression "the third function of the law."[66] Still, like Melanchthon and the other Continental reformers whose emphasis upon the law's so-called "third function" was far more explicit, Luther clearly deemed it necessary for Christians to look to the biblical commands and prohibitions as to a criterion by which to know what sort of "good works" God requires.[67] "In the New Testament," Luther wrote, "all those things are shown which ought to be done and ought not to be done."[68] What the Scripture commands, therefore, the Christian "must" do; what is therein forbidden, he "must" omit.[69]

Luther and the other mainline Continental reformers were also very much aware, however, that the biblical commands and prohibitions did not cover the whole of Christian life and worship. In the remarks of Jesus about the levity of the Christian burden of obedience, in Jesus' show of liberty over against the ancient Jewish traditions, and especially in the Pauline doctrine concerning the ceremonial and judicial content of the old Judaic law, the reformers recognized, in other words, that according to the New Testament, there obtains a wide realm of things and actions which, because, as Melanchthon put it, the presence of the Spirit of God cannot be dependent upon observance of the sort of distinctions of places and times, persons and things, they implied, have been "neither commanded, nor forbidden" in themselves, and need not, therefore, be observed "by necessity."[70] And it was precisely such matters, and only such matters, which the Continental reformers understood as being "things permitted," and to which, therefore, they applied the term adiaphoron.[71]

That such matters were not to be considered "sources of justification" was presupposed. But contrary to the impression left by some scholars,[72] this had nothing immediately to do with their definition as "adiaphora" or "things permitted." Their theologically adiaphoristic character was derived rather from the fact that such matters had been "neither commanded, nor forbidden" by the divine law revealed in the New Testament.[73]

With such a restricted theological definition of adiaphora even those many early English reformers who, like Henry VIII himself, did not subscribe to the doctrine of solafideism,[74] could and did also concur. It in no way challenged their repeated insistence upon obedience to the biblical commands and prohibitions,[75] but, in fact, brought the latter all the more clearly into focus. Thus, like their colleagues across the channel, the English adiaphorists could deny that matters commanded or forbidden in Scripture are indifferent,[76] and proceed to define adiaphora precisely in terms of their having been "neither commanded, nor forbidden." "Thinges indifferent," Thomas Starkey wrote, "I call all suche things which by goddis worde are nother prohibyted nor commanded."[77] Equally explicit in this regard was the 1537 *Bishops' Book*: "The greatest part of these rules or canons consisteth only in . . . such things as be of themselves but mean and indifferent things (that is to say, neither commanded expressly in Scripture, nor necessary contained or implied therein, nor yet expressly repugnant or contrary thereunto)."[78] The vast majority of other adiaphoristic assertions during the early stages of the English Reformation gave expression to, or at least implied, the same theological definition of adiaphora.[79]

By thus conceiving of adiaphora sometimes as those things left uncovered by the biblical commands and prohibitions, the English adiaphorists were eventually confronted with the problem of having to specify exactly what it was that Scripture had "neither commanded, nor forbidden." The solution offered to that problem by some of the more radical English reformers will be seen in a subsequent chapter to have altered considerably their definition of adiaphora. Here, however, the concern has been primarily to determine in what sense the term adiaphoron was understood by the mainline, so-called "conformist," English reformers. It has been seen that their definition of adiaphora was principally a theological one, and represented to a great degree simply an extension of the New Testament notion of "things permitted."[80] To that extent their version of adiaphorism also came to be linked up with the thought of many earlier theologians like Tertullian, John Wyclif, and others, who, although they never employed an explicitly adiaphoristic terminology, will be seen to have had very much to say about the biblical "permissions." It has also been seen, however, that thanks mainly to Erasmus, the English adiaphorists also sometimes employed the term adiaphoron in its original philosophical sense. For the English adiaphorists to have designated certain traditional ceremonies or laws adiaphora, therefore, could have meant either that the latter were to be considered "neither commanded, nor prohibited," or "neither good, nor evil," or, in some cases, both.

The overall net result of such a designation was to "free" or "neu-

tralize" the matters so designated. To appreciate so broad an implication of the adiaphoristic appraisal of the ceremonies, however, its negative and positive components must first be investigated separately.

NOTES

1. "Epistola D. Joannis Aepini Superintendentis Hamburgensis ad Illyricum," *OLS*, sig. R, fol. 5(v).

2. The term "puritan" will be applied throughout this study to the likes of Turner, Bale, and Hooper on the assumption that their dissatisfaction with official church policy regarding ceremonial matters was approximate to that of "the original anti-vestment party" of the Elizabethan period, whose members have sometimes been classified by historians as "original Puritans," "vestment Puritans," "episcopal Puritans," and "conforming Puritans," so as to distinguish them from later Puritans of a "separatist" and "presbyterian" bent (See Trinterud, *op. cit.*, pp. 9–11). For further discussion of the term "puritan," see: H. Davies, *Worship and Theology in England from Cranmer to Hooker 1534–1603* (Princeton, 1970), I, pp. 41–44; J.N. New, *Anglican and Puritan: The Basis of Their Opposition, 1558–1640* (London, 1964); P. Collinson, *op. cit.*, pp. 26–28; Dickens, *English Reformation*, pp. 313 ff.

3. See Diogenes Laertius, *Lives of Eminent Philosophers* vi, 11, 63, 71–73, 105. The term adiaphoron is derived etymologically from the Greek verb *diapherein*, meaning "to differ."

4. See Laertius, *Lives*, vi, 23, 24, 46, 72, 73, 104.

5. See *Ibid.*, vi, 55, 71, 74, 78.

6. *Ibid.*, vii, 2.

7. *Ibid.*, vii, 128. See also: Cicero, *De Officiis* iii, iii, 11–13; J.M. Rist, *Stoic Philosophy* (Cambridge, 1969), pp. 7–10; M.E. Reesor, "Indifferents in Old and Middle Stoa," *Transactions and Proceedings of the American Philological Association*, LXXXII (1951), pp. 106–10; E.V. Arnold, *Roman Stoicism* (London, 1958), p. 292.

8. Laertius, *Lives*, vii, 88.

9. *Ibid.*, vii, 87.

10. *Ibid.*, vii, 89. See also: Clement of Alexandria, *Stromata* II, 21: *PG* 8, 1075.

11. Laertius, *Lives*, vii, 88.

12. *Ibid.*, vii, 89.

13. See Cicero, *De Legibus*, i, 12, 33; *De Natura Deorum*, i, xiv, 36.

14. Laertius, *Lives*, vii, 101. See also: H.F.A. von Arnim, *Stoicorum Veterum Fragmenta* (Lipsiae, 1921), I, pp. 191–96, 559–62; III, pp. 117–23.

15. Laertius, *Lives*, vii, 105, 106. Examples given are natural ability, health, strength, wealth, and noble birth.

16. *Ibid.*, vii, 105, 106. Examples given are lack of ability, death, disease, and poverty. The Stoics also recognized a class of absolute adiaphora—i.e., things, like the number of hairs on one's head, that are altogether neutral, entirely lacking in the power to stir inclination or aversion (See *Ibid.*, vii, 104). It may be noted that Ariston, one of Zeno's students, rejected this Stoic differentiation of adiaphora, and returned to the Cynic position, declaring that everything outside of virtue and vice was equally indifferent (*Ibid.*, vii, 160; von Arnim, *op. cit.*, II, pp. 333–403).

17. Laertius, *Lives*, vii, 108, 109. A third class of entirely neutral actions is also admitted (*Ibid.*).

18. When St. Paul, for example, used the term *nomos* it was almost always exclusively in reference to the Mosaic Law (See J.A. Fitzmyer, "Saint Paul and the Law," *Jurist* 27 [1967], pp. 19–20).

19. Irenaeus, *Cont. Haer.* I, xxv, 5: *PG* 7, 685; II, xxxii, 1–2; *PG* 7, 826–28; I, xxvi, 3: *PG* 7, 687; II, xxxii, 2: *PG* 7, 828.

20. *Stromata*, II, 21; IV, 5: *PG* 8, 1071–72; 1231.

21. For Clement, see: *Ibid.*, VII, 3: *PG* 9, 422; IV, 26: *PG* 8, 391, 394, 406, 410–32, 490–98. For Origen, see: *Comm. in Matt.* XI, 12: *PG* 13, 939; *Comm. in Ep. B. Pauli Ad Rom.* IV, 9: *PG* 14, 994; *Ibid.*, X, 3: *PG* 14, 1253; *De Principiis* iii, ii, 7: *PG* 11, 313; *In Numeros Homilia* XVI, 7: *PG* 12, 696; *Contra Celsum* IV, 45: *PG* 11, 1102; *Ibid.*, V, 49: *PG* 11, 1238. Origen, it may be noted, cited the *Sentences of Sextus* to support his adiaphoristic views (See *Ibid.*, VIII, 30: *PG* 11, 1559; see also: H. Chadwick, *The Sentences of Sextus* [Cambridge, 1959], Sentence 109).

22. *Stromata* IV, 6: *PG* 8, 1251.

23. See *Quod Non Opporteat Peccata Fratrum Evulgara* 2: *PG* 51, 355; *Hom. in Ep. I ad Cor.* XVII, 1: *PG* 61, 139–40; *Hom. ad Rom.*, XI: *PG* 60, 483 ff.; *Hom. ad Eph.* XIII: *PG* 62, 93 ff.; *Hom. ad Tim.* XII: *PG* 62, 559, 563; *Hom. ad Col.* XII: *PG* 62, 384; *Ad Illuminandos Catecheses* II, 3: *PG* 49, 235–36.

24. *Collatio* XXI, 12–16: *PL* 49, 1185–91; *Collatio* VI, 2–12: *PL* 49, 648–64.

25. See *De Sermone Domini in Monte* II, 18: *PL* 34, 1296–97.

26. *LTK* I, 146; see also J. Mausbach, *Die Ethik des hl. Augustin* (Freiburg, 1909) I, pp. 219–21.

27. *Contra Julianum* IV, 21: *PL* 44, 749.

28. *De Sermone Dom. in Monte* II, 18: *PL* 34: 1296.

29. "Quaedam sunt pura bona; quaedam pura mala . . . inter haec sunt media quaedam, quae pro modo, loco, tempore vel persona, et mala possunt esse, et bona" (*Ep.* VII, 4: *PL* 182, 95).

30. "Veluti operum nostrorum actiones, cum in se sint indifferentes, ex intentione tamen, ex qua procedunt, bonae dicuntur aut malae" (*Dialogus inter Philosophum, Judaeum et Christianum: PL* 178, 1652; see also: *Scito Te Ipsum: PL* 178, 652, 644).

31. *Libri IV Sententiarum* II, d. XL, 3: *PL* 192, 750.

32. See O. Lottin, "Le Problème de la Moralité Intrinsèque D'Abélard A Saint Thomas D'Aquin," *PEM* ii, pp. 424 f.

33. *Ibid.*, pp. 426 f.

34. *Ibid.*, p. 430.

35. *ST* I–II, 18, 8. The fact that Thomas and almost all the medieval theologians in one way or another applied the term "indifferent" to certain human acts considered in themselves does not mean, however, that all the same theologians granted the existence of indifferent acts in the concrete. As a matter of fact, the majority did not. On this question, see O. Lottin, "L'Indifférence des actes humains chez Saint Thomas D'Aquin et ses prédécesseurs," *PEM* II, pp. 469–89; also: J.W. Melody, "Acts Indifferent," *CE* I, pp. 116–17; F. Copleston, *A History of Philosophy, Medieval Philosophy* (Garden City, 1962), Vol. 2, Part II, pp. 269–70.

36. *ST* I–II, 18, 8.

37. See Lottin, *PEM* II, p. 461.

38. At one point he defined adiaphora in precisely that sense: ". . . et possunt etiam indifferentes dici omnes illi actus qui sunt vel parum boni vel parum mali" (*ST* I–II, 92, 2).

39. For John Pupper's views in this regard, see: C. Ullmann, *Reformers Before the Reformation*, trans. E. Menzies (Edinburgh, 1863), I, pp. 72–74.

40. Hus, *De Ecclesia*, pp. 175, 176, 178, 188. On this whole question, see also: J. Hus, *Super IV Sententiarum* II, d. XL, ed. V.W. Fljshaus and M. Kominkova (Osnabruck, 1966), pp. 354–56.

41. See: Gansfort, *De Dign. et Pot. Eccl., Opera*, p. 756; Luther, *In ep. Pauli ad Gal. comm., 1519, WA* II, 565, 566; *In ep. Pauli ad Cor. I, WA* XII, 127–28; "Luther an den Propst," *END* IV, p. 4; Melanchthon: *Loci Communes* (1521), *MW* II/1, pp. 160 f.; Zwingli: *Von Erkiesen und Freiheit der Speisen, SW* I, pp. 98, 126; *In Epist. ad Rom. Annot., ZO*, Vol. 6, t. 2, p. 130; *Von dem touff, SW* 4, p. 256; Bullinger: *Decades*, d.V, s. IX, t. III, pp. 414–24; *Confessio Helv. prior*, in P. Schaff, *op. cit.*, p. 228; Bucer, "Brief an Zwingli, April 4, 1524," *CR* 95, 171–79; "Bucer to à Lasco," Strype *EM*, 2.2, pp. 445, 447; "Bucer to Hooper," *Ibid.*, pp. 459–62; Calvin, *Institutes* III,XIX, 7–9; IV,XVII, 43.

42. On several occasions, Zwingli expressed his distaste for the term adiaphoron because of its philosophical (i.e., "pagan") origins (*Von Erkiesen, SW* I, p. 98; *Apol. Archet., SW* I, p. 312).

43. See, for example, Melanchthon's discussion of the retention or rejection of adiaphora in view of the "end" to which they are directed (*Com. ad Rom., MW* V, p. 331).

44. "Letter to Paul Volz, Aug. 14, 1518," *EE* III, p. 370; *Enchiridion Militis Christiani, EO* V, 25, 27, 30.

45. J.K. McConica tends to overstate the Erasmian influence upon English adiaphorism (See McConica, *op. cit.*, pp. 151, 159–163, 235, 271).

46. The term was used so frequently that it would serve no purpose to attempt a comprehensive listing of all such references, but for some of the earlier and more important uses of the term, see: W. Tyndale, *Expositions and Notes*, pp. 113, 327, 329; Tyndale, *Answer to More*, p. 126; Tyndale, *Doctrinal Treatises*, p. liv; John Frith's translation of *The Revelation of Antichrist* (See Foxe, *Acts and Monuments*, V, pp. 583–91); J. Frith, *The Articles Wherefore John Frith Died, WER*, pp. 451, 454; J. Frith, *A Mirror or a Looking Glass, WER*, pp. 292–94; Robert Barnes, *A Supplication* (1531), sig. P, fol. vii(v); (1534): Q, iv(v); *Marshall's Primer* (*Three Primers Put Forth in the Reign of Henry VIII*, p. 72); Thomas Starkey, *An Exhortation*, especially sig. B, fol. ii(v); "Henry VIII to Bishops, Nov. 19, 1536," in Gilbert Burnet, *The History of the Reformation of the Church of England* (Oxford, 1829), I, ii, p. 539; Thomas Cranmer, *Miscellaneous Writings and Letters*, p. 77.

47. Clement: *Paedagogus* II, 1: *PG* 8, 391; Origen: *Com. ad Rom.* X, 3: *PG* 14, 1253.

48. See Chrysostom, *Hom. in Epist. I ad Cor.* XVII, 1: *PG* 61, 139–40.

49. This exchange with Jerome concerned the proper interpretation of Galatians 2:11–14: See Augustine, *Epistolae* XXVII (*PL* 33, 111 f.); XL (*PL* 33, 154 ff.); LXXII (*PL* 33, 243 f.); LXXIII (*PL* 33, 245 ff.); LXXV (*PL* 33, 251 ff.); LXXXII (*PL* 33, 275 f.); CLXXX, 5 (*PL* 33, 779).

50. See Augustine, *Ep.* LIV (*PL* 33, 199–204); LV (*PL* 33, 204–23); XXXVI (*PL* 33, 136–51).

51. "Illa vero quae indifferenter se habent respectu horum, puta comedere hos vel illos cibos, in his non est regnum Dei" (*ST* I–II, 108, 1, ad 1).

52. Writing about law in general, Thomas Aquinas, for example, stated: "Praecepta autem legis sunt de actibus humanis, in quibus lex dirigit... sunt autem tres differentiae humanorum actuum. Nam... quidam actus sunt boni ex genere... et respectu horum, ponitur legis actus praecipere vel imperare... Quidam vero sunt actus mali ex genere... et respectu horum, lex habet prohibere. Quidam vere ex genere suo sunt actus indifferentes; et respectu horum, lex permittere, et possunt etiam indiffer-

entes dici omnes illi actus qui sunt vel parum boni vel parum mali" (*ST* I–II, 92, 2).

Such an assertion by Thomas need not have meant that to his view a perfect coincidence obtained between adiaphora and things permitted by divine positive law, but such at least was the thrust of medieval thought. It may be noted that already Origen had written that it is fitting for the divine lawgiver to forbid those things which tend to vice, and to permit those things which are by nature indifferent (*Com. in Matt.* XI, 12: *PG* 13, 939; also: *Com. in Ep. B. Pauli ad Rom.* IV, 9: *PG* 14, 994).

53. In other words, actions like adultery and fornication were said to be forbidden because they are evil by nature, and not vice versa (See William of Auxerre's remarks in this regard: Lottin, *PEM* II, p. 427).

54. Briefly, it was Marsilius' definition of the operation of law solely in terms, not of its rationality, but of its formal element of coercion (*Defensor Pacis*, ed. C.W. Previte-Orton [Cambridge, 1928], II, ix, 3), and Ockham's subordination of God's *potentia ordinata* to his *potentia absoluta* (*Quodlibet*, VI, q. 1) which led to the breakdown or reversal.

55. The following exposition will center chiefly upon the thought of Luther and Melanchthon. For an introduction to the solafideism of other mainline Continental reformers, see especially: C. Gestrich, *Zwingli als Theologe* (Stuttgart, 1967), pp. 161–86; G.W. Locher, *H. Zwingli in Neuer Sicht* (Stuttgart, 1969), pp. 219–22, 233–39; J. Muller, *M. Bucers Hermeneutik* (Gütersloh, 1965), pp. 150–68; 207–11; F. Wendel, *Calvin, The Origins and Development of His Religious Thought*, trans. P. Mairet (New York and Evanston, 1963), pp. 255–63. On the Anabaptist position on this question, see: J. Hillerbrand, "Anabaptism and the Reformation: Another Look," *Church History* 29 (1960), pp. 404–23.

56. *Loci Communes* (1521), *MW* II/1, pp. 125–32; *De Lib. Christ.*, *WA* 7, 49; *Epist. ad Rom.* (Die Scholien), *WA* 56, 493. See, in general, Martin E. Marty, "Luther on Ethics: Man, Free and Slave," *Accents in Luther's Theology*, ed. H.O. Kadai (St. Louis, 1967), pp. 199–227.

57. See Marty, *op. cit.*, pp. 215–16, 220–22; Paul Althaus, *The Theology of Martin Luther*, trans. Robert C. Schultz (Philadelphia, 1966), pp. 302–3, 134–36; P. Althaus, *The Ethics of Martin Luther*, trans. R.C. Schultz (Philadelphia, 1972), pp. 39, 36–42; *De Lib. Christ.*, *WA* 7, 49.

58. Althaus, *Theology of Luther*, pp. 267, 270; *Ethics of Luther*, pp. 30–32.

59. W. Joest, *Gesetz und Freiheit* (Gottingen, 1968), pp. 62–63, 58–59, 62–64, 65–77; Althaus, *Ethics of Luther*, pp. 112–54; Althaus, *Theology of Luther*, pp. 242–44, 268, 269.

60. See in general: Joest, *op. cit.*, pp. 71–77; Althaus, *Theology of Luther*, pp. 270–73; F. Böckle, *Law and Conscience*, trans. M.J. Donnelly (New York, 1966), pp. 32–35; H. Fagerberg, *A New Look at the Lutheran Confessions*, trans. C.J. Lund (St. Louis, 1972), pp. 79–87; E. Schlink, *Theology of the Lutheran Confessions*, trans. P. Koehneke and H. Bouman (Philadelphia, 1961), pp. 105–22.

61. Althaus, *Theology of Luther*, p. 270.

62. *Ibid.*, pp. 271–72; Joest, *op. cit.*, pp. 72–77.

63. Luther wrote that apart from the Ten Commandments no work can be pleasing to God, no matter how worthy it may seem to men (*Grosser Katechismus* 311, *BEK*, p. 639). According to Melanchthon, it is simply inconceivable that the Spirit of God "can be in the human heart without fulfilling the Decalogue" (*Loci, MW* II/1, p. 133).

64. Althaus, *Ethics of Luther*, pp. 30–32; 36–42; 83–160.

65. Fagerberg, *op. cit.*, pp. 80, 86; Joest, *op. cit.*, p. 74; Althaus, *Theology of Luther*, p. 271 n.

66. Althaus notes that although Luther, unlike Melanchthon, did not use the expres-

sion *tertius usus legis,* "in substance it also occurs" in his thought (*Theology of Luther,* p. 273). See also: W. Elert, *Law and Gospel,* trans. E.H. Schroeder (Philadelphia, 1967), pp. 38 ff.; Joest, *op. cit.,* p. 72.

67. Fagerberg, *op. cit.,* p. 86.

68. WA 7, 760, as cited in Althaus, *Theology of Luther,* p. 271 n.

69. It may be noted that according to the Formula of Concord (1580), it is permissible for Lutherans to use the term "necessary" in reference to the new obedience of the just man, so long as one understands thereby, not the constraint of the law, but the impulse of a free and spontaneous spirit (Art. IV, in P. Schaff, *op. cit.,* p. 123).

70. *Loci,* MW II/1, p. 133.

71. See references cited above in II, footnote 41.

72. After asserting that "if one insists that justification is by faith alone, everything else is adiaphoristic," C.L. Manschreck, for example, has concluded in reference to Melanchthon's adiaphorism, that "external observances are adiaphora so far as righteousness is concerned; they are not necessary to justification" (Manschreck, "The Role of Melanchthon in the Adiaphora Controversy," *Archiv* XLIX [1957], p. 165). Similarly, T.W. Street, in an unpublished study of John Calvin's adiaphorism, has attempted to establish a distinction between Calvin's understanding of adiaphora and that of Luther and Melanchthon on the grounds that the latter located the indifference of external acts in their not being "sources of justification" ("John Calvin on Adiaphora, An Exposition," pp. 255–57). Underlying such conclusions, as Manschreck's remarks especially make clear, was the false impression held already in the sixteenth century by the Tridentine Fathers that it was Luther's view that "outside of faith everything is indifferent." At its sixth session the Council of Trent declared: "Si quis dixerit, nihil praeceptum esse in Evangelio praeter fidem, cetera esse indifferentia, neque praecepta, neque prohibita, sed libera, aut decem praecepta nihil pertinere ad Christianos: anathema sit" (*Concilii Tridentini Actorum,* ed. S. Ehses [Friburgi Brisgoviae, 1911], t.V, p. 799, canon 19). The Tridentine canon, with the exception of the word "*indifferentia*", was the same as the charge brought against the Lutherans some fifteen years earlier by John Eck in his *404 Articles* and the *Confutatio Pontificia* (See *The Augsburg Confession, A Collection of Sources,* ed. J.M. Reu [St. Louis, 1966], pp. 108, 338). Ehses notes that the phrase "*cetera esse indifferentia*" was inserted into the Tridentine canon by Cardinal de Monte (Ehses, *op. cit.,* p. 516). Both Eck and the Tridentine Fathers did, it should be noted, associate the reformers' use of the terms "free" and "indifferent" with the formula "*neque praecepta, neque prohibita.*" See also: B. Verkamp, "The Limits Upon Adiaphoristic Liberty According to Martin Luther and Philip Melanchthon," *TS* 36 (March, 1975), pp. 52–76.

73. On occasion the reformers gave explicit expression to the "neither commanded, neither prohibited" formula, as, for example, when Luther wrote in his *Wider die himmlischen Propheten*: ". . . die Christliche freiheit durch die zweierlei gebrochen wird, wenn man gepeut, zwingt und dringt zu thun, das doch nicht gepoten noch erzwungen ist von Gott, oder wenn man verpeut, weret, und hindert zu lassen, das doch nicht verpotten, noch geweret ist von Gott . . . einer felt zur lincken seiten, der ander zur rechten seiten, und bleibt keiner auff der rechten freien strassen . . . wir aber gehen auff der mittel ban und sagen, es gillt widder gepietens noch verpietens, widder zur rechten noch zur lincken, wir sind widder Bepstlich noch Carlstadisch, sondern frei und christlich" (*WA* 18, 111f). See also Luther's Commentary on the First Letter of Paul to Timothy (*WA* 26, 67–75). More often than not, however, it must be culled from the general context of their discussion of "things permitted." See: Luther: *Pred. des. Jah. 1522, WA* 10^{III}, 11f.; *Von Menschenlehre zu meiden, WA* 10^{II}, 72–92; *Epist. ad Rom.,*

WA 56, 493–94; *Vom Missbrauch der Messe*, WA 8, 484; *Vorlesung über die Briefe an Titus und Philemon*, WA 25, 9; *Vorlesung über I Mose*, WA 42, 510–12; *On Monastic Vows*, LW 44, 310; *De Lib. Christ.*, WA 7, 70 ff.; Melanchthon: *Loci*, MW II/1, p. 160 ff.; *Comm. ad Rom.*, MW V, p. 33; *Augs. Konf.*, Arts. XXVI, XXVIII, BEK, pp. 100–107, 126–29; Zwingli: *In Epistolam ad Rom. Annotationes*, ZO VI, t. II, pp. 126–30; *Von Erkiesen*, SW I, pp. 91–98, 126, 134; Letter to Erasmus Fabricius, SW I, pp. 142–54; *Die 67 Artikel Zwinglis*, SW I, p. 461; *Usslegen und Grund der Schlussreden*, SW II, pp. 244–46; Oecolampadius: *Die Erste Baslerconfession von 1534*, AS p. 469; Bullinger: *Decades*, d. III, s. IX, t. II, pp. 310–11; *Confessio Helvetica Post.* XXIV, in Schaff, *op. cit.*, pp. 299–300; Bucer: *Grund und Ursach*, BDS I, p. 219; *Benfelder Predigten*, BDS VII, p. 43; *De Regno Christi* II, LV, MB, pp. 354–57; Calvin: *Institutes*, III, XIX, 7–16.

74. See J.J. Scarisbrick, *Henry VIII*, p. 407.

75. Insistence upon obedience to the Decalogue was a commonplace among the early English reformers. Some explicitly stated that the moral commands and prohibitions had not been abrogated by Christ (See, for example, *The Works of Nicholas Ridley*, ed. H. Christmas [Cambridge, 1843], p. 84; Stephen Gardiner, *The Oration of True Obedience*, in *Obedience in Church and State, Three Political Tracts by Stephen Gardiner*, ed. Pierre Janelle [New York, 1968], p. 85; this latter volume hereafter cited as Gardiner, *Tracts*).

76. "Al suche thinges as in Christis gospel, by expresse commandment, eyther of our master Christie, or of his holy apostles and disciples be to us given and taught, all such be of mere necessitie, and not indifferent" (Starkey, *Exhortation*, sig. L, fol. iii[v]).

77. *Exhortation*, sig. B, fol. ii(v).

78. Charles Lloyd, *Formularies of Faith Put Forth by Authority during the Reign of Henry VIII* (Oxford, 1825), pp. 114–15.

79. See especially: Tyndale, *Expositions*, p. 113; Frith, *A Mirror*, p. 292–94; *Marshall's Primer*, p. 72; H. Latimer, *Sermons and Remains*, ed. G.E. Carrie (Cambridge, 1845), p. 353; Latimer, *Sermons*, ed. G.E. Carrie (Cambridge, 1844), p. 48; Cranmer, *Misc. Writings and Letters*, p. 81, 145; *Ten Articles*, in Lloyd, *op. cit.*, p. xvi; Cuthbert Tunstall, *Reply* [to Germans] in Burnet, *op. cit.*, I, ii, pp. 496–97, 522–23; Henry VIII's marginal notes on Tunstall's letter regarding auricular confession (Burnet, *op. cit.*, I, ii, 543–47); Myles Coverdale, *Remains*, ed. G. Peason (Cambridge, 1846), p. 338; *The Rationale of Ceremonial*, pp. 3–4; Peter Martyr, *The Commonplaces . . . with a large addition of manie theologicall and necessarie discourses*, trans. A. Marten (London, 1583), II, p. 166; N. Ridley, *Reply to Hooper*, in *Writings of Bradford*, ed. A. Townsend (Cambridge, 1853), p. 375.

80. For a further and more recent discussion of the relation of the term adiaphoron to the notion of "things permitted" see: Wolfgang Trillhaas, "Adiaphoron, Erneute Erwägungen eines alten Begriffs," *Theologische Literaturzeitung* 79 (1954), 457–62; W. Trillhaas, *Ethik* (Berlin, 1959), pp. 63–71; N.H. Søe, *Christliche Ethik* (Munich, 1965), pp. 150–56; Paul Althaus, *Grundriss der Ethik* (Gütersloh, 1953), p. 84: Dietrich Bonhoeffer, *Ethics*, trans. N.H. Smith (New York, 1967), pp. 326–27; F. Lau, "Adiaphora," *Die Religion in Geschichte und Gegenwart*, I, 93–96. See also: I. Kant, *Die Religion innerhalb der Grenzen der blossen Vernunft*, hgb. K. Vorländer (Hamburg, 1956), p. 21; F.E. Schleiermacher, "Grundlinien einer Kritik der bisherigen Sittenlehre," *Werke* (Leipzig, 1910), I, pp. 135–38; Schleiermacher, "Über den Begriff des Erlaubten," *Werke*, I, pp. 417–44.

CHAPTER 3

NEITHER GOOD, NOR COMMANDED

IN A SERMON addressed to their convocation on June 9, 1536, Hugh Latimer called upon his fellow English bishops to prove themselves "children of light," who "put all things in their degree, best highest, next next, the worst lowest, [and] extol things necessary, Christian and commanded of God."[1] Not long thereafter, Sir John Cheke wrote in his *Treatise on Superstition* that in the sweep of Henry VIII's reform program "such things as are great [shall] be reckoned as they are . . . there shall be no confusion of things, but things of different natures shall be distinguished."[2]

Whether the hierarchical arrangement to which Latimer and Cheke here referred was ever achieved during the early stages of the English reformation may be debated, but certainly they were right in pointing to it as an ideal underlying the Henrician program. Above all else, the early English reformers were intent upon restoring a proper balance between the fundamentals and non-fundamentals of the Christian religion.

Central to the realization of such an ideal was a reduction of the ceremonies—in their evaluation primarily, but also to some extent in their number, insofar as the weight attached to the ceremonies naturally influenced their proliferation, and vice versa. And it was out of a concern to effect such a reduction that the English reformers first turned to the theory of adiaphorism. Their primary interest in the term adiaphoron lay, in other words, in the negative reductive connotations it could bring to bear upon the ceremonial matters to which it was applied. Among such connotations are to be noted in the first place those implied by the Erasmian philosophical conception of adiaphora.

Viewed from what he considered the height of Christian perfection, Erasmus' adiaphoristic appraisal of the ceremonies implied above all that ultimately such matters are altogether useless and superfluous. In the final analysis, according to Erasmus, it is only charity which counts, only charity that makes one a Christian, only charity that wins for one salvation. But charity, he said, does not consist in "frequent visits to churches, in numerous prostrations before statues or saints, in the lighting of candles, in repeating a number of designated prayers," or in the performance of any other external ceremony. On the contrary, charity is first and last something "spiritual." Although it must find concrete expression within the external limits set by divine law, it lies ultimately in the interior disposition, and as such transcends the visible, sensible, compound particulars of that external realm to which ceremonies belong. For the Christian who has reached the "end" or the height of perfection, therefore, ceremonies have no meaning. Having advanced "from the body to the spirit, from the visible to the invisible, from the sensible to the intelligible, from the compound to the simple," the mature Christian has altogether outgrown his need for such matters.[3]

For the Christian still on the way toward perfection, this meant that ceremonial matters were not to be considered "ends in themselves." To "stop at" ceremonies, to conceive of them as the "beginning and end of sanctity" or the "sum of religion," to afford them priority over charity, to cling to them as if one's Christian identity depended upon them, or to put one's trust in them as if they held the key to one's salvation, would be "sublime stupidity," Erasmus said. Being adiaphora, ceremonies are at best "what philosophers call imperfect goals," which, as such, may be "used" to further piety and to help one reach the final goal of spiritual union with Christ, but are never to be performed merely for their own sake, or apart from the spirit of love.[4]

Couched in such general terms, this reductive thrust of the Erasmian adiaphoristic appraisal of the ceremonies found its clearest expression during the Henrician period of reform in England in the "25 Injunctions" issued by Thomas Cromwell in 1535. While making no explicit use of the term adiaphoron, the Injunctions cautioned the monks (to whom they were addressed) not to "stick" to their external practices, as though they could thereby perfectly fulfill "the chief and outmost of the whole true religion." "True religion," Cromwell noted, "is not contained in apparel, silence, fasting, uprising in the night, singing and such other kind of ceremonies, but in cleanness of mind, pureness of living, Christ's faith not feigned, and brotherly charity, and true honoring of God in spirit and verity." At best, he said, the external practices "be none other things than as the first letters or principles, and certain introductions to true Christianity," and were "instituted and begun that [Christians] being first exercised in those [external practices], in process of time might ascend to those as by certain steps, that is to say, to the chief point and end of religion." Performance of the ceremonies holds no promise of "reward" at all, Cromwell concluded, except that it be referred beyond itself to Christ.[5]

As such remarks make clear, and as will be further elucidated in a subsequent chapter, the Erasmian appraisal of the ceremonies along adiaphoristic lines did not preclude their conception or use as "means" to some higher end. But it certainly did imply that such matters are "not necessary to salvation."

The latter expression was applied repeatedly by the English reformers to those matters they designated adiaphora. It was an expression, however, that admitted of a variety of interpretations, not all of which were deducible from a purely Erasmian adiaphoristic frame of reference.

In the first place, to say that something is "not necessary to salvation" could have meant that such a matter was lacking in what theologians today call a "necessity of means." This would have meant, in turn, that such a matter lacked an essential, intrinsic relation to salvation, and that its performance or omission could not, therefore, in itself and apart from any positive legislation in its regard, have any essential bearing upon whether or not one is eventually saved. The Erasmians clearly meant to imply as much about those matters they designated adiaphora. That they did, need hardly have caused the Roman party any alarm. For no medieval theologian had ever ascribed to any external ceremonies, except for the most important sacramental rites, a necessity of means. And, in theory at least, the Roman party was no less concerned over the correction of superstitious beliefs than were the Erasmians.

To say that something is "not necessary to salvation" could also have meant, however, that such a matter lacked a "necessity of precept," or, in other words, a necessity arising out of a positive will of the superior or legislator. To have challenged the necessity of the traditional ceremonies in such a sense would have struck at the very heart of the ceremonial system of the medieval church, for, as has been seen, that system had been erected to a very great extent upon the assumption that church and civil officials enjoy jurisdiction over men's consciences.

Erasmus' position on this question, as on so many others, was rather ambivalent. In the first place, he clearly recognized the right of church and civil authorities to oblige their subjects to obedience of their legislation. When the butcher in his colloquy *Ichtuophagia* asks "wherein the force of obligation in human laws lies," Erasmus has the fishmonger reply: "In the words of St. Paul, '"Be obedient to those that are set over you'" (Rom. 13:1). "On this basis," then, the butcher concludes, "the ordinance of a bishop or a magistrate binds all the people." Consistent with traditional doctrine, the fishmonger replies, "Yes, so long as they are just and lawfully made."[6]

In a 1522 letter to the theologians of Louvain, however, Erasmus noted that the plight of Christians is indeed a hard one if any and every episcopal regulation binds under pain of damnation, the implication being that many do not. Which episcopal ordinances do or do not so bind might best be determined, Erasmus told the Louvain theologians, by the Pope. But in his *Ichtuophagia*, Erasmus has the fishmonger suggest that "it does not lie within the legislator's power to determine to what extent a law should be binding." "The legislator has the prerogative of making the law," the fishmonger concludes, "but how far it does or does not oblige must be left up to God." Here Erasmus would appear to be suggesting that Christians would do best not to worry about the whole question, and that, in fact, is exactly what he concluded in his *Spongia adversus aspergines Hutteni* when he included the question "whether episcopal ordinances can bind under mortal sin" among those many matters that are to be considered non-essential to Christian faith.[7]

At another point in his *Ichtuophagia*, however, Erasmus suggested yet another line of approach to the question. He draws a distinction between the "obligation" and the "manner of obligation" of a law, and has the butcher conclude that "the manner of the obligation is not so much to be derived from the legislator as from the law's content or matter."[8] The butcher makes this assertion in reference to the cessation of the obligation of certain laws, divine included, in cases of "necessity." But its emphasis upon the law's content also suggests something of the more general attitude taken by Erasmus toward human laws and their obligation within the context of the spiritualistic thrust of his adiaphorism.

As has been seen, underlying Erasmus' adiaphorism was the conviction that the Christian religion is primarily a spiritual affair, consisting before all else of an interior disposition of charity whereby the Christian tries to make the "mind of Christ" his own. Expanding on the traditional notion of epiky, Erasmus suggested that it is precisely this "mind of Christ" which must be sought out in all human laws, and made the criterion for determining to what extent one or another human law is binding.[9] In his *Ichtuophagia*, however, Erasmus has the butcher suggest that "for the most part human laws concern corporal matters,"[10] implying thereby that on the whole human laws only very remotely inculcate the "mind of Christ." In his *Ratio verae*

Theologiae, Erasmus noted that this is even more so the case with civil laws than with church laws, for even the "grossest content of papal constitutions," he said, approaches more closely to the "purity of Christ" than does the "most divine" content of the Emperor's or magistrate's laws, since the latter deal only with the most profane affairs, and have the effect of making man "not good, but only less bad."[11] Given their "corporal" content, human laws are at best, Erasmus has his "butcher" say, "the schoolmasters of piety."[12] Their content being generally adiaphoristic in nature, they can help to put or keep one in the "mind of Christ" by checking or restraining one's external conduct, but they are not to be considered ends in themselves, as if obedience of them has any value at all apart from their reference beyond themselves to the higher, spiritual goal of Christian life. Hence, apparently, the impression sometimes left by Erasmus that it would suffice for Christians to think of human laws as binding only in the sense of "counsels."[13] Hence also and especially the conclusion drawn by Erasmus' "butcher" that "mature" Christians need feel no greater obligation to observe human laws than is necessary to avoid scandalizing the "weak."[14]

In a letter to Paul Volz, Erasmus warned in this latter regard that mature Christians must take care lest their exercise of liberty become a pretext for "sensuality." But he also cautioned "those in power" not to be alarmed by the mature Christian's show of liberty, for no good father, Erasmus concluded, should ever want his children always to remain infants.[15]

While Erasmian adiaphorism did not, therefore, imply an outright rejection of the traditional view regarding the necessity and obligation of human laws, it certainly did tend to undermine the same, and its influence during the early stages of the English Reformation was undoubtedly felt along such lines also. As noted, however, the English brand of adiaphorism was not exclusively or even primarily of an Erasmian sort, being rather more theological in its thrust. And it remains now to be seen whether and to what extent the English reformers called into question the binding force of human laws by way also of their adiaphoristic appraisal of the ceremonies along theological lines.

The very definition of adiaphora along theological lines as those things which had been "neither commanded, nor forbidden" by Scripture, implied that so far at least as the immediate will of God was concerned such matters were lacking in any necessity of means or precept, and to that extent could not, in themselves and apart from any legislation in their regard by church or civil officials, be considered necessary to salvation. But, of course, the heart of the matter lay elsewhere. The more critical question was whether things which by theological definition were adiaphora and "not necessary to salvation" might upon legislation by church or civil officials lose their adiaphoristic character and become necessary to salvation by at least a necessity of precept.

Some early English reformers would seem to have thought that they could not. In his 1534 *Supplication* to Henry VIII, Robert Barnes, for example, wrote:

> All lerned men, that ever wrote, dothe grante that there be two maner of thynges in this world. Some be called *Res necessarie,* thynges that be necessary, and must be done, because that God has commanded them. And these thynges no man is able to make indifferent, so they must nedes be necessarily done. Other thynges there be, whiche learned men calleth, *Res medie,* thynges that be indifferent, and these may be done, and may be lefte without synne. Nowe is the nature of these, contrary to the other, for they cannot, nor may not be changed into thynges necessary. For that is against theyr nature as S. Paule declareth to the Romans, and in other diverse places... Wherefore it standeth with no lernynge, that mans lawe should change the nature of this thynge [virginity] and make it unto any man a thynge necessary, where as after Gods commandment, it is a thynge but indifferent. For that were as moche, as bothe to change Gods ordinance, and also the nature of the thynge. The whiche standeth with no lernyng. For as the Pope, and all the world cannot make of Gods commandment a counsell, no more can they of Gods counsell make a precept.[16]

But other English reformers would seem to have thought otherwise. Notwithstanding G.R. Elton's contention that Thomas Starkey's *An Exhortation to Unity and Obedience* contained "remarkably little about the obedience dutifully mentioned in the title,"[17] Starkey, in fact, was so emphatic about the obedience due the "common authority's" legislation of adiaphoristic matters that he concluded that "suche thynges as by their owne nature be indifferent, are made thereby [i.e., by their legislation] to our salvation necessary," and "binding under peine of damnation."[18]

Given the apparent contradiction between the views expressed here by Barnes and Starkey, one might be inclined to conclude that the English reformers reached no agreement on the question at hand. It should be noted, however, that while Barnes' assertion was made in reference to the authority of *church* officials over an adiaphoristic matter of a primarily *ecclesiastical* sort (i.e., clerical celibacy), Starkey's concerned the jurisdiction of *civil* officials—the King and Parliament, over adiaphora in general, civil as well as ecclesiastical. Perhaps, in the light of such distinctions, their views will prove less at odds than they might at first blush seem to be. In any event, such distinctions suggest that to appreciate the answer of Barnes, Starkey, and other English reformers to the question about whether adiaphora can become necessary to salvation and binding in conscience by virtue of human legislation in their regard, several lines of inquiry will have to be pursued. For what the English reformers concluded about the legislation of adiaphora by church officials need not necessarily have concurred with their conclusions about such legislation by civil officials, and what they thought of the latter's legislation of adiaphoristic matters pertaining to the secular order could very well have differed from their thoughts on the King's and Parliament's legislation of ecclesiastical adiaphora. Needless to say, the mixture of the secular and spiritual powers, or the combination of civil and ecclesiastical jurisdiction within one person, as it still prevailed in the sixteenth century, will render our inquiry of such matters all the more complex.

To start with, some notice should be taken of the fact that throughout the late middle ages there had been a growing tendency to challenge the binding force in conscience of all purely human laws—civil as well as ecclesiastical, but especially the latter.

It will be recalled from the first chapter that according to Thomas Aquinas and most high medieval theologians disobedience of human authorities was mortally sinful. In making such an assertion, Thomas understood disobedience in the sense of "contempt" of the law, and did not therefore mean that any and every transgression of a human law was a mortal sin.[19] Furthermore, it is to be noted that Thomas' assertion referred to the "precepts" of superiors; "not everything contained in the law," he said elsewhere, "is handed down through the manner of precept." Some things found in the law "are proposed through the manner of a certain ordinance or statute obliging to a definite penalty." And not all these "ordinances" or "statutes," Thomas concluded, bind under mortal sin.[20]

By these non-preceptive contents of the law, Thomas probably had in mind the sort of directives or constitutions issued in 1236 by the General Chapter of his Dominican Order with the proviso that they were to oblige "not *ad culpam,* but *ad poenam,* unless on account of precept or contempt."[21] Some ten years after Thomas' death, Henry of Ghent would conclude a discussion of the reasonableness of penal laws in religious orders with the assertion that "it is also thus with the statutes of princes and prelates in similar cases."[22] And in 1355, the

Provincial Council of Toledo would extend the concept of a purely penal law into the realm of ecclesiastical legislation, by declaring:

> Lest they be burdened with the weight of guilt through the violation of the provincial constitutions, the faithful, upon whom the divine compassion has deigned mercifully to impose a sweet yoke and a lighter burden, we, with the approval of this Council, ordain that the provincial constitutions of our predecessors, and those which will be established in the future—unless expressly stated in the constitutions to be established—oblige not as regards the guilt but only as regards the penalty.[23]

Some have suggested that Thomas himself favored such an extension of a purely penal law theory into the realm of civil and ecclesiastical law.[24] But if he did, it would only have been in the sense that he perceived certain ordinances or statutes as not really being laws, for where it was a question of genuine human laws, Thomas left little doubt but that, so long as they are just, human laws impose upon man an obligation in conscience.[25]

Underlying this Thomistic conclusion was the long historical development which led both church and civil officials to conceive of themselves as acting *in loco Dei,* promulgating a law which itself was defined primarily in terms of its expression of the divine will. Within such a frame of reference, the fear of earthly punishment was viewed as merely an instrument of the law, and not as being a constitutive element of the law itself. The latter was rather to be located in the law's obligation in conscience.

The broadest assault upon such an understanding of human law came from Marsilius of Padua. As Alan Gewirth has pointed out,[26] Marsilius completely reversed Thomas' conception of law, defining it not so much in terms of the ethical quality of its content, as in terms of its "coerciveness." On such terms, Marsilius added, the Gospel cannot, properly speaking, be called a "law." Nor may its advocates [the clergy] be called "judges." According to Marsilius, in other words, genuine law falls altogether outside the purview of clercial jurisdiction. Unless they enjoy the sanction of civil authorities, therefore, episcopal regulations touching upon external matters are altogether impotent. Civil legislation, on the other hand, is genuine law. It carries "force" because it arises out of the will of the people and incarnates, so to speak, popular wrath. It is also binding in conscience, at least in the sense that the people's governance of their earthly affairs is in accordance with God's own will as expressed in Scripture.[27]

Another challenge to the Thomistic high medieval conception of the binding force of human law came from William of Ockham. To be sure, some Nominalists, like Gabriel Biel, will be seen to have been no less vigorous in championing the prerogative of human authorities to bind their subjects in conscience than were the Thomists. All the same, Ockham's sharp differentiation of God's *potentia absoluta* and *potentia ordinata*[28] did weaken considerably the assumption based upon the high medieval synthesis of faith and reason that a just or "reasonable" human law was automatically in accord with the divine will. As expounded by some Nominalists, this came to mean that the only assurance one could have ultimately that a human law was binding in conscience was the fact that it had in one or another way been "revealed" by divine positive law.

To some extent, such a conclusion had already been anticipated by Durandus of St. Pourcain (1275–1334). In his commentary on Lombard's *Sentences,* Durandus concluded that no one makes himself worthy of damnation except insofar as he sins against the Eternal or the Evangelical Law.[29] The late medieval theologian Jacques Almain (1480–1515) understood Durandus to have meant thereby that a purely human law cannot bind *sub gravi.*[30] Perhaps, as Josef Schneider has claimed, Almain read too much into Durandus' assertions.[31] But at the very least Durandus brought into focus the need to locate the obligation of human law within the perspective of divine revelation, and to that extent pointed ahead to the position on this question later embraced by the Nominalist theologian, Jean Gerson.

As noted earlier, Gerson was of the opinion that the canon lawyers of his day had made "of the light yoke of Christ and the law of liberty an iron yoke and heavy burden pressing upon the necks of Christians," by trying to have all their own laws and regulations accepted as the precepts of divine law.[32] To relieve Christians from this impossible burden, he proposed to bring into clear focus "that law, the transgression of which removes the spiritual life afforded by Baptism and renders a man worthy of eternal death."[33] A purely human law, he said, cannot carry such weight.[34] What is said of the Religious Rules—namely, that they do not as such bind under pain of eternal damnation, but only to the penalty attached to them—ought to be axiomatic for all purely human laws, Gerson concluded.[35] Only the divine law can bind *sub gravi.* Since God alone has the power to infuse grace, he alone has the power to remove it. No one, therefore, will lose grace, or bring upon himself the guilt of eternal damnation, except to the extent that he has transgressed a precept of divine law. Thus, the omission of canonical hours, the transgression of church fasts, or the breaking of any other ecclesiastical statute, regulation, or canon, is never a mortal sin, except insofar as the same may be shown to have offended divine law. The prelates of the church have no more power to bind their subjects to something not contained in the Evangelical rule professed by all Christians than have abbots to bind religious beyond their own professed Rule. According to Gerson, then, the prelates and canon lawyers have no right simply to assume that their laws are binding in conscience. Indeed, if there is any doubt as to whether one or another law enjoys the sanction of divine law, one must assume, Gerson said, that it does not, for one has no right to make sport over the danger of sin.[36]

The question remains, however, about how, according to Gerson, one is to determine whether or not this or that particular precept belongs to divine law. In general, Gerson said that for a human precept to qualify as belonging to divine law, it must be shown to have been in one manner or another specially revealed and given to believe for the sake of attaining the goal of beatitude.[37] In itself, this general criterion would seem a rather difficult one to meet, locating as it does the essence of divine law in its "necessity to salvation," and not merely in its "revelation."[38] And one would think, therefore, that Gerson would have rejected the obligation *sub gravi* of most of the church laws obtaining in his time. But in his explanation of the above criterion Gerson distinguished so many ways in which it might be met,[39] that there actually remained few laws which could not be shown to contain at least something of the divine law.[40] And, as a matter of fact, Gerson himself continued to insist that the traditional laws concerning fasting, abstinence, the annual confession, the Sunday Mass, the Breviary, the prohibition of communion under both species, and so forth, were all binding *sub gravi*.[41] For all that, however, his argument that purely human laws cannot oblige *sub gravi* remained significant, in that it required of church officials that they at least subordinate their laws to the divine will, and to the extent that it established a principle which in the hands of one less ready to see in existing church rules a connection with divine law could very easily become a major force of reform. Furthermore, although Gerson himself only seldom used the term adiaphoron, his contention that only divine law can oblige *sub gravi* closely paralleled and undoubtedly added momentum to the view that adiaphora, theologically conceived as those things "neither commanded, nor forbidden" by divine law, are not binding in conscience.

The most vehement assault upon the high medieval view that human laws bind in conscience, and the one feeding most directly into the mitigation of that view along theologically adiaphoristic lines, was the insistence by the likes of Wyclif, Hus, and Gansfort upon the sufficiency of Scripture. Gerson had also championed the sufficiency of Scripture for all that was "necessary to salvation," but somehow included therein, he said, is also that "extrascriptural revelation given to the apostles and handed down by them to the church."[42] This was one reason why, for all its theoretical significance, Gerson's emphasis upon the distinction between divine and human law lost much of its bite when applied concretely. For, if one or another ceremony or law could be shown to belong to "extrascriptural revelation," it could thereby claim some share in the divine law, and therefore also enjoy the binding force of divine law. Wyclif, Hus, and Gansfort, however, understood the sufficiency of Scripture in a far stricter sense. As Heiko Oberman has noted, their *sola scriptura* doctrine did not exclude Tradition "understood as the ongoing interpretation of Scripture,"[43] but it certainly did imply that the law of God as revealed in Scripture is alone sufficient for the determination of those matters necessary to salvation.

"All law and all ethics are in Holy Scripture," Wyclif wrote.[44] To say "that Holy Writ is not sufficient to rule Holy Church," would amount to saying that Christ's law is not complete, and that, Wyclif argued, would be "to put a foul heresy on Christ."[45] "Let us look, then," he said, "and see what is enjoined and commanded

> by the Lord, in the law of perfect liberty, and observe it, and abstain from what is forbidden, and from giving attention to laws newly ordained, and this will be enough. Accordingly, what is over and above, is not only evil in its origin, but is itself evil, and blinds numbers."[46]

It was undoubtedly a passage such as this that inspired the biblical reductionism of the Lollards. But Wyclif himself had prefaced the same passage with the remark that "if the injunctions of Scripture are attended to, it follows that the man who lives to the end the life so prescribed, will be saved." The operative phrase here was: "will be saved." When, therefore, Wyclif spoke of that which is added "over and above" the commands and prohibitions of Scriptures as being "evil," he meant simply that Scripture is entirely sufficient as regards those things which are "necessary to salvation," and that anything commanded or prohibited over and above the Scriptural injunctions as "necessary to salvation" is to that extent "evil." If, therefore, a law like the one requiring auricular confession was intended to bind Christian consciences as "necessary to salvation," it is "evil," for "no one can believe that a man may not be saved without confession of this kind, because otherwise, all the dead from Christ's ascension to the time of Innocent III are lost—a horrible thing to believe."[47]

Wyclif, it should be noted, did not call practices like auricular confession adiaphora. But, it is clear from the above that he did conceive of them as "not being necessary to salvation" because they were "neither commanded, nor forbidden" by Scripture, and such precisely were the terms in which most subsequent adiaphorists would theologically define adiaphora.

With Jan Hus, the question of the binding force of church laws was linked still more clearly with their adiaphoristic character. On February 6, 1413, eight members of the theological faculty of the University of Prague issued a *Consilium* claiming that the cause of dissension among the people of Bohemia was the fact that the Hussite reform party refused to accept what the rest of the Czech clergy held as manifest truth. After contrasting the views of "the majority" and the reform party over such matters as the primacy of Rome and the place of Scripture, the *Consilium* went on to state:

> The clerical community in the kingdom of Bohemia, along with the whole community of the clergy in the world and of the entire Christendom, has held and faithfully believed as the Roman Church does and not otherwise, that according to the evangelical and apostolic doctrine as well as that of the holy doctors, the inferiors must be obedient to the Apostolic See, the Roman Church, and the prelates in all things whatsoever, where they do not prohibit anything purely good or prescribe anything purely evil, but the intermediate . . .[48]

In support of this opinion, the *Consilium* cited St. Bernard's letter to the monk Adam,[49] in which Bernard had stated that in matters indifferent the subject never has the right to oppose his own will to the commands of his superiors.[50] The *Consilium* then charged the reform party with agitation for the opposite opinion,[51] as indeed was the case.

To determine what obedience the subject owes his superior in things indifferent, Hus said, a variety of factors, like the reasonableness of that which is comanded,[52] the time and place the command is supposed to be fulfilled, and the capacity of the subject to perform that which is commanded, must be taken into account.[53] Most of all, however, consideration must be given to the person issuing the command. Only God, Hus said, is beyond erring, and Christians therefore ought to be "on guard lest it be thought that if the Roman pontiff or a prelate commands anything whatsoever, it is to be done as though it were a mandate of God." God's law as revealed in Christ and the Scripture is sufficient, and is in no essential need of papal law. Thus, it would be foolish, Hus said, to think that inferiors are bound to obey under pain of mortal sin their prelates' legislation of adiaphora.[54] Worldly pos-

sessions and marriage, for example, are things indifferent in themselves, but no Roman pontiff, Hus concluded, may command under
pain of mortal sin that one or another of his subjects marry or not hold
private property.[55]

Wessel Gansfort was equally explicit in asserting that ecclesiastical
legislation of adiaphora cannot be made binding *sub gravi* in conscience. If the statutes of the church are received as though they were
God's commandments, Gansfort wrote, "the yoke of the Gospel would
be heavier than the yoke of the Law." But Christ himself had warned
against affording too much authority to church laws by asking the
Pharisees why they broke the commandments of God to cling to their
traditions. The Christian, then, must pay close heed to the nature of
the command given by a superior. If the command is in "accordance
with Christ," then the command must be heeded "as though Wisdom
herself were speaking." He was quick to add, however, that "they [the
prelates] are not simply to be heeded on account of their pastoral
authority." That the pope or council commands something essential
to the inner law adds nothing to its obligatory character, for the Christian "is sufficiently bound by God's command and there is no need for
any greater obligation."[56]

As for the commands of church authorities regarding adiaphora,
Gansfort stated quite flatly that these cannot bind Christians under
pain of mortal sin: "hence in indifferent matters the faithful are not
made liable to a sin unto death solely because it pleases the pope."[57]
Christians are "servants of God, not of the pope," Gansfort insisted,
and therefore, while they are bound in conscience to obey papal commands when these are "in harmony with Moses," whatsoever popes
say "beyond or against this is not especially binding upon the faithful
against the law of perfect liberty."[58]

The late medieval theologians whose views have been outlined in
the preceding brief survey did not, of course, necessarily reflect the
official or even the predominant position of the Roman church on such
matters. Many, in fact, came into open conflict with church authorities. And few, if any of them ever enjoyed the stature of Gabriel
Biel. But Biel, notwithstanding his Nominalist bent and association
with the Brethren of the Common Life, evidenced little sympathy for
either the adiaphorism or the depreciation of human laws advocated by
the likes of Gerson and Gansfort. Biel admitted that the definitions and
precepts of the supreme pontiff bind no one, if they are issued against
canonical Scripture or divine law.[59] But for Biel, this was largely a
hypothetical case.[60] Furthermore, it was his opinion that before rejecting the papal decrees, one must be certain that the pope is in error; if

only doubt exists, obedience must be given. As a general rule, Biel stated that all the faithful are subject to the rule of the pope "and bound for their salvation to follow his voice as that of the true shepherd and to obey his precepts and commands." Admitting, for example, that the celebration of the Eucharist could be essentially completed without all the ceremonial laws being heeded, he insisted all the same that anyone contemptuously or knowingly disobeying them undoubtedly sins mortally.[61]

Now and then during the first half of the sixteenth century one or another theologian from the Roman party could be heard questioning the traditional view on the obligation in conscience of human laws. A Franciscan monk by the name of Alfonso de Castro, for example, was at work on a "purely penal" conception of civil law.[62] Another Franciscan, Kasper Schatzgeyer, voiced agreement with Gerson's opinion that purely human laws cannot oblige in conscience, and had in mind thereby to question especially the binding force of church laws.[63] Even so eminent a figure as Cardinal Cajetan at one point called for the relaxation of the *sub gravi* obligation of some church laws.[64] But such views were exceptional on the Roman side, and most theologians continued to assert that church laws can, often do, and generally should bind the Christian under pain of mortal sin.[65] Similarly, while some sixteenth-century Roman theologians were inclined to argue, albeit rather confusedly at times, that Scripture contains all that is "necessary to salvation,"[66] their point of view was not the predominant one, and according to Yves Congar, "was not shared by the majority of the [Tridentine] Fathers."[67] Many Roman theologians continued to subscribe to the notion of "unwritten traditions,"[68] and to conceive of Tradition itself as being a separate but equal source of revelation alongside Scripture,[69] so that even though one or another ceremony enjoyed no sanction in Scripture it could still be said to be an "invention of the Holy Spirit," and to that extent "necessary to salvation."[70]

As has already been seen, Erasmus was inclined within the context of his adiaphoristic views to challenge the binding force of church laws, and even more that of civil laws. By contrast, most sixteenth-century Protestant reformers, both Continental and English, ascribed a stricter obligation to civil laws than to church laws. Almost all the Continental reformers appealed to Romans 13:5 to insist that Christians are obliged to obey just civil laws not only for fear of punishment but also for conscience's sake.[71] Only Calvin challenged this traditional interpretation of Pauline doctrine. Calvin admitted that Romans 13:5 would seem to imply that "consciences are also bound by civil laws." But were that actually the case, he said, it would follow that church laws also bind under conscience—a conclusion which Calvin, of course, would not admit. To solve this problem, Calvin suggested that a distinction be drawn between "genus and species," and concluded therefrom that while the Christian is bound by God's general command to respect civil authority, and must strive to fulfill the "general purpose" or "ends" of civil legislation, he is not bound in conscience to obey the specific laws promulgated by the secular authorities.[72]

Calvin included this interpretation of Romans 13:5 in only the later editions of his *Institutes*,[73] and apparently none of the earlier English reformers were aware of it. The Pauline passage itself, however, was cited time and again by the latter to the effect that just civil laws are to be obeyed not only *"propter iram,* but also *propter conscientiam."*[74] Such citations of Romans 13:5 were generally made by the English reformers, and for that matter by most of the Continental reformers also, without any qualifications being added about the intention of the lawgiver or the gravity of the matter covered by civil legislation.[75] In the case of Hooper and other "puritans," this may have been due to the assumption that adiaphoristic matters are altogether beyond legislation.[76] But such an assumption was certainly not shared by the majority of English reformers, and the impression one is left with in their regard, therefore, is that civil legislation was considered binding in conscience, albeit not necessarily *sub gravi,* even when it dealt with adiaphora, or at least those adiaphoristic matters which were of a purely secular nature.[77] Some English reformers even contended that civil legislation of ecclesiastical adiaphora is binding *sub gravi* in conscience. Stephen Gardiner, for example, argued against Martin Bucer at their Ratisbon encounter in 1541, that "by me mariage of prestes was no sin before God til the Kingis Majesti made it sin before God."[78] Perhaps Starkey's blunt assertion that the legislation by the "common authority" of adiaphora converted the latter into things necessary to salvation was also intended to apply to the civil legislation of ecclesiastical adiaphora. But if Starkey did share Gardiner's view, few other English, or Continental, reformers did.[79]

As a matter of fact, the civil officials of the English church themselves went out of their way to point out that their legislation of ecclesiastical adiaphora was not binding in conscience or necessary to salvation.

Henry VIII's own Preface to the Ten Articles made a special point of noting that while the first five articles concern matters "such as be commanded expressly by God, and be necessary to our salvation," the last five are to be obeyed for the sake of decorum, although they be not expressly commanded of God, nor necessary to our salvation."[80] Cromwell's "Injunctions to the Clergy," issued shortly after promulgation of the Ten Articles, made the same point, and advised the clergy to explain the Ten Articles to their parishioners in such wise "that they maye playnly knowe and discerne, which of the said articles be necessarie for their salvation, and which of the same doo but concerne the decent and politique order of the said church."[81] After Cranmer reported to Henry VIII that "the prior of the black-friars at Canterbury" continued to preach "that the laws of the church be equal with God's laws,"[82] and other rumors of discontent over the Ten Articles reached the King, Henry wrote a letter to the bishops, reminding them once again that they were "in no wise contentiously to treat of matters indifferent, which be neither necessary to our salvation . . . nor yet to be in any wise contemned."[83]

Finally, it may be noted that the Forty-Two Articles, which bring the period under discussion to a climax, declared that anyone "willingly and openly" breaking those "traditions and ceremonies of the Church" which are not contrary to Scripture and have been approved by the common authority, "ought to be rebuked openlie (that other maie feare to doe the like) as one that offendeth against the common ordre of the churche, and hurteth the auctoritie of the Magistrate."[84] Especially noteworthy about this passage is first of all its rebuke of "open" and "contemptious" disobedience while saying nothing about the sort of "secret" disregard of some such laws evidenced by Cranmer and others in their clandestine marriages. Once again, it is offense to the common order and not disobedience of particular laws as such, that seems to be the central concern. It is also noteworthy that nothing is said about any obligation in conscience to heed the traditional ceremonies, although Article 38 reiterates Romans 13:5 in respect to obedience of magistrates in general.[85] All that is said is that those who break the ceremonies ought to be rebuked so that others may "fear" to do likewise—language which would suggest that the laws in question were considered purely "penal" in character.

The preceding assertions from the Henrician and Edwardine periods need not have implied that civil officials could not, if they so desired, make their legislation of ecclesiastical adiaphora binding in conscience. But even if they had, it is doubtful that many English reformers would have accepted the civil laws on such terms. Otherwise, it would certainly be hard to explain how Thomas Cranmer, the Archbishop of Canterbury, and other Englishmen could enter clandestine marriages, even though they knew very well that they were acting all the while contrary to a law of the land which Henry VIII himself thought enjoyed divine sanction.[86]

In the final analysis, however, it must be admitted that the reformers' response to this whole question of the binding force of civil law, and especially as it touched upon adiaphoristic matters, left much to be desired so far as clarity was concerned. More often than not their assertions in the latter regard were made within a context that mingled a discussion of secular and spiritual authority to such an extent that it is almost impossible to determine at any given point whether it is civil or ecclesiastical laws, or both, that are under discussion. The confusion resulting therefrom was, of course, simply a reflection of the concrete state of affairs obtaining in the relationship of the church and state at the time in England and throughout Christendom.[87]

In any event, whatever the Continental and English reformers thought about the binding force of civil legislation of adiaphora, they clearly were of the opinion that the legislation of adiaphora by the pope, the bishops, or any spiritual authorities, acting either alone or in unison, cannot be considered binding in conscience or necessary to salvation.

Luther had based his opinion in this regard to some extent upon the conclusion that while secular government enjoys a genuine *potestas* or jurisdiction, ecclesiastical government does not—its operation resting instead solely upon the love, equality, and freedom of all believers.[88] A similar rationale may be detected in the writing of some early English reformers also.[89] But to judge from the *Bishops' Book,* most English bishops themselves thought otherwise,[90] and their reason, as well as that of other English and Continental reformers, for concluding that ecclesiastical laws are not binding in conscience or necessary to salvation arose principally out of the conviction that the content of such laws, being adiaphoristic, lacked the sanction of Scripture, which is entirely sufficient for the determination of what is or is not necessary to salvation.[91]

Having argued for the prerogative of bishops to make laws for the church, the *Bishops' Book* went on to say that in as much as the content of such laws consists mostly "of such things as be of themselves but mean and indifferent things," no other obedience is to be expected in their regard than that men "may lawfully omit or do otherwise than is prescribed by the said laws and jurisdiction, " so long as they do so without contempt, have a good reason for doing so, and cause no scandal thereby to their neighbor. Failure to recognize this Christian liberty over against church laws explains why in the past, the *Bishops' Book* concluded, some Christians had developed greater "scruples in conscience" over the non-observance of "men's traditions" than over obedience of God's own commands.[92] The section of the *Bishops' Book* containing these remarks was omitted from the *King's Book*.[93] This omission was undoubtedly prompted by Henry VIII himself, not because he thought the bishops had been too humble in the estimation of their own authority, but just the opposite. As his marginal comments on the *Bishops' Book* suggest, the King was reluctant to grant the bishops any jurisdictional authority at all.[94] If anything, therefore, the omission from the *King's Book* represented a still further diminution of episcopal legislative authority. Furthermore, the *King's Book* does include a vehement protest against the papalists' claim that "whosoever disobeyeth or transgresseth . . . certain laws and ordinances of the church of Rome . . . committeth deadly sin,"[95] and one might well surmise therefrom that the bishops had in mind to imply that the laws of any "particular" church touching upon ceremonial matters must be viewed as less than binding *sub gravi*.

The 1549 *Prayer Book* noted that "the breaking of a common order and discipline is no small offense before God." But it added also that "the keeping or omitting of a ceremony (in itself considered) is but a small thing," the implication being that when no offense is done to the community, disobedience of one or another law dealing with adiaphoristic matter is not sinful.[96]

Article Five of the 42 Articles of 1553 once again reasserted the view that "Holie Scripture containeth all things necessarie to salvation," and that whatever is not contained therein may not be reputed as "requisite to the necessitie of salvation," even though it may be "profitable for an ordre, and comelinesse." Consistent with the same doctrine, Article Twenty-One stated that the Church may not "enforce anything to be believed for necessitie of Salvation" which is "besides Scripture," and Article Twenty-Two asserted that General Councils may not ordain anything as necessary to salvation "onlesse it maie be declared that thei be taken out of holie Scripture."[97]

Notwithstanding such disclaimers by the English bishops of any intention to have their laws received as obligatory under pain of damnation, John Hooper accused the bishops of having made the appointed vestments "things of necessity."[98] But this charge was quickly and with good reason branded by Nicholas Ridley—Hooper's chief antagonist from the episcopal ranks during the 1550 vestiarian controversy—a "slanderous lie!"[99]

In addition to the bishops' own remarks, a host of other English theologians could be cited to the effect that church authorities have no right to make their legislation of adiaphora binding *sub gravi* upon Christian consciences.[100] Typical was Peter Martyr's conclusion that while the church has power to make laws regarding adiaphora, such laws ought not to be made "in such sort . . . that if a man, without offense and contempt, doo not observe them, he sinneth deadly."[101]

Such then, to summarize, were the major negative connotations of the adiaphoristic appraisal of the traditional ceremonies along both philosophical and theological lines by early English reformers. To the extent that the ceremonies were said to be adiaphora, it was generally concluded that they were not to be considered ends in themselves, necessary to salvation, or binding in conscience, not even when legislated by church or civil officials. By bringing such negative connotations into focus, the English adiaphorists hoped to effect a qualitative reduction of the ceremonies in such wise as would restore priority once again to the Gospel and God's own commandments by way of checking the superstitious confusion of values which to their view had arisen out of the so-called "evil of superfluity" plaguing the late medieval church. Such a qualitative reduction of the ceremonies did not, however, negate altogether the value and role of the latter. Because it was pursued along adiaphoristic lines, what negation it implied was always limited and held in balance by the positive connotations of the term adiaphoron, to which we must now turn our attention.

NOTES

1. Hugh Latimer, *Sermons,* p. 48.
2. John Strype, *The Life of Sir John Cheke* (Oxford, 1821), p. 21 f.
3. *Paraphr. in Matt.* 11:30, EO VII, 63; *Enchiridion, EO* V, 35–36; *De Libero Arbitrio, EO* IX, 1222 ff.; "Letter to P. Volz," *EE* III, p. 370; *Enchiridion, EO* V, 27–39; 38–39.
4. *Ibid.,* 25; 34–36; 30–31; *"Letter to Volz,"* EE III, 373; *Ichtuophagia, EO* I, 793.
5. Burnet, *op. cit.,* I, ii, p. 221.
6. *EO* I, 798.
7. *EE* V, p. 93; *EO* VI, 1055; *EO* I, 796; *EO* X, 1663.
8. *EO* I, 796.
9. See Guido Kisch, *Erasmus und die Jurisprudenz seiner Zeit* (Basel, 1960), pp. 108–32; Bainton, *Erasmus,* p. 115.
10. *EO* I, 799.
11. *Ratio seu Compendium verae Theologiae* (Basel, 1519), pp. 27–28, as cited in Kisch, *op. cit.,* p. 129.
12. *EO* I, 799.
13. See, for example, *De Amabili Ecclesiae Concordia, EO* V, 504–5.
14. *EO* I, 799.

15. *EE* III, p. 374; see also: *Ichtuophagia, EO* I, 791.

16. Robert Barnes, *Supplycatyon* (1534) sig. Q, fol. iv(v).

17. G.R. Elton, *Policy and Police* (Cambridge, 1972), p. 194.

18. Starkey, *Exhortation*, sig. B, fol. iv(v); sig. T, fol. ii. Later in the *Exhortation*, Starkey told his countrymen that this obedience to the authorities "shall be to you euer a just defence, whereby you shall auoyde all blame and damnable reprofe, bothe before man here in polycie, and before god hereafter whan you shall comme to counte before his maiestie" (*Ibid.*, sig. Z, fol. ii[v]).

19. *ST* II-II, 105, 1, ad 1.

20. *ST* II-II, 186, 9, ad 2.

21. See Matthew Herron, *The Binding Force of Civil Laws* (Paterson, 1958), p. 34.

22. *Ibid.*

23. As cited in *Ibid.*, p. 35.

24. For a review of some of the arguments concerning the interpretation of Thomistic doctrine for or against the purely penal law theory, see especially: Herron, *op. cit.*, pp. 89–98; D.C. Bayne, *Conscience, Obligation, and the Law* (Chicago, 1966), pp. 79–81; 85–91; E. Dunn, "In Defense of the Penal Law," *TS* 18 (1957), pp. 50–51.

25. See *ST* I-II, 96, 4; I-II, 96, 4, ad 1.

26. A. Gewirth, *Marsilius of Padua, The Defender of Peace* (New York, 1956), I, p. 134.

27. Marsilius, *Defensor Pacis*, I, x, 4; II, ix, 3; I, ix, 5; I, xii, 6; II, ix, 9.

28. *Quodlibet* VI, q. 1; see also: E. Iserloh, *Gnade und Eucharistie in der Philosophischen Theologie des Wilhelm von Ockham* (Wiesbaden, 1956), pp. 67 f.; H. Oberman, *The Harvest of Medieval Theology* (Cambridge, 1963), p. 92 f.; F. Copleston, *op. cit.*, Vol. 3, Part I, p. 117.

29. *In 2. Sent.*, d. 24, q. 5, corp. n.9, as cited in J. Schneider, "Die Verpflichtung Des Menschlichen Gesetzes Nach Johannes Gerson," *ZKTh*, 75 (1953), p. 46.

30. *Ibid.*, pp. 44–45.

31. Taken in the context of Durandus' broader argument that mortal sin can occur only when one is acting with a knowledge of "revealed"—and not merely "natural"—principles, his assertion that no one makes himself worthy of damnation except insofar as he sins against the Eternal or the Evangelical Law, will not mean, Schneider says, that in order to commit a mortal sin, the binding force of the law one breaks must first have been "materially" expressed in revelation, but only that mortal sin is possible once one has formally recognized the obligation of the law in the light of revelation (*Ibid.*). In support of this interpretation, Schneider has shown that as a matter of fact Durandus afforded to human law in itself the power to bind under pain of mortal sin (*Ibid.*, pp. 47–53). Repeatedly, Durandus denied that one or another positive law is binding under pain of mortal sin, but always on the basis that the human lawgiver did not wish to bind *sub gravi*. Thus, for example, he will say that although the church has forbidden the exercise of marital rights during certain holy seasons, the use of those rights at such times is not a mortal sin, because in his opinion the church had no intention of setting a trap for the faithful, which would have been the case had she laid down the prohibition under pain of mortal sin (*In 4 Sent.*, d. 32, q. 1, corp. ns. 4 and 9, as cited in *Ibid.*). Whether, therefore, a human law does or does not bind *sub gravi* will depend, according to Durandus, upon the intention of the lawgiver. And it is clearly his opinion that the church did indeed intend for some of her laws to bind in such wise, as was evidenced by his assertion that as a general rule the church's law of Fast and Abstinence binds under pain of mortal sin (*In 4 Sent.*, d. 15, q. 9, corp. n. 6, in *Ibid.*).

32. *Liber de Vita Spirituali Animae, Opera* III, III, 16.

33. *Ibid.*
34. *Ibid.*, 38. For further discussion of Gerson's position in this regard, see: Schneider, *op. cit.*, pp. 6–12; T.J. Bouquillon, *Theologia Moralis Fundamentalis* (Brugis, 1903), p. 334.
35. *De Vita Spirit. Animae*, 68.
36. *Ibid.*, 37–38; 40; 39; 42.
37. *Ibid.*, 21.
38. See Schneider, *op. cit.*, p. 6.
39. These distinctions are presented and discussed in Schneider, *op. cit.*, pp. 4–25, and in J.B. Morrall, *Gerson and the Great Schism* (Manchester, 1960), pp. 48–51; Louis B. Pascoe, *Jean Gerson, Principles of Chruch Reform* (Leiden, 1973), pp. 50–68.
40. Schneider, *op. cit.*, p. 38.
41. *Ibid.* It should also be noted, however, that there were some laws and ceremonies to which Gerson in fact ascribed no divine connection, and which, therefore, in his view, could not be considered binding *sub gravi* (See *De Vita Spirit. Animae*, 41–42; also: Schneider, *op. cit.*, pp. 20–21).
42. See Oberman, *Harvest*, pp. 385, 387.
43. *Ibid.*, p. 377.
44. *De Veritate Sacrae Scripturae* I, 22, as cited in J. Stacey, *John Wyclif and Reform* (Philadelphia, 1964), p. 80.
45. *De Conversatione Ecclesiasticorum, TT*, p. 21.
46. *Trialogus* IV, *TT*, p. 179.
47. *Ibid.*
48. See Matthew Spinka, *Jan Hus' Concept of the Church* (Princeton, 1966), p. 142, 143; see also Hus, *De Ecclesia*, XVII, p. 148.
49. Hus, *De Ecclesia*, XVII, p. 148.
50. *Ep.* VII, 4: *PL* 182, 95.
51. Hus, *De Ecclesia*, XVII, p. 183.
52. *Ibid.*, XX, p. 186; XXI, pp. 194–206. This would include the reasonableness of asserting the adiaphoristic character of one or another matter commanded. In the concluding two chapters of his *De Ecclesia*, Hus attacked the claim of the Prague theologians that the excommunication, suspension, and interdict brought against him and those harboring him were indifferent matters and therefore supposedly wholly within the prerogative of Rome. Hus retorted that it is absurd to label indifferent, acts whereby the innocent are deprived of the sacraments and Christian burial (*Ibid.*, XXIII, pp. 231–32).
53. *Ibid.*, XXI, pp. 195, 198–99, 202; XX, pp. 186–87; XXI, p. 199.
54. *Ibid.*, XXI, p. 194; XIX, p. 176; XX, p. 188; see also Oberman, *Harvest*, pp. 376, 377.
55. *Ibid.*, XX, pp. 185 f. Hus cites Boniface IX's decree ordering Kings Wenceslaus and Sigismund to resign rule of their respective kingdoms as a blatant example of over-extension of papal authority in things indifferent (*Ibid.*).
56. *De Dignitate et Potestate Ecclesiastica, Opera*, pp. 750, 755; *De Sac. Poenit., Opera*, p. 804.
57. "Unde in rebus neutris... non obligantur fideles peccare mortaliter propter solum beneplacitum Papae" (*De Dign. et Pot. Eccl., Opera*, p. 756).
58. *Ibid.*, p. 760.
59. *Defensorium Obedientiae Apost.*, I, 8, p. 114.
60. *Ibid.*, p. 52.

61. *Ibid.*, I, 9, p. 118; I, 3, p. 86; G. Biel, *Canonis Misse Expositio*, ed. H. Oberman and W.J. Courtenay (Wiesbaden, 1963), pp. 116–17.

62. See Bayne, *op. cit.*, p. 92.

63. Like Gerson, Schatzgeyer argued that human laws can oblige man in conscience only to the extent that they inculcate the divine law (K. Schatzgeyer, *Scrutinium Divinae Scripturae* [1522], c. IX, i, 18 [Münster, 1922], *CC* 5, pp. 126 ff.; see also: H. Klomps, *Kirche, Freiheit und Gesetz bei dem Franziskaner theologen Kaspar Schatzgeyer* [Münster, 1959], pp. 131–68).

64. In 1530, Cajetan recommended that a general decree be issued by the pope "to the effect that the commandments of the church regarding the reception of the sacraments and the feast and fast days were not binding under grave sin" (H. Jedin, *A History of the Council of Trent*, trans. E. Graf [Edinburgh, 1957], I, p. 274). Cajetan's canonist colleague Accolti, however, thought it necessary to warn the pope against granting such a concession to the Protestants (*Ibid.*).

65. See, for example: J. Eck, *Defensio contra Amarulentas D. Andreae Bodenstein Carolstatim invectiones*, ed. J. Greving (Münster, 1919), *CC* I, p. 80; J. Eck, *Enchiridion locorum communium adversus Lutherum et alios hostes Ecclesiae* (Paris, 1559), pp. 122–32; J. Chichtove, *Compendium veritatum* (Paris, 1529), ch. 5–7; J. Cochlaeus, *Drei Schriften gegen Luthers Schmalkaldische Artikel*, ed. P.H. Volz (Münster, 1932), *CC* 18, p. 57; T. More, *Responsio ad Lutherum, The Complete Works of Thomas More*, ed. J.M. Headley (New Haven and London, 1969), p. 424; and the opinion expressed by one Richard Smith in Strype, *Memorials of Thomas Cranmer* (Oxford, 1840), pp. 795–96.

66. Josse Clichtove, for example, wrote that "the Gospel of Christ is indeed sufficient to lead a good life and it contains precepts that suffice to salvation; yet not all things that we have to do to reach salvation are explained in it in all particulars and details" (*Antilutherus*, fol. 29[v], as cited in George Tavard, *Holy Writ or Holy Church* [London, 1959], p. 160).

67. Congar, *Tradition and Traditions*, p. 513.

68. See, for example, B. Latomus, *Zwei Streitschriften gegen M. Bucer*, ed. L. Keil (Münster, 1924), *CC* 8, pp. 106–7; J. Eck, *Enchiridion*, pp. 66–69; J. Cochlaeus, *De authoritate ecclesiae et Scripturae* (n. p., 1524), I., iv, sig. B, fol. 4; I, viii, sig. E, fol. 2; T. More, *Responsio ad Lutherum*, pp. 92, 98, 210, 242; Henry VIII, *Assertio Septem Sacramentorum*, ed. L. O'Donovan (New York, 1908), pp. 279, 357; John Fisher, *Opera Omnia* (Wurzburg, 1957), 132, 385; *The English Works of John Fisher*, ed. J.E.B. Mayor (London, 1876), pp. 333–34; Bishop John Stokesley, as quoted in Alex. Alesius, *Of the Authoritie of the Word of God agaynst the Bishop of London* (London, 1538), sig. B, fol. vi–vi(v). The English reformers' position on this question of "unwritten verities" will be taken up in a subsequent chapter. On the widespread belief in "unwritten traditions" in the early and medieval church, see Congar, *Tradition and Traditions*, pp. 50–54, 87–88; R.P.C. Hanson, *Tradition in the Early Church* (London, 1962), pp. 130–44, 176–86; H. Oberman, *Harvest*, pp. 368 ff.; G. Tavard, *Holy Writ or Holy Church*, pp. 9 ff. Hanson especially emphasizes the fact that in the early church the "unwritten traditions" were viewed as possessing only secondary value (*op. cit.*, pp. 51, 97, 99, 137, 146, 156, 184).

69. Thomas More, for example, wrote: "Sacramenta septem: id reliquos articulos fidei: partim scripto, partim non scripto, sed tamen dei verbo fulciri: utrumque verbum ex aequo verum, ex aequo certum, ex aequo venerabile" (*Responsio ad Lutherum*, p. 242). The so-called *"partim . . . partim"* theory of the relation of Scripture and Tradition to which More here gives expression found strong support at the Council of Trent, but

was by no means "defined" by the Tridentine Fathers (See J.R. Geiselman, *Die Heilige Schrift und die Tradition* [Freiburg, 1962] pp. 111 ff.). Edward Surtz, it may be noted in passing, has tried to exonerate More's colleague, Bishop John Fisher, of this theory (*The Works and Days of John Fisher* [Cambridge, Mass., 1967], pp. 112, 459 n.).

70. See, for example, More, *Responsio ad Lutherum*, p. 372.

71. See Luther's *Lectures on Romans*, LW 25, p. 110; for a further discussion of Luther's political thought, and an extensive bibliography thereupon, see especially: *Luther und die Obrigkeit*, ed. Gunther Wolf (Darmstadt, 1972); F.E. Cranz, *An Essay on the Development of Luther's Thought on Justice, Law and Society*, Harvard Theological Studies, 19 (Cambridge, Mass., 1959), pp. 159–72. Melanchthon's clearest citation of Romans 13:5 to the effect that it is a mortal sin to break civil laws appeared in his 1532 *Commentary on Romans*: ". . . Ergo peccatum mortale est violare edicta magistratuum" (*MW* V, pp. 320–21); see also: *Apol. der Konf., BEK*, p. 308; the 1521 *Loci Communes* (*MW* II/1, p. 159), and similar citations in subsequent editions of the same work. On Melanchthon's political thought in general, see especially: Rolf B. Huschke, *Melanchthons Lehre vom Ordo politicus* (Gütersloh, 1968). For examples of Zwingli's and Bullinger's citations of Romans 13:5 and their comments thereupon, see Zwingli, *De Vera et Falsa Religione* (*SW* III, pp. 884–85), and Bullinger, *A Treatise or Sermon . . . concernynge magistrates and obedience of subjectes* (London, 1549), sig. D, fol. vi(v).

72. *Institutes*, IV, X, 3 and 5; III, xix, 15; IV, X, 5.

73. The 1550 edition of the *Institutes* was the first to include it (*CR*, XXIX, 841).

74. For some examples, see: W. Tyndale, *Obedience of a Christian Man, DT*, p. 174; Robert Barnes, *A Supplication* (1531), sig. O, fol. viii(v)–sig. P, fol. i; Barnes' 1540 recantation sermon: Foxe, *Acts and Monuments*, V, Appendix, No. VII, or Burnet, *op. cit.*, I, ii, pp. 369–71; John Lambert's Reply to the "45 Articles" put to him by Archbishop Warham (Foxe, *Acts and Monuments*, V, pp. 181–83); Thomas Becon, *A New Catechism*, p. 300; T. Becon, *The Fortress of the Faithful* (London, 1550), sig. C, fol. iv(v); *The Bishops' Book*, Lloyd, *op. cit.*, p. 121; *The King's Book*, Lloyd, *op. cit.*, p. 287; John Hooper, *Annotations on Romans XIII, Later Writings of Bishop Hooper* (Cambridge, 1852), pp. 108–9.

75. By contrast, it may be noted, that the anonymous Elizabethan pamphlet entitled *Whether it be mortall sinne to transgresse civil laws* qualified its affirmative answer to that question by quickly noting that "this sentence touching the precepts of magistrates must wisely be understand, namely of those precepts, which byd us not to do against the commandments of God," (Sig. A, fol. iii[v]), and concluding that while such precepts are "made for necessitie," there are others which "are not made so much for necessitie, as for comlyness", and whose binding force can only be determined by looking to "the mynde of the lawmaker" (sig. A, fol. iv).

76. In his remarks concerning Romans 13:5, Hooper seems to imply that the content of civil laws is either in accordance with the word of God and natural law or not, and takes no cognizance of any civil laws touching upon adiaphoristic matters (*Later Writings*, pp. 102–3).

77. Thomas Becon, it may be noted, after citing Romans 13:5 to ground the binding force in conscience of civil law, did caution civil magistrates to "take heed that we clog no man's conscience, nor make that a thing of necessity which is mere voluntary" (*Catechism* p. 300). But his subsequent discussion makes clear that the "voluntary" matters he has in mind are ecclesiastical ceremonies.

78. *The Letters of Stephen Gardiner*, ed. James A. Muller (Cambridge, 1933; Westport, Conn., 1970), p. 491.

79. Typical of the Continental reformers view in this regard was Luther's advice to

George Bucholzer in 1539: "In regard to the things of which you complain, the cowl and surplice in the procession on feast days, and the walking round the churchyard on Sundays and at Easter... this is my advice: If your lord, the Margrave and Elector, allows you to preach the gospel of Christ purely (etc.)... then in God's name go round with them, carrying a silver or gold cross, and cowl or surplice of velvet, silk or linen. And if one of these be not enough, then put on three, as did Aaron... And if your lord the Elector be not satisfied with one procession, then go round seven times... for such things, if not abused, neither add to nor take from the gospel, but they must never be regarded as necessary nor made a matter of conscience" (*Letters of Martin Luther*, sel. and trans. M.A. Currie [London, 1908], pp. 378-79). In his *De Regno* Martin Bucer encouraged Edward VI to work for the restoration of the "discipline of fasting", but warned that "the degree of abstinence... must be freely commited to individual consciences" (*MB*, p. 254), and that it is "anti-Christian to prescribe fasting for Christians as something necessary in itself to salvation" (*MB*, p. 253).

80. Lloyd, *op. cit.*, p. xvi.

81. *Life and Letters of Thomas Cromwell*, ed. R.B. Merriman (Oxford, 1902), p. 29.

82. Cranmer, *Writings and Letters*, p. 327.

83. Burnet, *op. cit.*, I, ii, p. 539.

84. C. Hardwick, *A History of the Articles of Religion* (London, 1852), Appendix III, Article 33, p. 294.

85. *Ibid.*, p. 300.

86. See *Infra*, chapter V, pp. 166-67, and Burnet, *op. cit.*, I, ii, p. 542; P.L. Hughes and J.F. Larkin, *Tudor Royal Proclamations* (New Haven, 1964), I, p. 274.

87. See Franklin Le von Baumer, *The Early Tudor Theory of Kingship* (New York, 1966), pp. 21-84.

88. See especially Luther's letter to Melanchthon, dated July 21, 1530 (*LW* 49, pp. 378-90; *WA*, Br 5, 492-95).

89. See, for example, Edward Fox, *The True dyfferens betwen the regall power and the Ecclesiastical power* (London 1548), sig. F, fol. iii(v). (Fox published a Latin version of this work in 1534).

90. *The Bishops' Book* clearly afforded the bishops not only a *potestas ordinis*, but also a *potestas jurisdictionis*, which included the power "to make and ordain certain rules or canons," so long at least as the King and Parliament consented thereto (Lloyd, *op. cit.*, pp. 107-14).

91. For the Continental reformers' rejection of the *sub gravi* obligation in conscience of church laws along these lines, see especially: "Si quid praeter scripturam statuerint in hoc, ut conscientias obstringant, non sunt audiendi. Nihil enim conscientiam obligat nisi jus divinum... Quidquid enim episcopi praeter scripturam imperant, tyrannis est. Nam imperandi jus non habent... Docendae libertatis gratia violare licet traditiones humanas, ut intelligant imperiti non peccari, etiamsi quid contra traditiones hominum admittunt" (Melanchthon, *Loci*, *MW* II/1, pp. 160-62; see also *Augs. Konf.*, Art. XXVIII, *BEK*, pp. 126-29). Luther made this point in many of his writings (See: *Ep. ad Rom.*, *WA* 56, 494; *Von Menschenlehre zu meiden WA* 10^II^, 76, 87-92; *De Capt. Babyl.*, *WA* 6, 535-36; *Vermahnung an die Geistlichen*, *WA* 30^II^, 347 ff.; *De Servo Arbitrio*, *WA* 18, 624), but one of his most thorough and incisive discussions of the question was the 1539 tract *Von den Konziliis und Kirchen* (*WA* 50, 488-653). After a lengthy discussion of the apostolic council at Jerusalem and the first four ecumenical councils, Luther concluded that "... hat ein Concilium nicht macht, neue Ceremonien den Christen auffzulegen, bei einer todsunde oder bei fahr des gewillens zu halten, als fastage, feiertage, speise, tranck, kleider" (*Ibid.*, 613). See also: Zwingli, *Apol. Arch.*, *SW* I, 305; *Die 67 Art.*, *SW* I,

p. 459; *De Vera et Falsa Religione, SW* III, pp. 895-97; Bullinger, "Letter to Robt. Horne *et al.*, May 3, 1566," as cited in *Whether it be mortall sin to transgress civil laws*, sig. C, fol. iv; Bucer, *Praelectiones ... Ephesios*, as cited in L. Trinterud, *Elizabethan Puritanism*, pp. 90-91; Calvin, *Institutes*, III, XIX, 3, 7, 14-16; IV, X, 3-5, 6, 27, 30, 31.

92. Lloyd, *op. cit.*, pp. 114-15, 115; 115-16.

93. See *Ibid.*, pp. 281-82.

94. For Henry's marginal notes, see Cranmer, *Writings and Letters*, pp. 97-99.

95. Lloyd, *op. cit.*, p. 247.

96. *Two Liturgies*, p. 155.

97. Hardwick, *op. cit.*, p. 256; 278; 278-80.

98. *Writings of Bradford*, pp. 388-90.

99. *Ibid.*, p. 389.

100. William Tyndale's and John Frith's assertions along these lines were usually in reference to doctrinal adiaphora, but they clearly meant the same to apply also to all ceremonial matters that had been "neither commanded, nor forbidden" by Scripture. See: Tyndale, *Answer to More*, pp. 26, 96; *Doctrinal Treatises*, pp. 381, 384; Frith, *An Answer*, pp. 361, 401; Frith, *A Disputation of Purgatory, WER*, pp. 181 ff.; Frith, *The Articles Wherefore John Frith Died, WER*, p. 450. For the denial by other English theologians that church laws can bind *sub gravi*, see especially: Robert Barnes, *Supplication* (1531) (sig. O, fol. viii-sig. R, fol. ii), wherein Barnes expanded on his thesis "that mens constitutions which are not grounded in Scripture, bynde not the conscience of men under the payne of deadly sinne," and concluded that if the bishops "will bynde us into indifferent thinges as unto a thynge of necessitie, then shall we not do it" (sig. R, fol. ii); Barnes, *Supplycatyon* (1534), sig. Q, fol. iv(v); Thomas Starkey, *Exhortation*, sig. M, fol. iv(v); C, i; T, i-T, iii; Thomas Becon, *A New Catechism*, p. 300; John Lambert, in Foxe, *Acts and Monuments* V, pp. 191, 196, 202, 203, 209; Myles Coverdale, *Remains*, pp. 336-38.

101. Martyr, *Commonplaces*, II, p. 172.

CHAPTER 4

NEITHER EVIL, NOR FORBIDDEN

IN FEBRUARY OF 1536, Thomas Cranmer, along with Bishops Nicholas Shaxton and Hugh Latimer, presided over one of the many heresy trials of John Lambert. A certain Thomas Dorset, "having nothyng to doo," happened to be present at the trial and reported that Lambert was charged with the opinion that "it was syn to pray to saintis." Anxious to avoid an open clash with Lambert's conservative accusers, the three bishops tried to get Lambert to moderate his views. They told Lambert, according to Dorset's report, that while they themselves "could not saye that it [praying to saints] was necessari or nedeful," still "he myght nott make syn of it." "Yf he wolde agree to that," Dorset concluded, "he [Lambert] myght have byn goan bye and bye, but he wold nott."[1]

Lambert's obstinacy was typical of the more radical early English reformers, who while endorsing wholeheartedly the adiaphorists' conclusion that certain traditional ceremonies were "not good" and "not commanded," were extremely reluctant to admit that the same ceremonies were also "not evil" and "not prohibited." This reluctance was indicative not so much of an outright rejection of the theory of adiaphorism, as of a desire to limit drastically the extent of its application. It reflected the view peculiar to some of the radicals on the aforementioned problem introduced by the theological conception of adiaphora, the problem, namely, of having to specify exactly what it was that Scripture had "neither commanded, nor forbidden."

This problem presented itself in the first place in regard to those matters concerning which Scripture had left neither commands, nor prohibitions, nor explicit permissions. How was this silence of Scripture to be interpreted? Already in the third century a controversy had arisen in the church over this question. Some Christians had argued then that attendance at the pagan "spectacles," or the wearing of the laurel wreath, were permitted because they had been neither com-

61

manded nor prohibited in Scripture.[2] It was their position, in other words, that "whatever is not forbidden is certainly permitted."[3] Tertullian argued otherwise. It is easy, he said, for someone to ask "where in Scripture are we forbidden to wear a crown?" But those who thus demand the support of a Scriptural text for a view they do not hold, ought to be willing to submit their own position to the same Scriptural text. Can they show a text, he asked, which says we should be crowned? But if they cannot, what is the rule to be? For his own part, Tertullian said, he rejects the position that "whatever is not forbidden is certainly permitted," and holds rather that "whatever is not clearly permitted is forbidden."[4]

Tertullian's position on this question found many adherents in subsequent centuries. The English Lollards, for example, apparently made it, by way of a reductionist interpretation of Wyclif's *sola Scriptura* principle, the basis for their incessant clamoring after the removal of most of the traditional church ceremonies. According to their earliest major antagonist, Reginald Pecock, the Lollards were always asking: "Where groundest thou it in the New Testament . . . or in the Old in such place which is not by the New Testament revoked?", the implication being, again according to Pecock, that what is not explicitly sanctioned by the Scriptural text must be considered not permitted or indifferent, but forbidden.[5] A radical branch of Hussites, known as the Picards, would seem to have stretched Hus' *sola Scriptura* principle to the same conclusion.[6]

Among the sixteenth-century Continental reformers, the most unequivocal expression of such biblical reductionism came from the Anabaptists, as was evidenced, for example, in the letter Conrad Grebel and other Anabaptists wrote to Thomas Müntzer in 1524. For all his radical inclinations, Müntzer had developed a liturgy for his Allstedt congregation which, while incorporating many changes, nevertheless retained much of the old order, including the practice of singing during the Eucharistic service.[7] Although the hymns introduced by Müntzer were in the vernacular, Grebel and his Anabaptist colleagues still found them offensive, and that precisely because they could "find nothing taught in the New Testament about singing, nor example of it."[8] And "what we have not been taught by clear words and examples," the Anabaptists concluded, "should be thought of as forbidden."[9]

Apparently, the biblical reductionist position also enjoyed considerable favor in some circles during the earlier stages of the English Reformation. Thomas Starkey attributed it to the extremist group he classified as being guilty of "blynd arrogance." This group, he said, wanted to "trede under foot all rytes and customes of the churche" because, among other things, they admit "nothinge at all, but that whiche is in Scripture expressely conteyned."[10] The "protestation" presented by the clergy of the lower house of the province of Canterbury to the Convocation in June of 1536 raised the same point. Among the sixty-seven *mala dogmata* claimed by the protestors "to have ben and now to be, within this realm, causes of dissenion, [and] worthy special reformation," was one to the effect that "all ceremonies accustomed in the Church, which are not clerly expressed in Scripture, must be taken away."[11] A popular ditty making the rounds late in Henry VIII's reign suggests how widespread the reductionist position had become:

Wil none in al this land,
Step forth and take in hand
These fellows to withstand,
the number like the sand ...
(who) taketh their authoritie
Out of the holy Evangelie:
Al customes ceremonial
And rites ecclesiastical
Not grounded on Scripture,
No longer to endure.[12]

The fit of iconoclasm which overtook the English church in 1547 was viewed by an irate Stephen Gardiner as having been inspired also by the opinion that nothing is to be allowed except that it be appointed by Scripture. Gardiner explicitly ascribed this latter view to the Lollards, and it was probably the Lollards also whom Starkey and the 1536 "protestors" had in mind. But the Lollards were not the only ones suspected. Not infrequently, Gardiner at least implied that the likes of William Turner and John Bale also were adherents of the biblical reductionist position.[13] Nicholas Ridley clearly thought that John Hooper's opposition to the vestments was based in part upon a conviction that for something to be allowed in the church it must be clearly sanctioned by Scripture.[14] And according to Cranmer, John Knox's opposition to the "kneeling rubric" of the revised Prayer Book of 1552 rested upon a similar rationale.[15]

Whether the early English "puritans" like Hooper and Turner were actually biblical reductionists will remain to be seen. But, in any event, there were, both on the Continent and in England, a considerable number of radical reformers who were inclined to believe that whatever had not been clearly permitted by the plain text of Scripture could not be considered indifferent or permitted, but had to be rejected as being evil and forbidden.

To the mainline Continental and English reformers such a position seemed nothing less than absurd.[16] Were one to contend that all is forbidden which is not explicitly permitted by Scripture, it would be necessary, Luther said, to observe the Eucharistic service nowhere but in Jerusalem, or even to refrain from it altogether, since the Scripture does not state whether red or white wine, wheat rolls or barley bread, had been used by Christ and the Apostles at the Last Supper. That being absurd, one is forced to conclude, Luther said, that there is no need for servile imitation of Christ's every action, and further, that what God has left unsaid—i.e., neither commanded, nor prohibited—should remain "free," as God himself has left it.[17]

Whatever may have been Zwingli's earlier position,[18] in his debate with the Anabaptists he clearly argued that those things not covered by the commands and prohibitions of Scripture, nor explicitly permitted therein, are to be treated as adiaphora. There are many things, Zwingli argued in his treatise on baptism, which lack a clear Scriptural text which men can determine for themselves without contradicting God's will. Take, for example, the Eucharistic celebration. Here, Zwingli said, we have the clear word of Scripture that the celebration is a memorial, and that it would be wrong to make anything else of it, since the fact that the celebration is a memorial is not an indifferent matter. But there are certain aspects of the celebration which enjoy no clear Scriptural text and are, therefore, left to man's own determination, as, for example, the admission of women to the Eucharistic celebration. Infant baptism is a matter of the same kind. Hence, just as we do not do wrong in admitting women to the Eucharistic service, so we do no wrong in baptizing infants, even though neither is clearly warranted by God's Word. Zwingli made the same point later in the treatise when he noted that the Scriptures give us no clear indication as to the standard and order according to which the Eucharist was celebrated among the apostles.[19]

In discussing the question of rebaptism, Zwingli once again appealed to the concept of adiaphora to challenge the Anabaptist position. It is certainly right and proper, he said, that Christians should live according to the Word of God. But if one does, then one will take care not to place obstacles in the way of one's brother in things which are external and indifferent; and even more so when it is a question of some external thing which lacks an explicit scriptural permission, such as rebaptism. There is a clear text in Scripture showing that the eating of meat is a free thing, but there is none regarding rebaptism. Yet, in a matter like rebaptism one ought to treat it as a thing indifferent; the same procedure should be followed as in the choice of meats.[20]

Oecolampadius and Bullinger voiced similar opinions. "The matter is indifferent," Bullinger wrote, "whether the churches take the supper sitting down, or going to the table; whether a man take the holy mysteries in his own hand, or receive it into his mouth at the hands of him that ministereth." Concerning the frequency of receiving the Eucharist, Bullinger added that "the apostles have given forth no commandment, but have left it indifferent unto every church's discretion." Likewise, he said, "it is an indifferent matter whether you use red wine or white in the supper," and much the same may be said about the use of leavened or unleavened bread, the time and place of celebration, the type of altar and vessels, the use of vestments, the use of songs, the type of prayers, the commemoration of feast days, and so forth. Ecclesiastical or civil regulations of all these matters, so long as they are not profferred as necessary to salvation, are themselves matters indifferent, even though they "be superadded to what is expressly prescribed in the Word of God."[21]

Oecolampadius, after a rather lengthy description of the form and manner of celebrating the Eucharist as established by Christ, immediately cautioned his readers not to think that the church today must follow literally every detail laid down in Scripture. The evening celebration of the Last Supper and the manner of sitting at the table were most suitable to Christ and the apostles, he said, but for the church today, the morning hour and the manner of going to the altar, there to receive the Eucharist while standing, are more convenient. Similarly, it is more expedient today, what with the large crowds in attendance, to have the bread cut and broken beforehand, rather than waiting for it to be done by the one distributing the bread. In brief, Oecolampadius concluded that the evangelists did not wish to limit or bind Christians to a definite rule in regard to these external things, but wanted only to recommend a respectable order, for it would be altogether impossible now to follow in every detail the original pattern. Otherwise one would also have to limit reception of the sacrament at any one time to twelve persons; all would have to receive it from one person only; and one could make use of the sacrament only in the evening.[22]

Writing in a similar vein, John Calvin noted that because "it was not Christ's intention to dictate in detail what Christians are to do in external discipline and ceremonies," the use of red or white wine, leavened or unleavened bread, kneeling or not kneeling during prayer, and all such matters are "things indifferent, left to the Church's discretion."[23]

Martin Bucer's and Peter Martyr's views in this regard found clearest expression during the 1550 Vestiarian Controversy in England. Writing against what they supposed was the biblical reductionist position of Hooper and à Lasco, both Bucer and Martyr contended that if it is argued that the appointed vestments must be considered forbidden because they lack the explicit sanction of Scripture, then a host of other ceremonies, like the celebration of the Eucharist in the morning, which also enjoy "no commandment of the Lord, nor no example of it," would also have to be rejected as forbidden. To avoid such an absurdity, Bucer and Martyr concluded that not only the vestments, but all such things as have been neither "commanded, nor forbidden," nor explicitly permitted by Scripture should be considered in themselves, things indifferent.[24]

Among the English reformers themselves, Stephen Gardiner, Nicholas Ridley, and Thomas Cranmer were especially explicit in their rejection of the biblical reductionist position. Citing Gregory of Nazianzen, Gardiner argued that it is not necessary to have the sacrament observed precisely as Christ administered it. And lest much confusion be introduced in this regard, it is necessary, he said, that the people take heed not to be deceived by the word "institution." The likes of Turner and Bale were always insisting, to the confusion of the "simple," that the Eucharist had to be celebrated according to the "institution" of Christ. Gardiner argued, however, that

> yf by the word institution shulde be signyfyed a precyse ordre, sette forth with all the circumstance, in the nature of a precyse lawe, sygnyfyenge that it must be frome thenceforth, so observed and none otherwise, whiche matter, the worde [institution] semeth to include, and soundeth so in common reason: there appeareth not in scripture, any institution of this nature, for we reede not in scripture, that Christe dydde prescribe any such precise ordre of receiuyng or ministryng.[25]

During the 1547 outbreak of iconoclasm, which he blamed on the Lollards, Gardiner again challenged the reductionist position. If the Lollard contention that images must be abolished "because Scripture appointed it not" is pursued to its logical conclusion, then, Gardiner said, a good part of the rest of the Church must also be rejected. "If ye allow nothing but Scripture, what say you to the king's rings . . . why doothe the king weare S. Georg on his brest . . . why kepe we S. George feast?"[26]

The same line of argument was employed by Nicholas Ridley in 1550 against Hooper's assertion that "there is nothing to be done in the

Church, but is commanded or forbidden by the word of God, Though not expressly, yet by necessary collection, etc." "This sentence is so far out of the way, and so erroneous," Ridley replied, "that it is intolerable; for it taketh away the most part

> of all due ceremonial circumstances, without the which, either after one manner or other, the very institutions of Christ cannot be observed. For is it possible [to] receive the holy communion, but thou either sit, stand, kneel, or lay? Thou must either take it at one time or another, fasting or after meat, clothed or naked, in this place or in another. Without the sum of these circumstances, it is impossible to do that the Lord biddeth thee. But none of all these circumstances are commanded in Scripture. Therefore, if the said sentence were true, none of them may be done; and so it must follow, that if we believe this doctrine, then can we not execute Christ's institutions.[27]

Thomas Cranmer's similar views in this regard found their clearest expression in 1552 when he sought to check the efforts of John Knox and other radicals to purge the revised *Prayer Book* of its "kneeling rubric."[28] These "unquiet spirits" argue, Cranmer wrote, that "it is not commanded in the Scripture to kneel, and whatsoever is not commanded in the Scripture is against the Scripture, and utterly unlawful and ungodly." But this, Cranmer added, "is the chief foundation of the Anabaptists and of diverse others." It is a "subversion of all order as well in religion as in common policy," and if it be true, then "take away the whole Book of Service; for what should men travail to set in order in the form of the service, if no order can be got but that is already prescribed by Scripture." If it cannot be found in Scripture "that Christ ministered the Sacrament to his Apostles kneeling," neither, Cranmer said, can it be found "in Scripture that he ministered it standing or sitting." As a matter of fact, "if we follow the plain words of Scripture," Cranmer concluded, "we should rather receive it lying down on the ground."[29]

As is clear from the above brief outline, Cranmer, Ridley, and Gardiner, as well as Bucer and Martyr, clearly meant to include early "puritans" like Turner, Bale, and Hooper under their condemnation of the biblical reductionist position. And until very recent times it was a common assumption among historians that the Puritans "held to the literal following of the Scriptures as an absolute in the sense that whatever was not expressly commanded in Scripture was unlawful."[30] John S. Coolidge, however, has recently challenged this assumption, arguing especially from an analysis of the Cartwright-Whitgift debate during the Elizabethan period, that while some "unschooled enthusiasts" among the Puritans may have subscribed to the biblical reductionist position, their more responsible spokesmen did not.[31]

The Elizabethan Puritans fall outside our immediate concern, but so far as their Henrician and Edwardine predecessors are concerned, Coolidge's conclusion, in its basic thrust at least, would seem to stand up. The likes of Turner, Bale, and Hooper were not, in any strict sense, biblical reductionists. To be sure, in their hot pursuit of the "Romishe Foxe," or the pope, whom they thought the English bishops were still harboring notwithstanding the king's attempt to drive him out of England,[32] these early "puritans" frequently spoke of the Scriptures as constituting a law book whose prescriptions were altogether sufficient for the determination of Christian life and worship. Against the bishops' defense of the canon law as the "law of the Church," Turner, for example, argued that the "most perfit law of the chirche [was] when and whersoever the most perfit chirch [was] in Christes tyme and the Apostelles tyme and in the tymes of the holy martyres." Canon law, however, was "not yit made in the Apostelles tyme," and could not therefore have been that "perfitest law of the chirche." Therefore, Turner concluded, "the chirche of Christ at all tymes hathe no other law but Christes word." Turner added that the "law of the gospell is a more perfit law for the Christen then the law of Moses was for the jewes." But since "the jewes neded no other law nor ceremonies than the law of Moses, then the Christen men nede no other law (as touchyng theyr soules) but the law of the gospel."[33] In a similar vein, John Hooper wrote that "God hath preserved in all captivities and persecution of the church miraculously one book, the holy Bible; delivered the same unto the church, and bound the church unto this book." In the Bible are all the "rules and canons" according to which reformation is to be made. This Scriptural "law" is "absolute, perfect, and never to be changed; nothing added unto it, nor taken from it."[34]

But such talk about the "law" of Scripture was commonplace among the Swiss trio of reformers (Zwingli, Oecolampadius, and Bullinger) who were most responsible for these early "puritans'" theological orientation.[35] And just as the remarks of the former in this regard need not have implied a biblical reductionist position, neither need the latter's be so interpreted. When Zwingli, for example, wrote that Christ's "testament" is no less sufficient than the law of Moses had been for the Jews, and that it stands in need, therefore, of no "addition or subtraction," what he meant was that nothing may be added over and above the Scriptural prescriptions as "necessary to salvation," not that the Church had to be reduced in every detail of its life and worship to literal accordance with its Scriptural model.[36] This was true of the early "puritans" also. They upheld the sufficiency of Scripture in the sense that therein is to be found all that is needed "as touchyng theyr soules," or in other words, all that is "necessary to salvation," and not in the sense that the Scriptural text provides a paradigmatic formula for any and every detail of Christian life and worship.[37] Their chief argument against the traditional ceremonies, therefore, rested not upon the fact that the latter enjoy no explicit sanction in the plain text of Scripture, but that, without any Scriptural warrant, such matters were supposedly being upheld as equal to the divine commands and as "necessary to salvation," or as binding under pain of mortal sin.[38] Turner, Bale, and Hooper all admitted that they were prepared to permit certain ceremonies which had not been explicitly prescribed by Scripture.[39]

Like the mainline reformers, therefore, the "puritans" also were opposed to the sort of biblical reductionism according to which nothing was to be allowed in the church except that it could be backed up by an explicit "proof-text" from Scripture. But the question arises then as to wherein precisely lay the difference between the "puritans" and the mainline English reformers on this issue of biblical authority and adiaphorism. On the basis of his study of the Whitgift-Cartwright debate, Coolidge would have us believe that their difference is to be located in this, that while the Puritans insisted that all ecclesiastical matters must be "according to" Scripture, the Conformists thought it sufficient that such matters be "not repugnant" to Scripture.[40] And there can be little doubt but that such a distinction does have a considerable bearing upon understanding the respective positions of the Puritans and Conformists. But there is also reason to believe, if our following analysis of early "puritan" thought is accurate, that Coolidge, following Cartwright's view of things, has misapplied the distinction and thereby has confused still further the relation between the Puritans and Conformists.

To start with, it should be noted that not only the Puritans but all the reformers were of the opinion that the church and its structures should be brought into "positive accord" with the New Testament. At the very least, this meant that the "essentials" of church life and worship must enjoy a sound and clear Scriptural basis. But it also meant that the church should strive, without becoming enslaved to the Scriptural text or the primitive model of the church, to regain as much as possible the sort of simplicity that had characterized the church of New Testament times. It was primarily in this sense that Luther, in his 1520 treatise on the Mass, after noting that Christ had celebrated the first Mass without chasuble, tonsure, singing, and the like, concluded that the closer the celebration of the Eucharist comes to Christ's first

Mass, the better it is, and the farther therefrom, the more dangerous.[41] Similar remarks by Zwingli,[42] Oecolampadius,[43] Bullinger,[44] Calvin,[45] Bucer,[46] Peter Martyr,[47] and a host of mainline English reformers[48] can best be interpreted in the same sense. Finally, the mainline reformers' insistence upon bringing the church into positive accord with Scripture also meant that all ecclesiastical matters, including those in whose regard Scripture has left no explicit commands and prohibitions, must be subjected to such criteria as arise out of the Scriptural dictates of faith and love.[49]

To say the very least, therefore, it would be misleading to suggest, as does Coolidge, that what differentiated the Puritan and Conformist positions was a disagreement over whether it is enough for church structures to be merely in a condition of "non-repugnance" to Scripture, or whether they must also be brought into "positive accord" with Scripture. Both parties insisted upon the latter. Where they disagreed was in the question about the point at which ecclesiastical structures, ceremonies, and the like, were to be subjected to this test of "positive accordance" with Scripture.

We have seen that both the mainline reformers and the Puritans rejected the Anabaptist and Lollard view that whatever is not explicitly permitted by the Scriptural text must be considered forbidden. From such a rejection of the biblical reductionist position, the mainline reformers moved on to the conclusion that whatever is not forbidden in Scripture must be considered "permitted"—permitted, not in the sense that such matters could or should under any and every circumstance be allowed to remain in the church, but in the sense that taken in themselves, abstractly, such matters tell neither for nor against the purity of Christ's religion, so that whether they are to be retained or rejected can only be determined by factors extrinsic to their abstract natures. In other words, it was the mainline reformers' view that whatever Scripture had not forbidden is to be considered permitted in the sense of being an adiaphoron. This was as much as to say that to qualify as an adiaphoron it is sufficient that one or another matter be "not repugnant" to Scripture.[50] Having thus identified the adiaphoristic nature of one or another matter, the mainline reformers sought, as will be seen in subsequent chapters, to bring their *use* of such matters into positive accord with Scripture.

The Puritans, on the other hand, or at least the pre-Elizabethan ones, were inclined to apply the test of "positive accordance" with Scripture to the very definition of adiaphora. This tendency was discernible already in the repeated challenges issued by Turner to the English bishops to provide some positive demonstration from

Scripture—albeit not necessarily an explicit text—for the "goodness" of those ceremonies which they wished to have retained on an adiaphoristic basis.[51] Neither Turner himself, nor John Bale, it should be noted, employed the term adiaphoron. Later Puritans might well have been wiser to have followed their example. But, for better or worse, John Hooper tried to reconcile the position of Turner and Bale with the adiaphoristic appraisal of the ceremonies by then so prevalent in the English Church.

The transition from Turner and Bale to Hooper may well have passed through the German theologian Matthias Flacius Illyricus. As part of his challenge to Melanchthon's collusion in the Leipzig Interim imposed upon German Protestants in 1549,[52] Flacius published a work entitled: *Liber De Veris et Falsis Adiaphoris*. Flacius frankly admitted the existence of many ecclesiastical adiaphora.[53] But he also insisted that a clear distinction be drawn between "true" and "false" adiaphora. Toward that end he introduced a variety of arguments which might have been lifted right off the pages of the works of Turner and Bale. Such, for example, were his arguments that the Roman ceremonies were the "main sinews of popery," or that ceremonies once abused by idolatry cannot be tolerated.[54] More relevant to the point at hand, however, were four other arguments propounded by Flacius to the effect that (1) "true" adiaphora take their origin ultimately from God himself, who directs them *in genere* toward the glorification of his own name, and the edification of his people;[55] (2) all things which are indifferent are such only to the extent that they serve to glorify God's name and edify the Church;[56] (3) adiaphora are no longer "true" when instituted tyrannically;[57] and (4) nothing can be truly adiaphoristic when it causes scandal.[58] As noted, all the mainline Continental and English reformers also insisted that adiaphora be used in such wise as to edify the Church and glorify God. But Flacius is saying something more here. To his view it is not simply a matter of adiaphora being used in an edifying manner. Rather, Flacius conceived of edification of the Church and glorification of God's name to be constitutive elements in the very definition of adiaphora.

It was not until 1566 that major portions of Flacius' *Liber* were translated into English and included in the anonymous Puritan publication *The Fortress of the Fathers*. But Hooper himself had been in exile on the Continent from 1547 to March of 1549, and had undoubtedly followed closely the Interim Controversy then raging in Germany. Furthermore, Charles V's harshness in implementing the Interim had sent a host of Continental reformers fleeing to England. Some of these refugees, and most notably John à Lasco, clearly shared Flacius' views, and lost little time in broadcasting them about the English realm. Significantly, à Lasco became Hooper's chief ally in the 1550 Vestiarian Controversy.

Already in his Lenten sermons of 1550, Hooper had taken the opportunity to deny the adiaphoristic character of several ceremonies required by the new *Ordinal,* including the wearing of a surplice and cope by the bishop-elect at his consecration.[59] Notwithstanding such outspokenness, Hooper was himself nominated to the bishopric, which he promptly refused to accept so long as the vestment rubric was to be required at his consecration. On October 3, 1550, he presented the Privy Council with a set of "Notes"[60] in which he tried to explain his reasons for such a refusal.[61]

During the months preceding issuance of his *Notes,* Hooper's position had been subject to some confusion, with some of his followers being left with the impression that it was Hooper who was championing the indifferent nature of the vestments against the denials of the other bishops.[62] But Hooper's chief antagonist in the controversy, Nicholas Ridley, eventually set the record straight. "All our controversy is in this," Ridley wrote in his reply to Hooper's *Notes,* "whether the vestments as they be now appointed . . . be things as of themselves indifferent, and not forbidden as sin against God's holy word or no." Hooper, Ridley claimed, was of the opinion "that they be not things indifferent, but very sin, for they be things forbidden by the word of God."[63] Hooper's *Notes* bear out the general accuracy of Ridley's appraisal of the controversy.

Hooper opened the argument of his *Notes* with the following syllogism:

> Nothing is to be used in the Church unless it enjoys the sanction of the express word of God, or otherwise is a thing indifferent in itself—i.e., a thing whose use is not profitable and whose non-use is not harmful.
> Uncommon and peculiar vestments in the ministry do not enjoy the sanction of God's word; nor are they things indifferent in themselves.
> Therefore, they are not to be used.[64]

Of particular interest at this point is Hooper's attempt to substantiate the second part of his minor premise, namely, that the vestments are not indifferent in themselves. To do so, Hooper proposed that for something to qualify as a thing indifferent it must meet four conditions. First, he said, "things indifferent must have their origin and foundation in God's word." Had Hooper meant thereby that to be designated indifferent, a thing had to enjoy the express sanction of Scripture, he would clearly have involved himself in a contradiction of his major premise wherein he had contrasted things indifferent with those things enjoying the express sanction of Scripture. And, in fact, his second "condition" makes it clear that he meant otherwise. While having its origin in Scripture, but being therein neither commanded, nor prohibited, but left free to be used or not used in accordance with individual conscience, an adiaphoron must nevertheless, Hooper noted, enjoy at least the implicit sanction of Scripture. To qualify as an adiaphoron, a thing must, thirdly, Hooper said, enjoy "a manifest and open utility, known in the Church," or, in other words, it must be "edifying." Finally, according to Hooper, "things indifferent must be instituted with levity and without tyranny, and those that are not, are no more indifferent." Because to his view the appointed vestments could meet none of these "conditions," Hooper concluded that they were not to be considered adiaphora.[65]

Hooper's whole argument, it should be noted, is shrouded in confusion. In an attempt to clear up some of his confusion, John Primus, in a study of the 1550 Vestiarian Controversy that is rather slanted in Hooper's favor, has suggested that Hooper's "four conditions" should be taken, not as Hooper himself argued, namely, as constitutive elements in the definition of adiaphora, but as "conditions" for the *usage* of adiaphora in the Church.[66] "It is when we keep in mind that Hooper makes this error," Primus says, "that we can properly understand what he is saying."[67] Primus contends that this is especially true of Hooper's third "condition." It will be recalled that in the opening syllogism of his *Notes,* Hooper had defined an adiaphoron as "a thing whose use is not profitable and whose non-use is not harmful." If, therefore, his third "condition" that "adiaphora must enjoy a manifest and open utility," is made to pertain to the definition of adiaphora, Hooper has blatantly contradicted himself, as indeed Ridley quickly pointed out to him.[68] According to Primus, however, "it is inconceivable . . . that a rational being, no matter how hot the controversy, could so obviously contradict himself in a document of comparatively small compass." Thus, Primus concludes, one must "view the statement in the original syllogism as a definition of an indifferent thing in the abstract," whereas "the third condition, on the other hand, establishes a principle basic in determining what is legitimate for church usage."[69]

But such a reconstruction of Hooper's thought would seem to make a shambles of his whole argument, by gutting it of any proof for the very point that he is trying hardest to demonstrate—namely, that the vestments are not to be used in the Church because they do not qualify as adiaphora. Hooper was, to be sure, talking about the "use" of adiaphora in the statement of his third "condition." But the point is that, like Flacius, he seems to be of the view that the vestments cannot be defined as adiaphora without some consideration being given to their use. À Lasco, it may be noted, was of a similar mind. "I call those things free [indifferent]," he wrote, which, among other things, "contain a manifest commodity to the Church."[70]

In making this last remark, à Lasco was obviously speaking of the "use" of adiaphora in the sense of their "usefulness." And it was probably in the same sense that Hooper understood his third condition. To qualify as an adiaphoron, in other words, a thing must, according to Hooper and à Lasco, prove "useful" toward the edification of the Christian community.

Now, so far as the retention or removal of one or another ceremony was concerned the mainline reformers also gave consideration to their "usefulness." In fact, as has been seen, it was an obvious corollary of especially the Erasmian adiaphoristic appraisal of the ceremonies that such matters were to be considered "intermediary goals" or "means" to some higher end beyond themselves. For all that, however, the mainline reformers, unlike Hooper and à Lasco, did not make the "usefulness" of the ceremonies a constitutive element in their definition as adiaphora, and could even on occasion speak of certain adiaphora as being "useless" things, and advocate their retention in the church on no other grounds than that their removal might "offend" the "weak" or disturb the peace.

One could also speak of the "use" of adiaphora, however, in the sense, not of their "usefulness," but of the "usage" to which they might at one or another time and place be put. It was in this sense that à Lasco had earlier tried to win Martin Bucer over to Hooper's cause by arguing that the "use" of the vestments had disqualified them as adiaphora. In a letter dated October 12, 1550, à Lasco told Bucer that according to Hooper, vestments, as "God's creations," are not *per se* evil, but that their present use is relatively impious to the extent that they represent the old Aaronic and papistical priesthood.[71] It is for this reason, à Lasco concluded, that Hooper denies the indifferent nature of the vestments.[72] When Bucer replied that he refused to accept the view that the vestments "in themselves" contain a "note or mark of Antichrist" or "a piece of Aaron's priesthood," and insisted that "in themselves" the vestments are "free things,"[73] à Lasco wrote Bucer another letter, charging him with having missed the whole point of the controversy. The argument, he said once again, is not over whether the vestments in themselves, as "God's creations," are good; everyone grants that; what is at stake is rather a certain "use and style" of the vestments, which "I think is an abuse and corruption of good things."[74]

Ironically enough, Nicholas Ridley had himself used a similar argument a few years earlier in an attempt to disprove the adiaphoristic character of "images" used in church. Ridley's main argument rested upon what he considered the biblical prohibition of images,[75] but he had also argued that "images placed in churches and set in an honourable place of estimation . . . and especially over the Lord's table, which is done . . . after the same manner and fashion which Papists used, especially after so long continuance of abuse of images, and so many being blinded with superstitious opinion towards them, cannot be counted a thing indifferent, but a most certain ruin of many souls."[76] This was almost exactly the same argument that Hooper and à Lasco were using to deny the adiaphoristic character of the vestments on account of their "usage." And Ridley's inconsistency did not escape Hooper's notice, pointing out as he did to Ridley that one could just as well defend the "images too, with as good authority as they [the bishops] defend the vestments."[77] Ridley's argument about the images, however, was exceptional. Most mainline Reformers who favored removal of the images because of their misuse in the past still conceived of them as being indifferent by nature.[78] So too with other things or ceremonies whose past usage was thought to warrant their removal. This is clear from the vestments controversy itself, for some who defended the indifferent nature of the vestments did so while still agreeing with Hooper and à Lasco that because of their past abuse the vestments might best be abrogated.[79]

What we have, then, is that while the mainline English reformers did not, on the whole, consider the use of external matters constitutive of their definition as adiaphora, the likes of Hooper and à Lasco did, so that a thing whose nature might at one time or place have been indifferent could conceivably have its nature altered at another time or place, depending upon the particular circumstances then obtaining. By thus rendering the use of externals constitutive of their definition as adiaphora, Flacius, Hooper, and à Lasco could and did bring to bear upon the adiaphoristic definition of externals, principles which the mainline English reformers were inclined to apply to such matters only after they had already been designated adiaphora—as, for example, the principle of positive accordance with Scripture. Hence, like Flacius and Hooper, à Lasco argued that to qualify as adiaphora, external matters must not only "contain a manifest commodity to the church," and "be void of tyranny binding men's consciences," but must also "have their original ground in the Scriptures."[80]

Finally, it may be noted in passing that given the popularity of Flacius' *Liber De Veris et Falsis Adiaphoris* among the Elizabethan Puritans, and their ready access to the writings of Turner, Bale, Hooper, and à Lasco, it would hardly be surprising to find a Thomas Cartwright pursuing much the same course as these earlier "puritans." And, in fact, Cartwright's "four general rules" for bringing into positive accord with Scripture those matters "as are not particularly mentioned of in the Scripture,"[81] would seem to amount to little more than a reiteration of the "conditions" laid down by Flacius, Hooper, and à Lasco for the definition of "true" adiaphora. Although it cannot be pursued here, the suspicion arises that Cartwright intended his "four general rules" to be applied in like manner.

To summarize, therefore, while the early "puritans" did not openly agree with the Lollard and Anabaptist contention that whatever Scripture had not explicitly permitted is forbidden, neither did they concur in the conclusion of the Conformists that whatever is not forbidden by Scripture is for that reason "permitted" or "indifferent." It was rather their view that among those matters concerning which Scripture is silent, only those which are in positive accord with the general directions of Scripture for the glorification of God, the edification of his people, and so forth, may be considered "permitted" or "indifferent" in themselves. Given the vigor with which they pressed for compliance with these general directives of Scripture, and the narrow interpretation they often put upon them, the early "puritans" in effect recognized no wider a realm of adiaphora than did the strict biblical reductionists. Except for those matters explicitly permitted by Scripture, like the choice of foods, the observance of days, and so forth, the early "puritans" were almost always reluctant to admit the adiaphoristic character of one or another matter that the biblical commands, prohibitions, and permissions had left uncovered, and more often than not spoke of such matters as being sinful or evil. Small wonder, then, that many of their contemporaries, and most historians ever since the sixteenth century, have been inclined to write the Puritans off as biblical reductionists. If such an appraisal of the Puritans was not entirely accurate, neither was it quite so absurd as Coolidge claims.[82] Be that as it may, however, the Puritan attitude toward biblical authority in either its apparent or actual form was unacceptable to the mainline English reformers, who, as noted, held to the position that whatever is not forbidden by Scripture qualifies for that reason alone as an adiaphoron, and as such may be used or not used depending upon the dictates of faith and love in any given situation.

The problem of having to specify exactly what it was that Scripture had "neither commanded, nor forbidden" presented itself to the English adiaphorists in a second way. For even though certain matters were recognized as having been permitted by Scripture either explicitly or by virtue of its "silence," the question remained whether "permissions" issued in Apostolic times were meant to obtain in all subsequent ages. This question arose most immediately over the ceremonial and judicial observances of the old Judaic code.

Against the Judaizers of New Testament times, the Apostle Paul had repeatedly insisted that in themselves the Judaic traditions mattered little. Whether one was circumcised or uncircumcised simply made no difference in itself (I. Cor. 7:19; Gal. 5:1–6; 6:15). A century or so later, Justin Martyr could still express much the same attitude.[83] By Justin's time, however, some were beginning to argue that since the Jewish customs were meant to prefigure Christ, their observance would imply that Christ had not yet come, and for that reason ought no longer be considered merely a matter of indifference.[84] One or another, more peripheral, Judaic observance, like the Quartodecimans' calculation of the date of Easter, was still tolerated,[85] or even explicitly designated adiaphoristic.[86] But that Pope Victor ever attempted in the first place to suppress the Quartodecimans suggests in itself something of the growing tendency to consider the observance of the Judaic ceremonies less than indifferent.[87] Augustine, who, as noted earlier, had insisted against Jerome upon an adiaphoristic interpretation of the Pauline observance of the Jewish ceremonies admitted to Jerome that imitation of the Apostle Paul's observance of the Jewish ceremonies would now be like "violating a sepulchre." Such ceremonies, Augustine said, were now, since the promulgation of the Gospel, not only "dead" but also "deadly."[88] Medieval theologians like Thomas Aquinas interpreted Augustine to have meant thereby that it would now be a mortal sin to observe the old Judaic ceremonies.[89]

Underlying such an argument about the final "burial" of the Jewish ceremonies was the implication that the "permission" of one or another matter in New Testament times need not mean that it must also be allowed in subsequent ages. It implied, in other words, that the biblical "permission" may have been nothing more than a "dispensation" or a "concession." Such an interpretation of the biblical permissions was often used both before and during the sixteenth century to downplay especially the Pauline "permission" to marry.[90] And as evidenced by the following remark made by Thomas More to Luther, it was used by the Roman theologians of the sixteenth century to undermine the Reformers' adiaphoristic appraisal of the Roman ceremonies:

> Now, as for what you bring up from Paul; suppose first of all that in that passage he clearly says what you say he says; what else have you yet proved from that passage than that the practice was then permitted? Do you conclude from it, after the king has proved to you that the Holy Spirit has willed the contrary for more than a thousand years already, that the same thing is permitted now because the apostle, by God's dispensation, permitted it then? As if the apostle did not at times permit certain things which shortly after even he himself prohibited; unless you now permit circumcision to all because Paul once circumcised Timothy.[91]

The fact was that Luther and other mainline Continental Reformers did indeed conceive of circumcision and other Jewish ceremonies as things indifferent, which may be used or not used so long as they are not proffered as necessary to salvation.[92] So too did many of the English reformers. William Tyndale, for example, wrote that

> There is no ceremony of Moses, but that I may keep it this day as an indifferent thing; howbeit, not as a thing so necessary unto my soul's health, that I should think that I sinned if I did not. But I may eat the Easter lamb of passover every year, when the time cometh, if I will. And I may circumcise myself for my pleasure, as well as pare my nails, if I list. And I may burn the blood and fat of oxen and calves unto this day without sin, as an indifferent thing.[93]

Peter Martyr and Nicholas Ridley tried to impress the same point upon John Hooper during the 1550 Vestiarian Controversy. It will be recalled that one of Hooper's arguments against wearing of the appointed vestments was that the latter belonged to the ancient Aaronic priesthood, whose ceremonial codes had been abrogated by Christ.[94] In his November 4, 1550, letter to Hooper, Martyr agreed that the vestments, as well as many other matters like tithing, the use of Psalms, and so forth, had their origin in the Aaronic priesthood. But that in itself, Martyr said, is no reason why they should now be considered evil and pernicious. To be sure, "no such store [should be] made of them as though they should bee necessarie to obtaine salvation," but apart from such superstition, they may be considered things indifferent, which may for one or another reason be retained.[95] For his part, Ridley agreed with Hooper that to set up any ceremonies according to their old Judaic "figurative" meaning, or to posit them as necessary to the worship of God, or to man's salvation, would indeed be sinful and a derogation of Christ's priesthood. But he denied that the vestments had been appointed on such terms, or that they were even similar to the ancient Aaronic vestiture, and concluded that in any event the appointed vestments were in themselves things indifferent.[96]

Such a conclusion also struck at the aforementioned argument often enunciated by the likes of Turner, Bale, and Hooper, to the effect that things once corrupted by idolatrous abuse can no longer be considered adiaphora.[97] For if the Jewish ceremonies could still be deemed less than "evil" in themselves, then there was no reason either why one or another ceremony ought to be designated evil rather than indifferent simply because it had suffered some abuse at Roman hands, or at the hands of any other "pagans." If the early Fathers of the Church could appropriate not only certain Jewish practices, but also a great number of temples, poems, plays, and like matters, which had formerly been used for idolatry by the Gentiles, then, Peter Martyr wrote Hooper, the Church may now also treat certain Roman ceremonies as adiaphora and restore them to their proper use.[98]

In the preceding pages of this chapter our concern has been chiefly with those sixteenth-century radicals who challenged an adiaphoristic appraisal of the traditional ceremonies by way of insisting that many such matters are "forbidden" primarily on the ground that they lack either the explicit or implicit sanction of Scripture or the Primitive Church. Before concluding the chapter, however, some notice must also be taken of yet another group of sixteenth-century Christian thinkers, the Spiritualists, who were inclined to consider the traditional ceremonies and, for that matter, all externals, evil in themselves on precisely the opposite grounds—on the grounds, namely, that the true Church, being purely "spiritual," cannot be tied down to the "letter" of Scripture, or to the sort of external ecclesiastical policy such as obtained in New Testament or other times. Like the Anabaptists, the Spiritualists were an extremely variegated group, and not all belonging to it were as dualistic in their thinking as the preceding remark would suggest. Of those who were, one of the most influential and outspoken was the one-time Roman Catholic priest and Lutheran convert Sebastian Franck. Franck's 1531 letter to John Campanus will suffice to illustrate the point at hand.

Franck admitted to Campanus that in New Testament times Christ had instituted certain external ceremonies for his church. This was done, however, not "for God's sake but rather for our own." "God permitted" such "outward signs to the church in its infancy," Franck wrote, in the same way "as a father gives something to a child so that it won't cry." No sooner had the Apostles died, however, than "the outward church of Christ was wasted and destroyed." The "outward ceremonies" became subject to the "Antichrist," and were thereby "not wiped out," but "misused and sullied." They became "tokens to Satan," who "seeks nothing other than the externals." But this degeneration of the "outward ceremonies," Franck said, was fully "anticipated" by "the holy and omniscent Spirit," so that while for fourteen hundred years most Christians, from Irenaeus and Augustine to Luther and Zwingli, have wallowed in the wasteland of externals, the God whose very "nature" is "spirit and inward," has been teaching, baptizing, and feeding "in the Spirit and in truth without any outward means," the true members of his "purely spiritual" church "in whatever part of the world they be," and under whatever name—Christian, Greek, Barbarian, or Turk—they go.[99]

According to Franck's neo-Joachimite view, in other words, the "fall" of the church marked the beginning of a new age of the Spirit, the maturation of Christianity. It was a signal from God for all his true disciples to come of age. That being the case, "what is the need, or why should God wish to restore," Franck asked, "the outworn sacraments, and take them back from Antichrist, yea, contrary to his own nature (which is Spirit and inward), yield to weak material elements?" "Does he wish now, just as though he were weary of spiritual things and had quite forgotten his nature, to take refuge again in the poor sick elements of the world and re-establish the besmirched holy days and the sacraments of both Testaments?" Quite the contrary. If one is a true "disciple of God" and "not addicted to the letter of Scripture," as are the papists, the Lutherans, the Zwinglians, and the Anabaptists, but in tune rather to the "God in [one's] heart," one will know that just as a father is pleased when his child matures and discards the playthings of its infancy, so God does not wish to have restored the outward ceremonies which he once gave to the infant church and has long since abandoned to the abuse of Antichrist.[100]

There was much, including use of the latter child–father metaphor, in this radical spiritualism of Franck and others which bore a similarity to elements in the thought of not only Erasmus, but of the mainline Continental and English reformers too, all of whom were inclined to one or another extent toward a re-emphasis upon the inner dimension of Christian life by virtue of their respective ties with the *devotio moderna,* humanism, the *theologia Germanica,* and the doctrine of solafideism. The similarity, however, was mostly of a superficial sort.

In the first place, however much Erasmus and the mainline reformers may have shared Franck's desire to see Christians come of age in the Spirit, unlike Franck they never conceived of such a process of maturation as releasing the Christian from *all* externals. For one thing, both Erasmus and the mainline reformers found altogether repugnant Franck's claim to a private revelation such as would render Scripture otiose. Though not incognizant of the difference between the "inner" and "outer" Word, or the "letter" and "meaning" of Scripture, they insisted that the external, written and audible, dimensions of God's Word remain essential to Christian faith no matter how advanced in the Spirit Christians individually or collectively might become.[101] And from the necessity of Scripture, they concluded also, and again notwithstanding their distinctions between the "spirit" and "matter," the "sign" and the "signified," or the "visible" and the "invisible," that such external ceremonies as enjoy the clear sanction of the biblical commands—like the outward rites of Baptism and the Eucharist— must also be considered essential even within a "mature" Christianity. Such externals, it was said, will always remain necessary under ordinary conditions for introducing one into the life of the Spirit, sustaining it, and bringing it into its proper Incarnational expression.[102]

Furthermore, even if Franck's views are applied only to those matters deemed non-essential by Erasmus and the mainline reformers, their similarity to the latter's views would still remain at best superficial. To be sure, Franck sometimes described the outward ceremonies in much the same language employed by Erasmus and the mainline reformers. But it is also clear that, unlike the latter, he did not really conceive of such matters as being anything less than evil and forbidden, and that for a variety of reasons. First, he seemed to be of the conviction that even if such matters were at one time permitted by God, *now*, because of their misuse by Antichrist for more than fourteen hundred years, and/or because it was a new age of the Spirit and a time for "maturity," they can no longer be considered good or even indifferent. But then it may be doubted whether Franck ever considered the outward ceremonies anything less than evil and forbidden in themselves, even prior to their misuse and the start of the new "spiritual" age. As has been seen earlier in the case of Tertullian and others, the divine permission of an earlier period could be interpreted in the sense of a "dispensation" to use for a time something that was basically evil in itself.[103] That the latter probably comes closest to Franck's own rationale seems likely. The overall impression he left when talking about the outward ceremonies was that Satan, in laying claim to such matters on the occasion of the Church's supposed "fall," was simply appropriating what belonged to him in the first place, namely any and everything that smacked of the material.

But whatever Franck's reasons for conceiving of the outward ceremonies as evil and forbidden, they ran counter to the adiaphoristic appraisal of such matters by Erasmus and the mainline reformers. As already noted, the latter were of the view that the misuse of externals could not rob them of their intrinsically adiaphoristic nature, and that whatever Scripture has not forbidden remains "permitted" in itself throughout all ages. These conclusions challenged the Spiritualists' position no less than that of the biblical reductionists. A more direct challenge to the dualistic thrust of Franck's Spiritualism, however, was presented by the adiaphoristic conception of the external cere- monies as "means" to spiritual advancement. Although never pre- cluded by the theological adiaphorists,[104] this conception emerged most immediately out of the adiaphoristic appraisal of the ceremonies along philosophical lines by the Erasmians.

In the spiritualist thrust of such an appraisal, Erasmus, as noted, concluded that the ceremonies, as adiaphora, cannot be deemed of such value as to constitute ends in themselves. Always concomitant to this negative implication of Erasmus' adiaphorism, however, was a positive one to the effect that those matters designated adiaphora can serve as "intermediary goals" or "means" to some higher end beyond themselves. This did not mean for Erasmus that to qualify as an adiaphoron one or another matter had to be proven "useful" or "mean- ingful." It meant simply that adiaphora were by nature such that they did not preclude an intermediary role in the pursuit of Christian per- fection.

For Erasmus himself and many of his Continental and English fol- lowers, this reference of the ceremonies beyond themselves often amounted to little more than a rehash of the sort of allegorization which the likes of Amalar, Durandus, and Gabriel Biel had pursued so passionately in previous centuries,[105] as was evidenced most clearly, for example, in the Church Regulations issued by Johann III in 1532 for the united dukedoms of Cleves-Mark and Julich-Berg,[106] in the 1540 Anglican *Rationale of Ceremonial*,[107] or in the *Bishops'* and *King's Book*, the "Edwardine Injunctions," and a number of writings by English reformers like Starkey and Becon, wherein emphasis was placed upon the role of ceremonies in bringing Christians into "re- membrance of some spiritual thing."[108] Those ceremonies which did not readily admit of such an allegorical interpretation were usually referred beyond themselves in terms of the "use" they might have in the service of one's neighbor.[109] Some Erasmians were also inclined to refer the ceremonies to God himself, and to conceive of them, there- fore, as being "meritorious," or "means to grace and the forgiveness of sin."[110] With this latter reference of the ceremonies beyond themselves, other Erasmians, like William Tyndale, who were of a basically Protestant persuasion, hardly concurred.[111] But be that as it may, it is clear that for all their own spiritualistic tendencies, the Erasmians were clearly at odds with the dualistic conclusions of Franck and his kind. Because they were, unlike Franck, adiaphorists, the Erasmians could subordinate the material to the spiritual, or the exterior to the interior, without at the same time setting the two realms in diametrical opposition. In brief, they could conclude that while "not good" in themselves, the outward ceremonies also are "not evil" in themselves.

Such then, to conclude, was the basic import of the English reformers' designation of certain ceremonies as "indifferent" and "permitted." Just as they meant to say thereby that such matters are not as good or obligatory as had traditionally been supposed, so they also had in mind to demonstrate that the same ceremonies were not as evil or proscribed as some were wont to claim. While this implied a limited qualitative reduction of such matters, and tended also to encourage their quantitative reduction to some extent, it neither precluded nor required, in itself, either the rejection or the retention of any one or all of the ceremonies. Whether, when, where, or how such matters were to be retained or rejected—these were questions which, according to the adiaphorists, could be decided only by way of considerations extrinsic to the ceremonies themselves. The first of such considerations to be taken into account is that of a concern for the "truth."

NOTES

1. "T. Dorset to Mr. Horsewell, March 13, 1536," in *Three Chapters of Letters Relating to the Suppression of Monasteries,* ed. T. Wright (London, 1843), p. 37. For an account of Lambert's earlier and later trials, see Foxe, *Acts and Monuments* V, pp. 181–225, 229–34.

2. See Tertullian, *De Spectaculia* 3: PL 1, 634; *De Corona* I: PL 2, 77.

3. "Sed quod non prohibetur, ultro permissum est" (*De Corona* 2: PL 2, 78).

4. "Imo prohibetur quod non ultro est permissum" (*Ibid.*). A similar argument was developed by Tertullian in his polemic against the possibility of a second marriage by his wife after his death. Nothing is to be sought after for the sole reason that it is not forbidden, he said, for even such things are, in a sense, forbidden, because other things are preferable to them (*Ad Uxorem* I, 3: PL 1, 1390–91). Nowhere does one find in the Gospel or the Pauline epistles permission for a second marriage, and since it must be acknowledged that a thing "is forbidden by God where there is no evidence that he permits it," marriage, Tertullian concluded, is to be contracted only once (*De Exhortatione Cast.* IV, 1: PL 2, 700).

5. R. Pecock, *Repressor of Overmuch Blaming of the Clergy,* ed. C. Babington, *Public Record Office (PRO* hereafter), Vol. 19 (London, 1860), I, p. 118. See also: W.W. Capes,

The English Church in the Fourteenth and Fifteenth Centuries (London, 1903), pp. 112, 190-92, 208; H.O. Taylor, *The English Mind* (New York, 1962), pp. 59-73.

6. See Luther's remarks in this regard: *Ep. ad Rom.*: *WA* 56, 494; also *The Reformation, 1520-1559*, ed. G.R. Elton; *The New Cambridge Modern History*, Vol. II (Cambridge, 1958), p. 191.

7. See G. Rupp, *Patterns of Reformation* (Philadelphia, 1969), pp. 305-323.

8. Thomas Müntzer, *Schriften und Briefe*, ed. G. Frantz (Gütersloh, 1968), p. 439.

9. "Was wir nit gelert werdend mit claren sprüchen und bispilen, sol unss alss wol verbotten sin" (*Ibid.*). The most extreme form of this biblical reductionism was practiced by the Anabaptists of St. Gall (See G. Williams, *Radical Reformation* [Philadelphia, 1962], pp. 127-34, 830). Grebel and his friends, it may be noted, also wrote to Müntzer that they were anxious to learn whether he was of the same mind as Karlstadt (Müntzer, *Schriften*, p. 441). Apparently it was their conviction that Karlstadt shared their opinion that what was not clearly permitted in Scripture was forbidden. And while there is some evidence to suggest that he occasionally did (See Rupp, *Patterns*, pp. 80-83), it should also be remembered that Karlstadt's "spiritualism" was eventually such that he could conclude that he did "not need the outward witness" of Scripture (G. Williams, *Radical Reformation*, p. 823).

10. *Exhortation*, sig. F, fol. iv(v); also: *Ibid.*, sig. G, fol. iv.

11. Strype, *EM* I, ii, p. 261.

12. *Ibid.*, II, ii, p. 333.

13. Muller, *Gardiner's Letters*, pp. 260-61, 273, 275, 484, 486.

14. *Writings of Bradford*, pp. 390-91.

15. See Cranmer's letter of October 7, 1552, to the Privy Council (in J.H. Blunt, *The Reformation of the Church of England* [London, 1882], II, pp. 104, 105). It may be noted that even before coming to England, Knox had been charged during an "examination" with such tendencies. His examiner at that time had asked: "Will ye bynd us so strait, that we may do nothing without the express word of God? What! and I ask a drynk? think ye that I synne? and yitt I have not Goddis word for me?" (J. Knox, *Works*, ed. D. Laing [Edinburgh, 1846], I, p. 196). Knox replied by admitting that Scripture has explicitly left certain things, like meats and drinks, "free," but he denied that a similar freedom obtains in the realm of worship: ". . . hear it is doubted, yf we may tack the same freedome in the using of Christis Sacramentes, that we may do in eating and drynking" (*Ibid.*). Citing Deuteronomy 4 to the effect that nothing may be added to or taken away from God's Word, he concludes: "Now unless that ye be able to prove that God has commanded your ceremonies, than his former commandment will dampne boyth you and thame" (*Ibid.*, p. 199). Knox's biblical reductionism also came to the fore when in April of 1550 he had been summoned before the Council of the North to answer for his attacks upon the Mass while doing pastoral work in the city of Berwick (See J. Ridley, *John Knox* [New York and Oxford, 1968], pp. 84-105). His reply consisted of a lengthy "Vindication," whose basic argument ran as follows: "All wirschipping, honoring, or service inventit by the braine of man in the religioun of God, without his own expresse commandment, is Idolatrie: The Masse is inventit by the braine of man, without any commandment of God: Thairfoir it is Idolatrie" (*Works*, III, pp. 34). In the process of proving his major, Knox at one point entered upon a discussion of the first Council at which the Apostles commanded Christians to abstain "from what is strangled and from blood" (Acts 15:20), and concluded that the precept upon which the Apostles based this prohibition was Christ's commandment of brotherly love, understood in the Pauline sense of bearing with the weak (*Ibid.*, pp. 45-46). To judge from that passage, one would think that Knox's major implied much less of a biblical reductionist attitude than would

at first blush seem to be the case. But such an attitude seems to come to the fore again when Knox later concludes that "Albeit that the Apostillis has made lawis other than the express word commandit, what aperteneth that to you?" (*Ibid.*, p. 46). Since God's law was sealed and confirmed in the days of the Apostles, it is the "maist extreame impietis ... to mak any alteratioun thairin" (*Ibid.*).

After the insertion of the "black rubric" into the 1552 Prayer Book, explaining that no adoration was implied by the kneeling rubric (*Two Liturgies*, p. 283), Knox encouraged his parishioners to submit to the "kneeling" rubric for the sake of charity and peace, since it was "so small a matter" (See R.W. Dixon, *History of the Church of England* [London, 1878] III, pp. 489–90), but he apparently still refused to admit that "kneeling" was indifferent. According to his own later account, Knox was asked, among other things, during a 1553 appearance before the Privy Council, "if kneeling at the Lord's table was not indifferent?" (Strype, *EM* II, ii, p. 72–73). To this question, Knox replied that "Christ's action was most perfect; and that it was most sure to follow his example: and that kneeling was man's addition and invention" (*Ibid.*, p. 73). The Council apparently took this to mean that Knox did not consider "kneeling" indifferent, for Knox says that there ensued a "great contention" between himself and the Lords of the Council (among whose number was Cranmer) over this question (*Ibid.*). Finally, after "long reasoning," the Lords expressed to Knox their good-will, but added that "they were sorry to know him of a contrary mind to the common order" (*Ibid.*). Knox claims to have replied that "he was sorry the common order was contrary to Christ's institution" (*Ibid.*).

16. As indeed it had earlier seemed to Reginald Pecock. To the oft-repeated Lollard question "Where groundest thou it in the New Testament?" Pecock had replied that there are many things which men are obviously permitted to do which have no explicit warrant in either the plain text of Scripture or the example of Christ and the Apostles (*Repressor, PRO* 19, I, pp. 118, 313). He denied that the Lollards could ground in the plain text of Scripture their own insistence upon a vernacular Bible (*Ibid.*, p. 119), or a variety of other obviously worthwhile actions (*Ibid.*, pp. 120–21). One is forced to conclude, therefore, Pecock wrote, that "al not forbodun bi Holi Scripture ... is not unleeful" in itself (*Ibid.*, II, pp. 435, 456), but has rather been left by God to be dealt with by man in accordance with his own rational judgment (*Ibid.*, I, pp. 10, 12–13, 17, 121, 125).

17. *Wider die himml. Proph.*, WA 18, 115; 112, 114.

18. Some scholars have been inclined to argue that at least prior to his confrontation with the Anabaptists, Zwingli subscribed to a "negative Scripture principle"—the principle, namely, that "what is not authorized in Scripture [is to be] rejected" (J.T. McNeill, *The History and Character of Calvinism*, (New York, 1967), pp. 32, 39, 43, 73, 74, 84). I have tried to show elsewhere that this was not the case (See B. Verkamp, "The Zwinglians and Adiaphorism," *Church History* 42 [December, 1973], pp. 486–504).

19. *Von dem touff*, SW 4: pp. 296–97, 288.

20. "Also soltend ir im gethon haben, den widertouff, ob er glych under die mitlen ding ghorte ... In andren dingen derglychen, als in erkiesen der spysen" (*Ibid.*, pp. 255–56).

21. *Decades*, d. 5, s. 9, t. 3, pp. 422, 424, 414, 410, 418–23, 421; d. 5, s. 5, t. 3, pp. 190–97, pp. 203 ff.; d. 5, s. 10, t. 3, p. 504; Bullinger to Humphrey and Sampson, May 1, 1566, *Zurich Letters*, p. 352. Although Bullinger lent Hooper some general support in his struggle against the appointed vestments (See Burcher to Bullinger, January 21, 1551, in *OL*, p. 676), he later made it perfectly clear that he considered the vestments things indifferent. Asked "whether the dress of the clergy is a matter of indifference," Bullinger replied: "It certainly seems such, when it is a matter of civil ordinance, and has

respect only to decency and order, in which things religious worship does not consist" ("Bullinger to Humphrey and Sampson, May 1, 1566," *The Zurich Letters*, ed. H. Robinson [Cambridge, 1842], 1: 349).

22. *Christliche Antwort. OS*, p. 251, 252, 254.

23. *Institutes* IV, X, 30; IV, XVII, 43.

24. "Bucer to à Lasco, October 20, 1550," Strype, *EM* II, ii, pp. 445–47, 449; "Bucer to Hooper, November, 1550," *Ibid.*, II, ii, pp. 459–62; "Martyr to Hooper, November 4, 1550," Martyr, *Commonplaces*, II, p. 120.

25. S. Gardiner, *A Detection of the Devil's Sophistry* (London, 1546), sig. Q, fol. iv(v); sig. R, fol. v(v); sig. R., fol. iii(v)–iv.

26. Muller, *Gardiner's Letters*, pp. 260–61.

27. *Writings of Bradford*, p. 390, 391.

28. The rubric read: "Then shall the minister first receive the Communion... and next deliver it... to the people in their hands and kneeling" (*Two Liturgies*, p. 279).

29. "Cranmer to Council, October 7, 1552," Blunt, *op. cit.*, II, pp. 104, 105. It should be noted that underlying the opposition of Knox and others to the kneeling rubric was also a desire to avoid any ceremony which might imply a belief in the physical presence of Christ in the Eucharistic elements.

30. See: F.C. Cross, *ODCC*, p. 654: H. Davies, *op. cit.*, I, pp. 51–54, 258–61; J.F. New, "The Whitgift-Cartwright Controversy," *Archiv* 59(1968), p. 206; Knappen, *Tudor Puritanism*, pp. 354–66.

31. John S. Coolidge, *The Pauline Renaissance in England*, p. 6.

32. See, for example, William Turner, *The Huntyng and fynding out of the Romishe Fox whiche more than seven yeares hath bene hyd among the bishopes of Englong after that the Kynges Hyghness had commanded hym to be dryuen out of hys realme* (Basel, 1543), sig. A, fol. ii–vi.

33. *Ibid.*, sig. B, fol. v–v(v); vii; sig. C, fol. ii(v).

34. *Answer* [to Gardiner's *Detection of the Devil's Sophistry*], *Early Writings*, p. 138; *Christ and His Office, Early Writings*, pp. 29, 24, 47, 82, 26. For Bale's views in this regard, see *Yet a Course at the Romyshe Foxe*, sig. C, fol. ii; C, v(v); C, viii(v); D, vi; D, viii; K, v(v); K, viii–L, i; L, iv; L, vii.

35. See, for example, Zwingli, *Apologeticus Archeteles*, *SW* I, pp. 304–5; Oecolampadius, *Christliche Antwort, OS*, pp. 246, 249; Bullinger, *Decades*, d. 3, s. 9, t. 2, pp. 352–53; Bullinger, *Zuschrift an Frau Anna, Leben und ausgewählte Schriften*, ed. G. Pestalozzi (Elberfeld, 1858), p. 552.

36. *Apol. Arch.*, *SW* I, pp. 304–5; *Von Erkiesen*, *SW* I, p. 134.

37. See, for example, W. Turner, *The Second Course of the Hunter at the Romishe Fox and Hys Advocate*, sig. E, fol. viii.

38. See: *Ibid.*, sig. D, fol. i; J. Bale, *Yet a Course*, sig. B, fol. i; C, v(v); C, viii(v); D, vi; D, viii; D, viii(v); K, v(v); K, viii(v)–L, i; L, iv; L, vii; Hooper, *Sermons upon Jonas, Early Writings*, p. 534; *Writings of Bradford*, pp. 388–90.

39. Turner, *Second Course*, sig. N, fol. iv; Bale, *Yet a Course*, sig. K, fol. vi(v); Hooper, *Christ and His Office, Early Writings*, p. 85.

40. Coolidge, *op. cit.*, pp. 6–12, especially p. 11.

41. *Ein Sermon von dem neuen Testament*, *WA* 6:354–55.

42. "Ac ubi euangelio conformia deprehenderimus, servabimus; ubi difformia, foras mittemus" (*Apol. Arch.*, *SW* I: 319); "Maiorum traditiones... quanto magis euangelicam et apostolicam doctrinam redolent, tanto magis suspicimus omnes; quanto longius ab hac recedunt, tanto magis fastidimus" (*Ibid.*, p. 300); "Ac ea que cum scrip-

tura canonica consentiunt . . . recipienda nimirum erunt, iis que dissentiunt reiectis" (*Ibid.*, p. 303).

43. "Wir können aber jenes Nachtmal des herrn auf keine Weise reiner halten, als wenn wir uns auf sorgfältigste nach der Einsetzung Christi und nach dem Brauche der Apostel richten" (*Christliche Antwort, OS,* p. 255).

44. According to Bullinger, God cannot be pleased with any attempt to alter "the most simple, most plain, best, and perfect form of the Supper delivered of the Lord himself" (*Decades*, d. 5, s. 9, t. 3, p. 407). To Frau Anna Roist, Bullinger wrote: "Die Kirche keine andere Form mache, sondern die von dem herrn und den Aposteln eingesetzte und aufgestellte fest und unverwandelt behalten soll . . . Wer sich aber dess nicht genügen lässt und etwas Anderes, gleich als was Besseres und hübscheres sucht, der verachtet und verwirft die Ordnung des Sohnes Gottes ist" (*Leben und ausgewählte Schriften,* p. 552).

45. See: Calvin, *Institutes,* IV, X, 14, 23; also Calvin's letter of October 22, 1548, to the Protector Somerset, in J. Burnet, *Letters of John Calvin* (Philadelphia, 1858), II, p. 194, or in *Opera* XIII (CR XLI), 87.

46. See Bucer's aforementioned letters to à Lasco and Hooper (J. Strype, *EM* II, ii, pp. 445, 450, 456, 464).

47. During the 1550 Vestiarian Controversy with Hooper, Martyr told the latter: "In ceremonies I would come as neere as might be unto the holie Scriptures, and would continue in the imitation of the better times of the Church" (*Commonplaces,* II, 133). In a letter to the ministers of the Church of Polonia, Martyr wrote that the administration of the sacraments should be such as "shall come nerest to the purenesse which Christ used with his Apostles" (*Ibid.*, I, p. 88).

48. The *King's Book,* for example, noted that "it is out of doubt that Christ's faith was then most firm and pure, and the scriptures of God were then best understand, and virtue did then most abound and excel. And, therefore, it must needs follow, that the custom and ordinances then used and made be more conform and agreeable unto the true doctrine of Christ, and more conducing unto the edifying and benefit of the church of Christ, than any customs or laws used or made by the bishop of Rome" (Lloyd, *op. cit.,* pp. 287–88). See also: *The Catechism of Thomas Becon with Other Pieces,* p. 299; *A Short Instruction into Christian Religion,* ed. E. Barton (Oxford, 1829), pp. 201–2.

49. This point will be documented in subsequent chapters.

50. This conclusion, it may be noted, applies to the Zwinglians and to Bucer no less than to those reformers of a Lutheran or Calvinist bent, and does not seem to have been taken into adequate account by those scholars who have tried to differentiate the respective positions of all these Continental reformers by suggesting that in contrast to the Lutherans and Calvinists, the Zwinglians and Bucer insisted, if not upon a literal accordance with the plain text of Scripture, at least upon more than a "non-repugnance" of ecclesiastical matters to Scripture, and to that extent were of the view that "strictly speaking", there are "no adiaphora" (See G.W. Bromiley, *Zwingli and Bullinger* [Philadelphia, 1953], p. 29; A. Lang's representation of Bucer as a "Wegbereiter des Puritanismus" would seem to rest upon the same mistaken assumption [A. Lang, *Puritanismus und Pietismus* (Darmstadt, 1972), pp. 21–22]).

51. See Turner, *A Second Course,* sig. E, fol. iii.

52. In 1530 Charles V had decreed that all "protestants" were to abide by the *Confutatio Pontificia,* the papalist reply to the *Augsburg Confession* prepared by John Eck and others. Due to a variety of reasons, mostly of a political sort, it was a long time, however, before the emperor could actually impose the sort of religious unity he wanted.

Finally, with the defeat of the Protestant forces at Mühlberg in 1547, his chance came. On May 15, 1548, he issued the Augsburg Interim. While attempting to meet the Protestant point of view on such questions as clerical marriage and the granting of the Eucharistic cup to the laity, it also undermined the doctrine of solafideism and was rejected by Melanchthon and other Wittenberg theologians. But because Charles V immediately proceeded to force the implementation of the Interim by banishing rebellious ministers and devastating uncooperative cities, Melanchthon and the German Protestants were faced with a serious dilemma. Finally, after extended and desperate negotiations, Melanchthon and others put together what has come to be known as the Leipzig Interim, which while retaining or re-instating most of the traditional ceremonies, nonetheless respected basic Protestant doctrine. This Leipzig Interim remained in effect from December, 1548, until Duke Maurice, whose earlier betrayal of his father-in-law, Philip of Hesse, had made Charles V's victory at Mühlberg less difficult, turned coat once again, and forced the Emperor to negotiate the Peace of Passau (1552). On these and other basic facts pertaining to the Interim, see: C.L. Manschreck, *Controversy,* pp. 165–81; Manschreck, *Melanchthon,* pp. 277–92; Manschreck, "A Critical examination and appraisal of the adiaphoristic controversy in the life of Philip Melanchthon," unpub. Ph.D. Dissertation, Yale University, 1948. For a listing and a rather jaded discussion of much of the polemical literature exchanged by the disputing Lutheran parties during the Interim, see: F. Bente, *Historical Introductions to the Book of Concord* (St. Louis, 1965), pp. 107–12). See also: R.A. Kolb, "Nicholas von Amsdorf, Knight of God and Exile of Christ. Piety and Polemic in the Wake of Luther," unpub. Ph.D. Dissertation, University of Wisconsin-Madison, 1973, chapter 3; Luther David Peterson, "The Philippist Theologians and the Interims of 1548," unpub. Ph.D. Dissertation, University of Wisconsin, 1974.

53. He cites I Cor. 7, 8, 10, 14 and Rom. 14 as ample proof thereof: *Liber de Veris et Falsis Adiaphoris* (Magdeburg, 1549), *OLS,* sig. X, fol. 2.

54. *Ibid.,* sig. Aa, fol. 8; sig. Z, fol. 1; sig. Y, fol. 8.

55. *Ibid.,* sig. X, fol. 3(v).

56. "Omnia enim, quae sunt Adiaphora, eatenus sunt Adiaphora, quatenus illis prioribus finibus (See sig. X, fol. 3[v]) serviunt" *(Ibid.,* sig. Y, fol. 5[v]).

57. *Ibid.,* sig. Y, fol. 6(v), and fol. 8.

58. See *Ibid.,* sig. Cc, fol. 3(v)–4; elsewhere Flacius wrote that "nihil est adiaphoron in casu confessionis et scandali" *(Regula generalis de Adiaphoris, OLS,* sig. C, fol. 2).

59. For the Ordinal ceremonies see: *The Two Liturgies,* pp. 169, 179, 182. For Hooper's remarks against them, see especially *Sermons upon Jonas, Early Writings,* pp. 477–79, 534, 549, 554.

60. Hooper's "notes" were rediscovered by Constantine Hopf and are printed in the *JTS,* 44(1943), pp. 194–99. M.M. Knappen had presented a rough draft of them in *Tudor Puritanism,* pp. 483–86. Some scholars still seem to be unaware of Hopf's discovery (See, for example: John Opie, "The Anglicizing of John Hooper," *Archiv,* 59[1968], p. 169n; H.C. Porter, *Puritanism in Tudor England* [Columbia, 1971], p. 58 n.).

61. Hooper to Bullinger, June 29, 1550, *OL,* p. 87; Hales to Gualter, May 24, 1550, *OL,* p. 187; Utenhovius to Bullinger, April 9, 1551, *OL,* p. 585.

62. Stumphius to Bullinger, June 1, 1550, *OL,* pp. 466–67; *Infra,* VII, n. 192.

63. *Writings of Bradford,* p. 375.

64. "Nihil est Ecclesiae in vsu habendum, quod non aut expressum Dei verbum habeat quo se tueatur, aut alioqui res sit ex se indifferens, quae facta, et vsurpata, nihil prosit, infecta vero et praetermissa nihil obsit.

Privata et peculiaris vestimenta in Ministerio, non habent verbum dei quo praecipiuntur, neque sunt res ex se Indifferentes.

Ergo non sunt in vsu habenda" (Hooper's *Notes, JTS,* 44[1943], p. 196).

65. *Ibid.,* pp. 196, 197; "Quare quum hac prima proprietate careant, quae in rebus indifferentibus requiritur, vestimenta ex Adiaphororum numero excludimus (etc)... (*Ibid.,* p. 198).

66. John H. Primus, *The Vestments Controversy,* (Kampen, 1960), pp. 18–19.

67. *Ibid.,* p. 18.

68. "But how agreeth this note with his (Hooper's) saying in the first that a thing indifferently used profiteth not... How shall he agree with another that cannot agree with himself" (*Writings of Bradford,* pp. 377–78; also: pp. 376, 385–86).

69. Primus, *op. cit.,* pp. 26–27.

70. As cited in *Fortress of Fathers,* Trinterud, *op. cit.,* pp. 110–11.

71. Text in C. Hopf, *Martin Bucer and the English Reformation* (Oxford, 1946), p. 149.

72. "Itaque hanc talem vestium istarum usum damnat Hoperus: Et medium atque indifferentem esse negat" (*Ibid.*).

73. "Bucer to à Lasco, October 20, 1550," in Strype, *EM* II, ii, pp. 447–49, 452.

74. "... sed de certo quodam illarum usu ac modo agitur, quem ego abusum et corruptionem bonarum rerum esse puto" (Hopf, *Bucer,* pp. 166–67).

75. N. Ridley, *A Treatise on the Worship of Images, The Works of N. Ridley,* p. 84.

76. *Ibid.,* p. 90.

77. *Writings of Bradford,* pp. 387–88.

78. Like the Wittenberg Articles, which had asserted that the use of images is "a matter of indifference," and that only the "misuse" of images is to be condemned (See N.S. Tjernagel, *Henry VIII and the Lutherans* [St. Louis, 1965], Appendix I, p. 285), the Ten Articles stated that images may be allowed, but are not to be used superstitiously (Lloyd, *op. cit.,* p. xxviii). The Bishops' Book included an assertion to the effect that "it were more seemly for Christian people to be without all images of the Father, than to have any of them," but that other images, while not to be worshipped, may be used for the sake of inspiration (*Ibid.,* pp. 135–36); even the rejection of the "images of the Father" was too much for Henry VIII (*Cranmer's Writings and Letters,* p. 101). The official sanction for the fit of iconoclasm in 1538 was in part politically inspired (see Hughes and Larkin, *op. cit.,* I, pp. 275–76, and Wriothesly, *Chronicle* I, pp. 86–87), and in part theologically motivated, but the latter only as an attack upon "superstitious idolatry," and not against the images in themselves (See Cromwell's Injunctions of Sept. 30, 1538: H. Gee and W.V. Hardy, *Documents Illustrative of English Church History* [New York, 1896], pp. 277–78; and the Royal Proclamation of November 6, 1538: Hughes and Larkin, *op. cit.,* I, pp. 270–76). The *King's Book* omitted the objection to "images of the Father" found in the *Bishops' Book,* and otherwise took the same adiaphoristic attitude toward images as had been evidenced in the latter (Lloyd, *op. cit.,* pp. 134–38, 299–301). During the years 1547 and 1548, and after Cranmer, Ridley, and William Barlowe had touched off another fit of iconoclasm by having preached against images (See Cranmer, *Writings and Letters,* p. 127; Dixon, *op. cit.,* II, p. 417; Muller, *Gardiner's Letters,* pp. 255–67, 273–75), Protector Somerset called for the removal of all images (Foxe, *Acts and Monuments* IV, pp. 28–30, 34–36), but at the same time admitted that the images could be useful as "books for the unlearned," and that it would be foolish to condemn them in themselves (*Ibid.,* IV, pp. 28–29). The Edwardine Injunctions called for the abolition of only those images that

smacked of superstitious abuse (*Visitation Articles and Injunctions*, ed. W.H. Frere, and W.M. Kennedy [London, 1910], pp. 105, 110, 115, 116, 119–20, 126–28). Consistent with Somerset's aforementioned views, the Privy Council wrote Cranmer on February 21, 1548, calling for the removal of all images (Foxe, *Acts and Monuments*, V, pp. 717–18), but in doing so did not term the images evil in themselves, but rather called them "things not necessary" which might best be removed for the sake of peace (*Ibid.*, p. 717). The same attitude was apparent in the Nuremburg *Catechism* whose English translation was commissioned and authorized by Cranmer in the summer of 1548 (*A Short Instruction into Christian Religion*, pp. 21, 22, 28, 29). Finally, it may be noted, that already in 1531 Hugh Latimer had declared that "it is lawful . . . to make use of images" so long as they are dealt with as "voluntary things" (*Sermons and Remains*, p. 331).

79. Bucer, for example, wrote to à Lasco that he would personally prefer "that no kind of vesture which the papists used were retained among us" (October 20, 1550, in Strype, *EM* II, ii, p. 445; see also: *Ibid.*, p. 450.; and Bucer to Hooper, November 1550,: *Ibid.*, II, ii, pp. 456, 464). Martyr wrote the same to Hooper (Martyr to Hooper, November 4, 1550, *Commonplaces*, II, p. 117).

80. As cited in *Fortress of Fathers*, Trinterud, *op. cit.*, pp. 110, 116.

81. As listed by Coolidge, Cartwright's "four rules" for "such cases as are not particularly mentioned of in the scripture" were as follows:

    1) That they offend not any, especially the church of God.

    2) That all be done in order and comeliness

    3) That all be done to edifying

    4) That they be done to the glory of God

(Coolidge, *op. cit.*, p. 5).

82. *Ibid.*, p. 6 n.

83. Justin Martyr, *Dialogus cum Tryphone Judaeo* 47: *PG* 6, 568.

84. *Ibid.*

85. See Eusebius of Caesaria, *Historiae Ecclesiasticae* V, xxii–xxv: *PG* 20, 489–508.

86. According to both Socrates and Sozomen, a fourth-century Novation synod declared the dating of Easter a "thing indifferent." Socrates, *Historia Ecclesiastica* V, xxi: *PG* 67: 623; Sozomen, *Historia Ecclesiastica* VII, xviii: *PG* 67, 1470.

87. In this same connection could be mentioned the increase in legislation against Sabbatarian observances (See J.H. Blunt, *Dictionary of Sects, Heresies, Ecclesiastical Parties and Schools of Religious Thought* [London, 1892], p. 509).

88. *Ep.* LXXXII, 16, 2: *PL* 33, 282, 280.

89. *ST* I–II, 103, 4; see also: Peter Lombard, *PL* 192, 110–14, 153, 158, 454; Marsilius of Padua, *Defensor Pacis*, II, ix, 10.

90. See for example: Tertullian, *De Monogamia*, III: *PL* 2,932; Tatian, as cited in Clement of Alexandria, *Stromata* III, xii: *PG* 8, 1182; Gregory I, as cited in Bede, *Ecclesiastical History*, p. 97. An almost identical interpretation of the Pauline permission was still being proffered in the sixteenth century by Jean Colet (See Colet, *An Exposition of St. Paul's First Epistle to the Corinthians*, trans. J.H. Lupton [London, 1874; Ridgewood, 1965], pp. 215, 216, 222, 224, 225, 227.).

91. More, *Resp. ad Luth.*, p. 421.

92. Luther, for example wrote: "Nunc vero sola opinio, fiducia et conscientia inter haec discernit, quae utraque (i.e., circumcision or uncircumcision) sunt licita, indifferentia, neutra, sicut et omnia alia opera legis . . . Post Christus igitur circumcisio nihil est, neutra tamen et licita, sicut quaecunque alia de diebus, cibis, vestibus, locis, hostiis etc." (*In epistolam Pauli ad Galatas commentarius, 1519*, WA II, 565–66). See also Luther's

comments on 1 Cor. 7:19 (*WA* XII, 127–28), and his Sermons of 1522 (*WA* 10^{III}, 19–20). For Melanchthon, see *Loci, MW* II/1, pp. 132–35; *CR* 7, 566. See also Eck's 404 Articles, the 154th and 155th of which refer to Luther's and Melanchthon's position on this point (Reu, *op. cit.,* p. 106). The Swiss reformers were generally less explicit in this regard, but at least Calvin clearly stated that the Jewish ceremonies should be dealt with from an adiaphoristic point of view (See *Comm. in Ep. Priorem ad Cor., Opera* XXXI [*CR* 77], 415, 428, 448).

93. Tyndale, *Expositions and Notes,* p. 327.

94. Hooper, *Notes,* p. 198; Hooper, *Sermons upon Jonas, Early Writings,* p. 554; *Writings of Bradford,* pp. 381–83.

95. Martyr, *Commonplaces,* I, p. 118.

96. *Writings of Bradford,* pp. 384–85, 389, 380, 375. Bullinger, it may be noted in passing, later wrote that "no one can reasonably assert that Judaism is revived" by the introduction of the disputed cap and gown ("Bullinger to Humphrey and Sampson, May 1, 1566, *Zurich Letters,* I, p. 347).

97. See, for example, Hooper, *Notes,* p. 197; Turner, *Second Course,* sig. N, fol. iv.

98. "Martyr to Hooper, November 4, 1550," *Commonplaces,* I, p. 119. See also Stephen Gardiner, *The Examination of a Proud Presumptious Hunter,* in Muller, *Gardiner's Letters,* pp. 482–83.

Not all the early Church Fathers, it may be noted, were so enthusiastic about appropriation of the "spolia Aegypti." Tertullian, for example, anticipated many of the sixteenth-century arguments against such an appropriation, as when he argued that it does no good to contend that the "spolia" are all creatures of God, and as such "good in se"; by having been superstitiously abused, he said, they have lost their quality of goodness, and now bear the mark of Satan (*De Spectaculis* II: *PL* 1, 632–33; also *De Corona* VIII: *PL* 2, 87–97).

99. "A Letter to John Campanus, by Sebastian Franck, Strassburg, 1531," *Spiritual and Anabaptist Writers,* ed. G.H. Williams (London, 1957), pp. 149–56.

100. *Ibid.,* pp. 149, 154, 155.

101. See, in general: Gordon Rupp, "Word and Spirit in the First Years of the Reformation," *Archiv,* XLIX (1958), pp. 13–26; P. Althaus, *Theology of Luther,* pp. 35–42; R. Bainton, "The Bible and the Reformation," *Studies on the Reformation,* pp. 10–12; G.W. Locher, *H. Zwingli in Neuer Sicht,* pp. 225–27; J.T. McNeill, "The Significance of the Word of God for Calvin," *Church History* XXVIII (1959), pp. 131–46; Calvin, *Institutes* I, VI, 2 and 3; G. Williams, *Radical Reformation,* pp. 821–28. For the best example of the mainline English reformers' views on this point, see Cranmer's 1540 "Preface to the Bible" (*Writings and Letters,* pp. 118–25), and sections of the treatise "A Confutation of Unwritten Verities," which has generally been ascribed to Cranmer (*Ibid.,* pp. 10, 17–19). On Erasmus, see: *De Libero Arbitrio, EO* IX, 1219; *Enchiridion, EO* V, 505.

102. By rejecting the outward ordinances of God like the external sign of Baptism and the preached Word of God, the Spiritualists, Luther wrote, are burning the very bridge by which the Holy Spirit can come, notwithstanding their incessant clamoring after the "spirit" (*Wider die himml. Proph., WA* 18, 137). There were major differences in the way Luther, Zwingli, and Calvin understood the relation of the "sign" and the "signified," and so forth, and the same shows up repeatedly in their respective sacramental theologies, Christologies, and ecclesiologies. But even Zwingli, who was the most "transcendental" in his thinking (See K. McDonnell, *John Calvin, the Church and the Eucharist* [Princeton, 1967], pp. 89, 93), and who on that account was extremely reluctant to admit a spiritual "efficacy" to anything "material," considered for example the external rites of Baptism and the Eucharist necessary in at least the sense of being

"covenant signs" or "pledges" (See *Von dem touff, SW* 4, 203 ff.). Erasmus also was of the view that the external, sacramental rites enjoyed little "efficacy," and, like Zwingli (and the Dutch Sacramentists, to whom both were indebted [See Williams, *Radical Reformation*, pp. 30–37, 86–89]), saw their value in primarily "symbolic" terms (See J. Etienne, *Spiritualisme Erasmien et Theologiens Louvainistes* [Louvain, 1956], p. 42). Whether Erasmus actually considered participation in the external sacramental rites necessary, and not merely "useful," is debatable (See especially *De Amabili Ecclesiae Concordia, EO* V, 502–6). But even if the latter were the case, he was still far from the disdainful attitude toward the outward, sacramental rites shown by Franck, and to one or another extent by Karlstadt, Schwenkfeld, and other Spiritualists (Williams, *Radical Reformation*, pp. 40–44, 101–3, 106–16).

For the English reformers' assertion of the "necessity to salvation" of the sacraments of Baptism, Penance, and the Eucharist, see: *The Bishops' Book* (Lloyd, *op. cit.*, p. 129); contrary to Jaspar Ridley's opinion that the *King's Book* eliminated the *Bishops' Book's* distinction between the three greater and four lesser sacraments (*Cranmer*, p. 239), the *King's Book* actually was less orthodox than the former in that by distinguishing between "Penance" and the "sacrament of Penance" it no longer considered "auricular confession" necessary to salvation (See Lloyd, *op. cit.*, pp. 257, 261), a development precipitated by Cranmer (*Writings and Letters*, p. 477; Strype, *Memorials of Cranmer*, p. 751; G. Burnet, *op. cit.*, I, ii, pp. 360, 362; *Ibid.*, III, ii, p. 227), and by Henry VIII himself (Strype, *Memorials of Cranmer*, p. 345; G. Burnet, *op. cit.*, I, ii, pp. 543–50). The *King's Book* did, however, still speak of Baptism and the Eucharist as being "necessary to salvation" (Lloyd, *op. cit.*, 257, 293).

103. Hence, for example, Hugo of St. Victor's assertion: "Deus permittit mala, et malus non est, quia malum ad bonum et decorem universi novit optime reformare" (As cited in G. Biel, *Canonis Misse*, p. 142).

104. As was evidenced, for example, by Luther's attitude toward "images" (*Wider die himml. Proph., WA* 18, 83), and by what was the general, pedagogical thrust of his liturgical reforms (See V. Vatja, *Luther on Worship*, trans. U.W. Leupold [Philadelphia, 1958], pp. 177 ff.).

105. See *Supra*, I, n. 18; G. Biel, *Canonis Misse* II, pp. 86–112; for an expression of Erasmus' own admiration for allegory, see *Enchiridion, EO* V, 28–31.

106. See: J.P. Dolan, *The Influence of Erasmus, Witzel and Cassander in the Church Ordinances and Reform Proposals of the United Duchees of Cleve During the Middle Decades of the Sixteenth Century* (Münster, 1957), pp. 15, 33, 46, 48.

107. See *The Rationale of Ceremoniale*, pp. 15–33. On Cranmer's opposition to this work, see: R.W. Dixon, *History of the Church of England*, II, pp. 311–13.

108. *The Bishops' Book*, Lloyd, *op. cit.*, p. 147. *The King's Book, Ibid.*, p. 311; *Articles and Injunctions*, p. 108; Starkey, *Exhortation*, sig. U, fol. i; Becon, *The Potation for Lent, Early Works*, ed. J. Ayre (Cambridge, 1843), pp. 110–17.

109. See, for example, W. Tyndale, *Exposition and Notes*, pp. 93–97; *Answer to More*, pp. 7, 73–74; *Doctrinal Treatises*, pp. 219, 362, 373.

110. See, for example, Erasmus, *De Amabili Ecclesiae Concordia, EO* V, 500; see also: R. Bainton, *Erasmus*, p. 188. Even Cromwell, it may be noted, left some room for a conception of the ceremonies in terms of "reward" (See G. Burnet, *op. cit.*, I, ii, p. 221).

111. See *Answer to More*, pp. 76–77.

CHAPTER 5

THE TRUTH OF ADIAPHORISTIC LIBERTY

IN THE YEAR 1550 or thereabouts, Thomas Becon proudly proclaimed that the English realm had already been "delivered from anti-Christ's tyranny."[1] However valid such a conclusion may have been, earlier English adiaphorists like Tyndale and Frith had found themselves in quite a different situation. The title "Defender of the Faith" conferred by Leo X upon Henry VIII in 1521 had been well earned. Henry's *Assertio Septem Sacramentorum* had been as passionate a defense of the Roman position as any pope could ever have hoped for, extolling as it did, among other things, the quasi-divine, obligatory character of papal law, and the ancient "unwritten traditions."[2]

Furthermore, although Henry's dramatic defiance of papal authority in the early 1530's was itself, at least according to Thomas Starkey's reckoning, a bold assertion of adiaphoristic liberty,[3] there would remain periods throughout Henry's reign when his appreciation of Christian freedom in the realm of adiaphora seemed even to the more moderate of his reform-minded subjects to have left much to be desired. And even when, either on his own or at the prodding of Cromwell and Cranmer, the king himself favored its advance, there were always around the likes of Edmond Bonner and a host of other, more or less prestigious champions of a "depapalized" *status quo,* who on the whole did all in their betimes considerable power to check the spread or implementation of adiaphoristic theory. Finally, and notwithstanding Henry's brutal execution of its best spokesmen, there was the recusant party, many of whose members could be counted on, either at home, or, as in Reginald Pole's case, from abroad, to show the same sort of hostility or apathy toward the theory of adiaphorism earlier evidenced by More and Fisher.[4]

While, therefore, Turner and Bale may have been hallucinating when they spied a "Romyish Foxe" lurking behind every medieval vestige of the English Church, the so-called "tyranny of Antichrist" remained throughout at least the duration of the Henrician period, a fact with which the English adiaphorists, willy-nilly, had to cope.

Furthermore, in addition to those who stood ready to suppress tyrannically the truth of adiaphoristic liberty, there were others, as John Calvin noted in 1536, who, while pretending "a Pauline prudence" and taking every precaution "to protect their own repose," wished "all mention of freedom to be buried."[5] Among the English reformers, Stephen Gardiner probably came closest to fitting this description. For, although Gardiner's opposition to the adiaphorists seemed at times to have been of a "tyrannical" sort, more often than not it took the form of an extreme skepticism about the wisdom of broadcasting adiaphoristic doctrine, even if it were "true"—as he himself on occasion was brought to admit.[6] This desire on Gardiner's part to quash any mention of adiaphoristic liberty arose primarily out of his fear that simple-minded folk would thereby be led to despise even the fundamentals of religion,[7] and his fear that the masses might also be encouraged thereby to such contempt of human law as to leave the ecclesiastical and civil community in a state of chaos.[8]

Confronted with a similar "timidity" in Erasmus, Luther once remarked that the truth "is not to be put under a bushel, even if the whole world goes to smash."[9] In making such a remark, however, Luther was referring to a doctrine—i.e., the "bondage of the will"— which to his view, but not to Erasmus', was a "fundamental" article of Christian faith.[10] And before trying to determine to what extent and how, according to Luther, Erasmus, and other adiaphorists, the "truth" of adiaphoristic liberty was to be defended or expressed in the face of "tyranny" and "timidity," some notice must first be taken of the possibility of their having considered their "doctrine" of adiaphoristic liberty itself something "indifferent."

Up to this point, only the slightest notice has been taken of any application of the theory of adiaphorism beyond the realm of liturgical and ethical matters. And, in fact, the English reformers would seem to have been the first to have made any extensive use of the term adiaphoron in relation to doctrine. Nonetheless, a variety of distinctions had been drawn by one or another pre-sixteenth century theologian which tended to favor some sort of hierarchical evaluation of Christian doctrine. Such, for example, had been the Pauline distinctions between the *keryma* and *didache,* and between the "milk" and "meat" of Christ's message, both of which distinctions were echoed repeatedly by the early Church Fathers, to some extent inspired the formulation of the Creeds, and by the time of Augustine, began to give rise to the more technical distinction between explicit and implicit faith, which, while presupposing the "unity of faith," did make allowances for the less mature Christians.[11]

Among the sixteenth-century, reform-minded theologians on the Continent, Erasmus especially was insistent upon establishing some sort of hierarchical evaluation of the plethora of doctrines then obtaining in Christian circles. The "sum of religion," he argued, "is peace and harmony." But the latter will never prevail, "unless we define as little as possible and in many things leave each one to his own judgment." In earlier times, Erasmus said, "faith was in life rather than in the profession of articles." As soon as the articles increased, sincerity decreased; contention grew hot and love grew cold. This was the first stage in the fall of the Church, and if unity is ever to be restored, he said, then instead of trying to define every last point pertaining to faith, "we will have to let do with what is clearly expressed in Scripture and is necessary to salvation."[12]

Consistent with such remarks, Erasmus stated in the preface to his treatise *De Libero Arbitrio* that his dislike for dogmatic assertions is so great that he prefers the views of the skeptics wherever the inviolable authority of Scripture and the decision of the Church are not at stake. His discussion of "free will" will not, therefore, he added, be an attempt to "dogmatize," but only an "inquiry." Even the latter, he noted, is a task he does not much relish having to perform. Men would do much better to leave the "darker" passages of Scripture to God, and be satisfied with what is clearly contained therein. All the laborious investigations about the Trinity, the Virgin birth, and other such matters, only lead men to love each other less. Furthermore, there are certain opinions which, even if true and intelligible, would be better left unexposed to the public.[13]

Erasmus obviously despised the inquisitorial mentality that would spot a heretic behind every bush. Only six months prior to publication of his *De Libero Arbitrio,* he had written the brief colloquy entitled *Inquisitio de Fide,* in which he as much as stated that as far as essential doctrines were concerned, Catholics and Lutherans were one.[14] In his reply to Ulrich von Hutten and elsewhere, Erasmus concluded that questions about the binding force of episcopal constitutions, or about whether papal primacy derives from Christ, whether Christ himself instituted the sacrament of penance, whether free will is important to salvation, whether faith alone contributes to salvation, and whether the Mass is a sacrifice, are matters that have no essential bearing upon Christian faith.[15]

There was little that was new in the criteria employed by Erasmus for the sake of establishing a hierarchy of truth.[16] Few, however, with the possible exception of Nicholas of Cusa, had ever applied them so broadly as did Erasmus and some of his followers like George Cassander (who built upon them his well-known notion of the "fundamental articles").[17]

In his Commentary on Romans, Luther wrote that faith consists of something indivisible; it is either a whole faith and believes all there is to believe, or it is no faith at all if it does not believe one part of what there is to believe.[18] Such an emphasis upon the "unity of faith," indications of which can be found in the writings of other mainline reformers too, brings into focus the correlation or interdependence which the reformers saw obtaining between all the articles of faith, and explains to some extent how they could speak of a variety of doctrines constituting, each in its own way, the very essence of Christian faith.[19]

This insistence upon the unity of faith did not, however, deter the reformers from a hierarchical evaluation of Christian doctrine.[20] In the first place, clear distinctions were drawn between the articles of faith and theological opinions,[21] and between the deposit of faith and its formulations.[22] Furthermore, they clearly differentiated between those doctrines contained in Scripture and those that were not. Scripture, they said, contains all the truths "necessary to salvation," and it is only such truths which the Christian is bound to believe. In one of the few explicit applications of the term adiaphoron to doctrinal matters by the Continental reformers, Luther wrote in his response to Henry VIII's Assertio that "whatever has been written outside the holy Scripture" should be considered "free and indifferent," because "necessary articles of faith" should not be fashioned from the "words of men."[23] But Scripture was not for the reformers the only material principle by which to evaluate doctrine. The Creeds, Patristic tradition, and the consensus ecclesiae were also sometimes appealed to for the sake of further specifying the core of Christian truth.[24] A number of formal principles were also brought into play. Chief among these was the doctrine of justification, which to almost all the reformers represented the sum and substance of Christian belief to such an extent that its connection with other doctrines was considered a decisive factor in the determination of their fundamentality or lack thereof.[25]

To demonstrate how all these criteria were correlated by the reformers would far exceed the scope of the present discussion. Suffice it to say that in one way or another their combined application led the reformers to the conclusion that not all Christian doctrines are of the same sort. Some, because of their place in Scripture, their necessity to salvation, their connection with the doctrine of justification, and so forth, are fundamental, while others are not. The former were deemed so necessary to salvation that they should be certain and unquestioned by all; the latter can go unknown without harm to the sum of religion, and without loss of salvation, and disagreement in their regard need not become a cause of schism.[26]

While, therefore, Erasmus and the Continental reformers only very rarely applied the term adiaphoron explicitly to doctrinal matters, there was much in their discussion of the latter which undoubtedly encouraged the English reformers to use the term more extensively in relation to doctrines. Among the first to do so were William Tyndale and John Frith.

In a letter he wrote to Frith in 1533, Tyndale stated that he "would have the right use [of the Eucharist] preached, and the [Eucharistic] presence to be an indifferent thing, till the matter might be reasoned in peace at leisure of both parties." He encouraged Frith to make his stand "in open necessary things," and "not to pronounce or define of hid secrets, or things that neither help or hinder, whether they be so or no." If a point of contention "be a thing that maketh no matter," Frith should "laugh and let it pass, and refer the thing to other men; and stick . . . stiffly and stubbornly in earnest and necessary things."[27]

At about the same time as he wrote this letter to Frith, Tyndale published a short treatise entitled *A Brief Declaration of the Sacraments,* in which he noted that it is the duty of those who profess the faith of Christ, and the love of his neighbor, to bear with each other's diverse opinions regarding the Eucharistic presence "as long as the other opinion is not plain wicked through false idolatry, nor contrary to the salvation that is in Christ, nor against the open and manifest doctrine of Christ and his apostles, nor contrary to the general articles of the faith of the church of Christ, which are confirmed with open scripture." It is wrong, Tyndale concluded, for a Christian who is "bound under pain of damnation to love his brother as Christ loved him, to hate, to persecute, and to slay his brother for blind zeal to any opinion, that neither letteth nor hindereth to salvation that is in Christ."[28]

Perhaps because he had witnessed the not always so charitable Marburg Colloquy of 1529, Frith wholeheartedly embraced Tyndale's advice, and in two of his last writings from the Tower—*An Answer unto Sir Thomas More's Letter* and *The Articles Wherefore John Frith Died*—insisted that any doctrine about the manner of Christ's presence in the Eucharist was to be considered "indifferent."

Frith himself, it may be noted, was inclined to Oecolampadius' "spiritual" or "commemorative" interpretation of the Eucharistic presence.[29] But having expounded his own view against the doctrine of transubstantiation, Frith quickly added that "I would not that any should count that I make my saying (which is negative) any article of the faith . . . I say again, that we make none necessary article of the faith of our part, but leave it indifferent for all men to judge therein, as God shall open his heart." In fact, Frith added, "if there were no worse mischief that ensued of this belief [i.e., transubstantiation] than it is in itself, I would never have spoken against it." But, unfortunately, the doctrine leads to "damnable idolatry, for through the belief that his body is there, men fall down and worship it, and thinking to please God, do damnably sin against him". But again, apart from this idolatry, belief of the doctrine of transubstantiation "is of itself not damnable, as it is not damnable to think that Christ is a very stone or a vine, because the literal sense so saith: or if you believe that you ought to preach to fishes, and go christen them another while, as ye do bells."[30]

On the other hand, however, neither can the denial of the doctrine of transubstantiation be said to be damnable. Just as it is a thing indifferent to assert the doctrine, so is it a thing indifferent to deny it. To prove this point Frith argued not so much from the fact that the doctrine of transubstantiation is without basis in the Scriptures (as he had earlier argued in reference to the indifference of the doctrine of Purgatory[31]), as from the fact that it is not included in the tenets of the Creed. Even if the doctrine could be shown to be "true" from Scriptures, Frith stated, that would not prove that it is "necessary to salvation," for there are "points contained in Scripture, although they be undoubted verities, yet may I be saved without them." This, he said, can occur in three cases: first, "in the case that I never heard of them"; second, when although "I hear of them, I cannot understand them nor comprehend them"; and third, when "I hear them and understand them, and yet, by the reason of another text, misconstrue them." On all the "truths" falling within these categories the Christian may dissent "without any jeopardy of damnation," and that includes, according to Frith, all "truths" that have not been included in the Creed. "The same faith shall save us," Frith stated, "which saved the old fathers before Christ's incarnation." "We are bound to believe no more under pain of damnation than they were bound to believe." But the "old fathers" were "never so mad as to believe that the manna was changed into Christ's own natural body, but understood it spiritually." Yet, they "did eat Christ in faith both before they had the manna, and more expressly through the manna, and with no less fruit when the manna was ceased." As for the specific content of their faith, Frith said that "there

is no point in our Creed but that they believe it, as well as we do."
These Creedal articles, and only these, Frith stated, are "necessary to
salvation: for them am I bound to believe, and am damned without
excuse if I believe them not." But as for the doctrine of transubstantiation, "it is no article of our creed, in the twelve articles whereof are
sufficient for our salvation; and therefore we may think that you lie,
without all jeopardy of damnation."[32]

Few English reformers would seem to have concurred in Tyndale's
and Frith's adiaphoristic designation of the doctrine of the Eucharistic
presence. But with the latter's doctrinal adiaphorism as such, subsequent English reformers did agree, with one doctrine especially—
that of purgatory—repeatedly being classified as an adiaphoron.[33]

Given, therefore, this implicit or explicit doctrinal adiaphorism of
Erasmus and the reformers, the question remains whether perhaps
they did not also consider their doctrine of adiaphoristic liberty itself
"non-fundamental" or "indifferent." None of them, it should be noted,
ever gave the question any formal attention. Nor did they ever attempt
to draw up any exhaustive listing of which doctrines they considered
"non-fundamental" or "indifferent," and which not. Any answer to the
above question will largely depend, therefore, upon which of their
variety of criteria for the differentiation of doctrinal matters is applied
to their doctrine of adiaphoristic liberty. Tested over against the material principle of the Creed sometimes favored by especially Frith, it
would seem that they would have been very hard pressed to have
denied the latter's own adiaphoristic character.[34] On the whole, however, and consistent with their theological definition of adiaphora as
those things which have been "neither commanded, nor forbidden" by
Scripture, the reformers were most inclined to draw their distinction of
adiaphoristic and non-adiaphoristic doctrines in accordance with the
material principle of Scripture. And to the extent, therefore, that they
considered their doctrine of adiaphorism clearly grounded in
Scripture—as they surely did—they would, as with all other Scriptural
doctrines, have considered it a truth of the sort, that "all true Christian
men ought and must most constantly believe, maintain, and defend."[35]
And that is precisely what the evidence suggests they did.

Those Continental and English reformers who were of a more
adiaphoristic bent than Stephen Gardiner were not oblivious to the
latter's concern for law and order. As will be seen in a subsequent
chapter, they took every precaution to guard against the possibility of
their doctrine being converted by libertine or antinomian forces into an
excuse for "carnal liberty." But their primary concern was for man's
freedom before God, and if the declaration of such freedom implied

some risk so far as man's external social order was concerned,[36] then, unlike Gardiner, that was a risk they were prepared to take. In brief, whatever concerns they may have had for worldly peace, they refused to bury their doctrine of adiaphoristic liberty under a bushel, but instead deemed it of the very essence of their Christian vocation to share their "knowledge" with those who supposedly still stood in the dark.[37]

This "labor for knowledge"—as William Tyndale, citing the Apostle Paul, was wont to call it[38]—was carried on chiefly from the pulpit. Some of the very best sermons of the whole reformation era—Luther's *Invocavit* series of 1522, or Zwingli's sermon at the height of the "sausage" controversy at Zurich in the same year, or Hugh Latimer's fiery sermons before the Convocation in 1536[39]—were those which sought to bring the Christian community into a mature awareness of its adiaphoristic liberty.

But the printed word was also used to good advantage in disseminating such "knowledge." Few books of the period were ever as exclusively concerned with expounding the doctrine of adiaphoristic liberty as were Zwingli's *Von Erkiesen und Freiheit der Speisen*, John Frith's *Articles*, or Thomas Starkey's *Exhortation to Unity and Obedience*. But almost every work published by Erasmus or the Continental and English reformers included some discussion of their adiaphoristic doctrine. Especially noteworthy among the latter, because of its semi-official authorship, was the 1537 *Bishops' Book*, which carried in its pages what must certainly be considered one of the most remarkably unequivocal expressions of Christian liberty ever produced by a body of Christian bishops, not only bewailing, as it did, the "want of the knowledge" of such liberty in previous ages, but also calling upon their subjects to "diligently learn" and to "study to preserve that Christian liberty, whereunto they be called and brought by Christ's blood and his doctrine."[40]

Letter-writing was probably at an all-time high in the sixteenth century, and not surprisingly their letters also became for the adiaphorists an important means of spreading their doctrine about adiaphoristic liberty. Tyndale's aforementioned letter to Frith, Starkey's persistent correspondence with Reginald Pole, Hugh Latimer's letters to Edward Baynton in 1531 or to Cranmer in 1532, Henry VIII's letter of November 19, 1536, to his bishops, Melanchthon's letters of 1539 to Cromwell and the king, Calvin's 1548 letter to Somerset, Cranmer's angry exchange with a Kentish magistrate in 1537, or his equally heated missive of October 7, 1552, to the Privy Council concerning the "kneeling rubric," and Bucer's and Martyr's aforementioned correspondence with Hooper and à Lasco about the vestments, were but a few of the countless attempts to carry on the "labor for knowledge" by epistolary means during the early stages of the English reformation.[41]

Contributing toward the same end—at least after Henry VIII's supposed "enlightenment," were many of the Articles, Proclamations, and Injunctions issued under the aegis of the King and Parliament from 1536 through 1552. Typical of many of these official documents promulgated during the Henrician and Edwardine periods of reform, was Cromwell's 1536 "Injunctions" calling upon the clergy "to instruct" their parishioners in such wise "that they maye playnly know and discerne" what is "necessary to salvation," and what is not.[42]

Needless to say, much of this effort on the reformers' part to share their "knowledge" of adiaphoristic liberty was expended in vain. Some in their audience were either too young or too "ignorant" to grasp its meaning, or did so in such moderate degree that, as Jean Colet put it, they could not be "induced to believe that [they] can meddle with [indifferent] things without peril". Distrusting what is "unusual and not seen before," such individuals, Colet added, "feel confident that what is approved of by their use will do no harm," but "shrink from other things as hitherto untried," and hence persist in differentiating times and other things pertaining to the external conduct of life.[43] The adiaphorists generally referred to individuals of this sort as "the weak."

Not to be confused with "the weak," however, were those individuals whom the adiaphorists called the "tyrants." By these latter folk were understood those "stubborn," "Pharaisaical," "hypocritical" individuals who, while knowing full well the "truth and liberty of the saints," nonetheless, because of their pride and lust for power, refuse to accept the truth and instead go about trying to subvert or to suppress it.[44] As will be seen, these "wolves"—as Luther described them,[45] could also be found, according to the reformers, outside the Roman camp. But initially at least, they were generally thought of as being representative of the latter.

Now, neither in the presence of the "weak," nor in the presence of the "tyrants," it was said, must the truth of adiaphoristic liberty be compromised. So far as the "weak" are concerned, every effort must be made to teach and strengthen them so that they will not forever be left on a diet of "milk" alone,[46] and "never come to the knowledge of the truth."[47] The "tyrants" on the other hand, should simply be "let go" in accordance with Christ's suggestion that such individuals are "blind leaders of the blind" who will eventually fall into a pit of their own making (Mt. 15:12–14).[48] Implicit to such a conclusion was the assumption that any further attempt to instruct such individuals would only be a waste of time and energy. Thus, when Henry VIII promulgated the Six Articles Act in 1539, decreeing among other things that clerical marriage is forbidden *de jure divino*,[49] Luther for example simply wrote the king off as a lost cause, explaining that "we do not consider ourselves obliged to instruct him yet again."[50] Also implicit to the decision to "let go" the tyrants, however, was the determination to stand up to them, just as the Apostle Paul confronted Peter when the latter tried to impose the Jewish ceremonies upon the Gentile Christians (Gal. 2:11). "Do not yield an inch unto them," John Frith advised. Their "obdurate ignorance," he said, must be resisted "in the face."[51]

Frith practiced what he preached. His death at the stake on July 4, 1533,[52] was as noble a defense of the truth of adiaphoristic liberty in the face of "tyranny" as any ever made. Unlike his fellow reformer and adiaphorist, Robert Barnes, who went to his execution in 1540 asking: "Is there here any man that knoweth wherefore I die?"[53], Frith was very lucid about the cause of his execution. He also recognized, however, that while he himself understood what his death was all about, many of his friends might not. To forestall their bewilderment, Frith spent his last days in the dungeon at Newgate writing an apology of his death—the aforementioned *Articles Wherefore John Frith Died*. The bishops "examined me," Frith began,

> but of two articles . . . whether there was a purgatory . . . and whether [Christ's] very natural body, both flesh and blood, is really contained under the sacrament, and there actually present, besides all similitudes.[54]

His answer to both questions, he noted, was negative. But he hastened to add: "I would not that any should count that I make my saying . . . any article of the faith," for while "it is true that I lay in irons when I wrote this . . . you may think the contrary without all jeopardy of damnation."[55]

Frith was obviously aware that his imprisonment and death would be self-defeating were others to conclude therefrom, and not without some logic, that a denial of purgatory and transubstantiation was essential to faith. On the other hand, Frith was also aware that if they agreed that such articles were "indifferent," then, his death would seem a contradiction: "I think many men wonder how I can die in this article, seeing that it is no necessary article of our faith." But, as a matter of fact, Frith goes on to say, he is not to die for a denial of the aforementioned doctrines. Rather,

> the cause of my death is this; because I cannot in conscience abjure and swear that our prelates' opinion of the Sacrament (that is, that the substance of bread and wine is verily changed into the flesh and

blood of our Saviour, Jesus Christ), is an undoubted article of the faith necessary to be believed, under pain of damnation.[56]

To admit otherwise, Frith concluded, would be to

damnably condemn all the Germans and Almains with infinite woe, which indeed do not believe nor think that the substance of bread and wine is changed into the substance of Christ's natural body.[57]

In making this defense of adiaphoristic liberty, Frith, it should be carefully noted, did not mean to suggest that to be true to their adiaphoristic liberty Christians would have to reject the "tyrants'" doctrines of transubstantiation and purgatory. In fact, as he explicitly stated, it was precisely to prove the contrary that he accepted his martyrdom. This point is very important for properly understanding what the Continental and English adiaphorists really meant by their doctrine of adiaphoristic liberty, and its expression, maintenance, and defense in the external forum.

No sooner had the likes of Erasmus, Luther, and Frith announced their adiaphoristic appraisal of certain matters, than Karlstadt and other radicals promptly concluded that Christians had no alternative but to break all such traditions in order to demonstrate to the world that they were indeed "free" men.[58] A similar view would seem to have been operative in Flacius Illyricus' opposition to the Leipzig Interim. For when one cuts through all his confusing, if not confused, arguments for proving that the Interim ceremonies were not "true" adiaphora, one comes, in the final analysis, to his conviction that, at least "in times of persecution and scandal," one cannot really be true to one's Christian liberty except that one actually reject those ceremonies which the "tyrant" is trying to impose. To illustrate his conviction in this latter regard, Flacius cited the example of the prophet Daniel's disobedience of the royal decree that no one was to make a petition of any god or man other than the king for thirty days (Dan. 6:6–10). Now, whether Daniel prayed before an open window or behind a closed window was in itself a thing indifferent, Flacius noted. But given the decree of the king, it was imperative, Flacius argued, that Daniel pray, as he did, before the open window, so as to show others than he would not obey the king's godless decree.[59] Flacius used this example to support his general conclusion that in times of persecution and scandal, there are no adiaphora, but he could just as well have used it to hold Daniel up as a true champion of "adiaphoristic" liberty. For, in the final analysis, his conclusion that the Interim ceremonies were not genuine adiaphora was merely the logical extension of the peculiar conception of "adiaphoristic" liberty he shared with Karlstadt and other radicals. Applied to Frith's case, Flacius' views would have meant that in order to be true to his adiaphoristic liberty, Frith would have had no choice but to have denied the papist doctrine of transubstantiation. But this in turn would have implied that the latter was not an adiaphoron. Flacius undoubtedly would have concluded as much—and all the more in that he could hardly have denied that such a doctrine was far more essential to "popery" than the many ceremonies which it had helped to spawn. Frith, on the other hand, as has been seen, suffered martyrdom to prove that such a doctrine was an adiaphoron, which as such might be held or not held without in any way jeopardizing one's quest for salvation.

That other mainline English reformers did not share Flacius' view in this regard may be demonstrated by way of their reaction to Henry VIII's legislation of clerical celibacy. Already in 1536 and 1538 royal proclamations had been issued forbidding clerical marriage in England.[60] Notwithstanding Christopher Mont's assurances to the German princes that these royal prohibitions had been inspired only by Henry's concern to avoid scandalizing the "weak,"[61] the king in 1539 personally engineered Parliamentary passage of the Six Articles, the third of which asserted that "by the law of God," priests may not marry after ordination.[62] Continental and English reformers alike were quick to protest this attempt to render "necessary to salvation" a matter which they considered clearly adiaphoristic. Simon Heynes, for example, expressed himself incredulous that "so learned a king, having such a great number of learned Bishops in H. Scripture," would think of suggesting that clerical celibacy and similar matters which have no express foundation in Scripture bind the Christian *ex jure divino*. "It were good to remember," Heynes warned, that

> if the King's Grace, with his Lords Spiritual and Temporal, etc. should establish these things to bee true *jure divino*, without authority of holy Scripture; or else by authority wrong understanded, [then] the Emperor and the Fr. King hath the same authority in their dominion that our master hath here; and therefore may in their councils decree other things to be true *jure divino*, of Scriptures likewise wrong understand . . . as for example . . . *Episcopus Romanus est jure divino Caput universalis Ecclesiae, juxta illud*.[63]

From the Continent, Melanchthon wrote the king that his Six Articles threatened to plunge England back into the dark ages when "men's traditions have been a yoke to good men's consciences." "You pretend to impugn and gainstand the tyranny of the Romish bishops," Melanchthon continued, but "in the meantime, you defend and maintain those laws of that Romish antichrist, which be the strength and sinews of all his power."[64]

In the prohibition of the Six Articles Act against clerical marriage, therefore, the reformers obviously considered themselves confronted with as blatant an example of "antichrist's tyranny" as any provided by Charles V during the Leipzig Interim. In fact, it was far more so, in that while most of the Interim ceremonies were imposed only on an adiaphoristic basis,[65] Henry's prohibition of clerical marriage, as noted, was projected on *jure divino* grounds, and to that extent went beyond even the thinking of a majority of the Tridentine Fathers.[66] If, therefore, the English reformers shared Flacius' view, they certainly had the chance to show it in 1539. But as a matter of fact, they did not.

For all their verbal protest against the "tyranny" of the Six Articles Act, the English reformers did not conclude therefrom, as Flacius undoubtedly would have, that clerical marriage was no longer to be considered a genuinely adiaphoristic matter. Nor did they emulate the prophet Daniel by rushing out to display publicly their contempt for Henry's legislation by actually marrying or by flaunting the marriages some had already entered into secretly.[67] If anything, they became more secretive than ever about the outward display of their adiaphoristic liberty to marry. Cranmer, for example, who had been keeping his marriage to the niece of Andreas Osiander's wife secret for over seven years, now, after passage of the Six Articles Act, took the further precaution of having her shipped back to her folk in Germany until such time (1543) as he deemed it feasible to have her return.[68] It was hardly the sort of reaction one would expect of the Archbishop had he been of Flacius' mentality. Flacius himself would undoubtedly have considered Cranmer's conduct in this affair an act of cowardice and a serious scandal. And perhaps Cranmer was motivated to some extent by the kind of fear Henry could so easily arouse in his subjects. But it is also conceivable, and indeed more likely, that Cranmer acted as he did out of a conviction that his marriage was and remained an adiaphoristic matter, or in other words, a matter between himself and God, which he was free to arrange in the external forum in whatever manner he deemed by the light of his Christian faith to be best for the Christian community.

As noted, Luther reacted to the Six Articles Act by simply concluding that Henry was a lost cause, who might best be "let go." According to all the mainline reformers, such a "letting go" implied, among other things, the possibility of emulating Christ's example of breaking the Jewish traditions (Mt. 9:12), or the Apostle Paul's example of refusing to circumcise Titus (Ga. 2:3), and boldly standing up to the "tyrants" by doing exactly the opposite of what they demand,[69] no matter how much "offense" they might "take" at the same,[70] it being one thing to "give" offense, and quite another to have it "taken."[71] Luther claimed that his marriage to Katherine von Bora was partly inspired by precisely such a concern—a concern, namely, to spite a "tyrannical" pope.[72] Similar examples of a bold display of their adiaphoristic liberty in public manner could be cited from all the mainline reformers, including Cranmer.[73] But such actions were not undertaken in the belief that no other alternative was open to them. If they did what they did, it was the result of prudential judgments based upon a set of principles which could at another time or place incline them to the very opposite course of action, along the lines of which they would, in accordance with Christ's own counsel, "turn the other cheek" (Mt. 5:39), or go yet a second mile with the tyrants who had forced them to walk the first (Mt. 5:41).[74] Cranmer's decision to suffer the inconveniences of a clandestine marriage, or even separation from his wife, can best be interpreted as an exercise in such forbearance of "tyranny," as can also Zwingli's similar action of keeping secret the fact of his marriage to Anna Rheinhart for over two years, or his action of refusing to partake of the sausage served at Frohschauer's infamous Ash Wednesday dinner at Zurich in 1522, or, finally, Melanchthon's action of choosing to suffer the "harsh servitude" of Charles V during the period of the Interim.

Other principles occasionally directing the adiaphorists down such a course of action will be taken up shortly. But it should be emphasized here that their concern for the principle of truth could itself incline them to accept with patience the external bonds of "tyranny." Just as it is sometimes necessary to do the very opposite of what the "tyrants" demand "lest many others be snared by their impious views,"[75] so, Luther wrote, it may on occasion be necessary to bear externally with "tyranny" in order to avoid having the essentials of Christian truth taken away from the faithful.[76] It was primarily for this reason that Melanchthon chose to accept the Leipzig Interim. Because the latter did not to his view compromise the essential Protestant doctrine of solafideism, the ceremonies it imposed could be tolerated on an adiaphoristic basis.[77]

Cranmer may well have been thinking along similar lines when he chose not to flaunt the fact of his marriage. Not to mention the excessive strain it would have put upon the "weak" grasp that many of his fellow countrymen then had upon the "truth," such a revelation before and for at least a few years after 1539 would probably have left Henry little choice but to have taken some direct punitive action against

Cranmer. Whether Henry could ever have brought himself to deal Cranmer, one of his closest friends, as fatal a blow as he did Cromwell in 1540, may be doubted.[78] But if Henry was anything, he was "unpredictable." And if Cranmer outlived Cromwell it may well have been because, unlike the latter, he never took the king for granted—at least not in public.[79] In any event, even if Henry's punishment of Cranmer would have stopped at exile, imprisonment, divestiture, or merely the loss of grace, the Protestant cause in England would have been seriously jeopardized. As it turned out, by successfully concealing his marriage until such time as even the king himself could receive news of it without going into a tantrum,[80] Cranmer was able to retain the king's ear and thereby eventually relax the latter's hostility toward the Protestants to such an extent that during his latter years Henry himself took the lead in setting the stage for the Protestant domination of the Edwardine period.[81] In other words, just as Melanchthon's adiaphoristically inspired compromise helped to keep Charles V from consolidating the victory he had gained over the German Protestants at Mühlberg in 1547,[82] so the flexibility evidenced in Cranmer's adiaphoristic maneuvers may well have been responsible for saving the Protestant cause in England.

When Luther, Melanchthon, Zwingli, Cranmer, or any of the adiaphorists spoke of compromising, or actually did compromise, on adiaphoristic matters for the sake of preserving the essentials of Christian doctrine, they did not, it should be emphasized, have in mind to suggest that the truth of adiaphoristic liberty itself was less than essential. Nor were they selling one truth to buy time on another. They strove to champion the truth of adiaphoristic liberty. But they refused to identify that truth with any one or another particular external mode of conduct in the realm of adiaphora. To them, adiaphoristic liberty was first and last an affair between God and man, or, as Calvin put it, something altogether "spiritual," whose whole force lies in quieting men's consciences before God about the use of things indifferent. That Christian will be true to his adiaphoristic liberty, therefore, who "knows" that such things in themselves can not make or break his relation to God. This "knowledge" *is* his adiaphoristic liberty. It does not need to be "proven," nor can it, ultimately, be "proven" in the external forum. The man who, for example, abstains from meat throughout his life cannot for that reason alone be considered any less free than the man who eats meat every day of his life.[83] So long as neither conceives of his action as being in itself of any importance to God, both can claim to be giving witness to the truth of their adiaphoristic liberty. For a Karlstadt or a Flacius Illyricus to insist to the contrary that certain external actions must of necessity be rejected as proof of one's liberty is but a new type of "tyranny,"[84] which must be opposed no less than the "tyranny of antichrist."[85]

How, therefore, the Christian is to exercise his adiaphoristic liberty in the external forum—whether he should retain or reject this or that traditional ceremony, use or not use his right to marry, eat or not eat any food of his choice, to believe or not to believe one or another peripheral doctrine—these were questions which could not, according to the adiaphorists, be decided solely on the principle of truth. The need for honesty, they said, cannot be overlooked. But honesty in the realm of adiaphora requires in a very special way, they added, that close consideration be given also to the dictates of love.

NOTES

1. T. Becon, *The Flower of Godly Prayers,* in Becon, *Prayers and Other Pieces,* ed. J. Ayre (Cambridge, 1844), p. 4.

2. Henry VIII, *Assertio Septem Sacramentorum,* pp. 221, 315, 356, 279, 357.

3. Arguing that papal supremacy was "not of the law of God, prescribed unto us for the necessity of our salvation, but yet it is a thing indifferent, the disobedience whereof, bringeth not to our sowles damnation" (*Exhortation,* sig. M, fol. iv[v]), Starkey concluded that the king was quite within his prerogative to decide that the papacy was no longer expedient (*Ibid.,* Sig. R, fol. iii[v]–sig. S, fol. iv).

4. Though a host to Starkey for a number of years at Padua, a correspondent with Erasmus, and an early supporter of the humanist reform program, Pole simply ignored Starkey's constant pleading that he recognize the adiaphoristic character of the papacy (S. Herrtage, *Starkey's Life and Letters,* pp. xvii–xx, xxxiv–xxv). When Pole's *De Unitate* reached England in 1536, Starkey concluded with great disappointment that its arguments "would make every old custom of the Church necessary to salvation" (As cited in the introduction to: R. Pole, *Pole's Defense of the Unity of the Church,* trans. J. Dwyer [Westminster, 1965], p. xxv). Apparently, Pole and Starkey had been in disagreement over "the things which pertain not of necessity to man's salvation" already prior to 1534, (see J.S. Brewer and J. Gardiner, *Letters and Papers, Foreign and Domestic of the Reign of Henry VIII* [London, 1862f.], XI, no. 73; Zeeveld, *op. cit.,* p. 126).

5. Calvin, *Institues* III, XIX, 12.

6. On June 29, 1548, Gardiner was made to prove his loyalty to Edward VI by preaching before the king on certain articles basic to Protestant belief, and on that occasion asserted, among other things, that despite the fact that he had often been called a "master of ceremonies and of outward things," he had always followed the opinion of Paul and Augustine, and esteemed ceremonies as "things indifferent" (Foxe, *Acts and Monuments* VI, pp. 91–92).

7. In an obvious reference to the adiaphorists' tendency to consider things "in themselves" or "abstractly," Gardiner, in his treatise *A Detection of the Devil's Sophistry,* attacked the "devilish sophistry" of "dividing and examing parts alone" (*A Detection,* sig. R, fol. vi). There are certain parts of the Christian religion which "if consydered several-

lye, be nothynge," Gardiner explained, and yet when "joyned togyther, be somewhat, and very necessarye . . . necessarye for oure estate, althoughe not necessarye in respecte of the pryncypall thynge" (*Ibid.*). If the relative necessity of these parts is to be respected, their interrelation must obviously be maintained, but that, according to Gardiner, was precisely what the devil seeks to break down. Thus, for example, it is asked "whether a shaven crowne maketh a priest?", or "whether a longe gowne . . . of that colour, or that facyon . . . maketh a priest?", or "shall forbearynge of meates save a man?", or "is the place cause why a man's prayer is good?" (*Ibid.*, sig. R, fol. vi[v]–vii[v]). And since to all of these questions—so put—the answer is "naye, Naye, Naye," the devil can ask "what nedeste thou comme to churche then?", or "why not eat all day long?", or "why wear a crown or cassock?" (*Ibid.*). In such a way, Gardiner concluded, "the deuyl robbeth simple men, euen of the substance by degrees of true religion" (*Ibid.*, Sig. R, fol. vii[v]).

8. See *Infra*, pp. 142–43, 164.

9. As cited in Bainton, *Erasmus of Rotterdam* (N.Y., 1969), p. 192; see also: *De Servo Arbitrio, WA* 18, 604–6.

10. *Ibid., WA* 18, 786.

11. See C.H. Dodd, *The Apostolic Preaching* (New York, 1962), pp. 8–17; Oscar Cullmann, *The Earliest Christian Confessions*, trans. J.K.S. Reid (London, 1949), pp. 33–38; T.W. Street, *op. cit.*, pp. 266–86; Congar, *Tradition and Traditions*, pp. 20–22, 27–28, 51, 109, 114, 509 n. 2, 510; Hanson, *op. cit.*, pp. 52–74; Henri de Lubac's introduction to Origen, *On First Principles*, trans. G.W. Butterworth (New York, 1966), pp. xix f.; A. Harnack, *History of Dogma*, trans. N. Buchanan (Boston, 1898–1903), V, p. 81; VI, pp. 165–67; VII, p. 7; J. Lecler, *Toleration and the Reformation*, trans. T.L. Westow (London, 1960), I, pp. 52–60, 79–101; M.D. Chenu, "Contribution à L'Histoire Du Traité De La Foi," *Mélanges Thomistes, Bibliothèque Thomiste* (Le Saulchoir, Kain, 1923), III, pp. 123–40; L. Hödl, "Articulus Fidei, Eine Begriffsgeschichtliche Arbeit," *Einsicht und Glaube*, ed. J. Ratzinger and H. Fries (Freiburg im Breisgau, 1962), pp. 358–76; H. Oberman, *Harvest*, pp. 75–89. Of all the pre-sixteenth-century theologians, Nicholas of Cusa would seem to have been the most insistent upon a distinction of "fundamental" and "non-fundamental" truths (See his *De Pace Fidei, Opera Omnia* VII [Hamburg, 1959], pp. 51–62).

12. Letter to John Carondelet, *EE* V, pp. 177, 180, 181; *EE* IV, p. 118.

13. *EO* IX, 1215, 1216, 1217.

14. *EO* I, 732.

15. *Spongia Adversus Aspergines Hutteni, EO* X, 1663; also: *Ad Timotheum* 1:13, *EO* VI, 926–28; *Catechismus, EO*, V, 1176, 1172–73, 1175, as cited in Bainton, *Erasmus*, p. 267.

16. Certainly his use of the material principle of Scripture in conjunction with the formal principle of "necessity to salvation" to differentiate doctrines was not new. Nor, of course, was his distinction of faith and its theological elaboration new. Roland Bainton has noted, however, that Erasmus would seem to have been the first to speak of "doctrines by which the Church stands or falls" (*Ibid.*, p. 186).

17. According to Cassander, so long as Roman Catholics, Lutherans, Calvinists, Zwinglians, and Orientals agreed on "the foundation of Apostolic doctrine . . . as contained in the brief Symbol of the Faith" they retained the *jus communionis* (See J. Lecler, *op. cit.*, I, pp. 272–73; also: R. Rouse and S.C. Neill, *A History of the Ecumenical Movement, 1517–1948* [London, 1954], p. 38).

18. *WA* 56, 246; see also: *Wider Hans Wurst, WA* 51, 516; *De Servo Arbitrio, WA* 18, 604.

19. See Manschreck, *Melanchthon*, pp. 258–59; Calvin, *Institutes* IV, II, 5; IV, I, 5; Althaus, *Theology of Luther*, pp. 224–25; U. Valeske, *Hierarchia Veritatum* (Munich, 1968), pp. 107–9.

20. For further discussion of the basic points to be presented here, see especially: F.W. Kantzenbach, *Das Ringen um die Einheit der Kirche im Jahrhundert der Reformation* (Stuttgart, 1957), pp. 40 ff.; U. Valeske, *op. cit.*, pp. 107–19; 129–30; Street, *op. cit.*, pp. 284–317; Althaus, *Theology of Luther*, pp. 224–25, 118; F. Hildebrant, *Melanchthon, Alien or Ally* (Cambridge, 1946), pp. 27–33, 78–98; G. Tavard, "Hierarchia Veritatum", *TS* 32 (1971), p. 286.

21. Of all the reformers, Melanchthon probably came closest to Erasmus' broad application of this distinction (See: Manschreck, *Melanchthon*, pp. 293–302. But, see also: Althaus, *Theology of Luther*, pp. 4–5; Calvin, *Institutes* I, XIII, 21; Street, *op cit.*, p. 315).

22. See Althaus, *Theology of Luther*, pp. 7–8; Calvin, *Institutes* I, XIII, 3–5.

23. "Neque enim ego vel usum, vel aucthoritatem hominum in totum negavi, sed libera esse volo, et indifferentia, quaecunque extra scriptura sanctas scripta sunt, tanquam articulos fidei necessarios fieri recuso ex hominum verbis" (*Contra Henricum Regem Angliae*, WA 10^{II}, 191). For the other reformers on this point, see: Valeske, *op. cit.*, pp. 109–10, 114–15, 118; Congar, *Tradition and Traditions*, pp. 512, 515; Zwingli, *Acta Tiguri*, SW I, 489–90; Melanchthon, *Loci*, MW II/1, p. 60. For similar assertions by some few Roman theologians during this period, see: Congar, *Tradition and Traditions*, p. 513. According to Tavard, Roman Catholic controversialists of the sixteenth century generally identified the material principle of Christian truth with "the universal teaching of the Church and its magisterium" (Tavard, *Hierarchia Veritatum*, p. 286).

24. See Valeske, *op. cit.*, pp. 107 ff.

25. See *Schmalkaldische Artikel* II, 1: *BEK*, p. 416; Zwingli, *67 Art.*, SW I, 458 f., arts. 2–5; Calvin, *Institutes* III, XV, 7.

26. Calvin, *Institutes* IV, I, 12; III, V, 9; Luther *De Servo Arbitrio*, WA 18, 605.

27. *Doctrinal Treatises*, pp. liv, lv, lviii.

28. *Ibid.*, p. 384; 381; 385.

29. Typical was Frith's assertion that the bread and wine "is ever consecrated in his heart that believeth, though the priest consecrate it not" (*An Answer*, WER, p. 415; also: *Ibid.*, pp. 325, 328–30, 356–60, 363, 370–73, 395–96, 415–17). For further discussion of Frith's views on the Eucharistic presence, see Clebsch, *op. cit.*, pp. 117, 122–27.

30. *Articles*, WER, p. 451, 454; *An Answer*, WER, p. 413.

31. To believe in the doctrine of purgatory as a necessary article of faith is, Frith said, far more dangerous than not believing it to be so, for there is "great peril to believe a thing for an article of the faith which is not opened nor spoken of in Scripture" (*A Disputation of Purgatory*, WER, p. 182). Still, "I count neither part a necessary article of our faith, necessarily to be believed under pain of damnation, whether there be such a purgatory or not" (*Articles*, WER, p. 450).

32. *An Answer*, WER, pp. 330, 330–31, 331, 325, 330, 329, 330, 410. See also: *A Book of the Sacrament of the Body and Blood of Christ*, WER, pp. 324, 325, 329, 330–31.

33. Thomas Starkey, for example, wrote: "For as to affirm purgatorie to be, there is no grounde of suretye, so it to denye hath moche lesse certaynte, for scripture giueth sure argument to nother of them both. Wherfore as to affirme hit to be, as an article of the faythe, and to the saluation of man to be of necessite, I think it great folye: so to deny it to be a holesome tradition to the conseruation of the christian lyfe moche conuenient, I juge it to be playn arrogancy" (*Exhortation*, sig. X, fol. i). Like Frith, Starkey considered the Creed sufficient as regards the necessary doctrines of Christian faith (*Ibid.*, sig. B,

fol. iii[v]). All other doctrines are "indifferent," "for menne, the whiche are of lernynge and letters, in suche matters neuer dydde yet accorde nor agree in unitie" (*Ibid.*, sig. B, fol. iv). Accordingly, the "unlearned" should hold to the "generalle poyntes and artycles of Christis faythe" and as for the rest, to follow the common authority, and let the learned "prove theyr wyttes after theyr owne pleasure, mynde, and lybertie" (*Ibid.*). For further expressions of a doctrinal adiaphorism, see: The Ten Articles, *The Bishops' Book,* and the *King's Book* (Lloyd, *op. cit.,* pp. xvi, xxxi, 61, 210–11, 226–27, 374–75), The Forty-Two Articles (Hardwick, *op cit.,* pp. 262, 278–80); "Hillis to Bullinger, 1541", *OL,* pp. 212–14; Cranmer, *Writings and Letters,* pp. 515–16.

34. It should be noted that in appealing to the Creed, Frith's main concern was to identify those doctrines he considered "necessary to salvation," and neither he nor any of the English reformers were ever altogether clear as to whether such non-necessity to salvation was itself enough to qualify a matter as adiaphoristic. For those reformers who favored Scripture, and not the Creed, as the sum of those doctrines necessary to salvation, this lack of clarity was of little significance. With Frith and his introduction of the Creed as a material principle, however, it makes for considerable confusion.

35. The Ten Articles, *The Bishops' Book,* and *The King's Book,* all make this assertion about Scriptural doctrines (Lloyd, *op. cit.,* pp. xvii, 61, 227). They also say, it may be noted, that the Creedal articles are all necessary to salvation, but they do not say that the Creeds contain all the doctrines necessary to salvation.

36. As Zwingli had noted, the preaching of the Gospel will inevitably upset the peace to some extent (*Von Erkiesen, SW* I, p. 112).

37. William Tyndale, for example, noted that according to the Apostle Paul (Eph. 4) it is for the very reason of bringing Christians to a "full knowledge" that "spiritual officers" are ordained (*Obedience of a Christian Man, Doctrinal Treatises,* p. 220.)

38. *Ibid.*

39. *Pred. des Jah.* 1522, WA 10ᴵᴵᴵ, pp. 1–64; *SW,* pp. 88–136, Latimer, *Sermons,* pp. 34–55.

40. Lloyd, *op. cit.,* p. 115.

41. Herrtage, *Starkey's Life and Letters,* pp. xiii–xvii, xviii–xxi, xxii–xxiii, xxiv–xxvi, xxviii–xxxi, xxxiv–xxxviii, xlv–xlvii; Latimer, *Sermons and Remains,* pp. 331, 353; G. Burnet, *op. cit.,* I, ii, pp. 539 ff.; *CR* III, 676–79; Strype, *EM* I, ii, p. 403; G. Burnet, *op. cit.,* I, ii, pp. 488–93; Foxe, *Acts and Monuments,* V, pp. 351–57; Calvin, *Opera* XIII, *CR* XLI, 64–90, or J. Burnet, *Letters of John Calvin,* II, especially pp. 186–97; Cranmer, *Writings and Letters,* pp. 350–56; J.H. Blunt, *History,* II, pp. 103–5.

42. Merriman, *Life and Letters of Cromwell,* p. 29.

43. J. Colet, *An Exposition of St. Paul's Epistle to the Romans,* trans. J.H. Lupton (London, 1873; Ridgewood, 1965), p. 208, 207–8.

44. See *De Lib. Christ., WA* 7, 71; Zwingli, *Von Erkiesen, SW* I, p. 125; Bullinger, *Decades* d. III, s. IX, t. II, p. 317; Calvin, *Institutes* III, XIX, 11; Frith, *A Mirror, WER,* pp. 293–95; Martyr, *Commonplaces,* II, p. 167.

45. See *De Lib. Christ, WA* 7, 71.

46. Zwingli, *Von Erkiesen, SW* I, p. 120; *Annot. ad Rom., ZO* VI, p. 127; Bucer, *Grund und Ursach, BDS* 1, pp. 218 ff.; Calvin, *Institutes* III, XIX, 13; Frith, *A Mirror, WER,* p. 292.

47. Martyr, *Commonplaces,* II, p. 173.

48. Melanchthon, *Loci, MW* II/1, p. 162; Zwingli, *Von Erkiesen, SW* I, p. 125; Bullinger, *Decades,* d. III, s. IX, t. II, p. 317; Calvin, *Institutes* III, XIX, 11; Martyr, *Commonplaces,* II, p. 167.

49. See Gee and Hardy, *op. cit.,* p. 306.

50. As cited in E. Doernberg, *Henry VIII and Luther* (Stanford, 1961), p. 118.

51. Frith, *A Mirror, WER*, p. 293.

52. For documentation of this and other facts about Frith's short career, see: Clebsch, *op. cit.*, pp. 78–98; J.F. Mozley, *William Tyndale* (New York, 1937), especially pp. 245–60.

53. Foxe, *Acts and Monuments* V, p. 435; see also: Edward Hall, *Hall's Chronicle* (London, 1809), p. 840; *OL* pp. 209–10. According to J.J. Scarisbrick, Barnes was an innocent victim of a plot conceived by Norfolk and Gardiner to get at Cromwell (*op. cit.*, pp. 380–83).

54. *The Articles, WER*, pp. 450–51.

55. *Ibid.*, p. 451, 454.

56. *Ibid.*

57. *Ibid.*, p. 455.

58. See Luther's remarks concerning Karlstadt in Luther's letters of 1524 to the Christians at Augsburg (*WA* 15, 391–97); also: *Wider die Himml. Proph.* (*WA* 18, 111–16); *Letter to William Provest* (1528) (*END* VI, p. 226). Calvin had the same type of individual in mind when he wrote of those who use their adiaphoristic liberty "as though it were not sound and safe if men did not witness it" (*Institutes* III, XIX, 10).

59. *Liber de Veris et Falsis Adiaphoris, OLS*, sig. Cc, fol. 3(v). Flacius also cited the example of Christ refusing to wash his hands ("in itself a thing indifferent") so as to avoid leaving the impression that he approved the Jewish traditions (*Ibid.*, sig. Cc, fol. 4).

60. G. Burnet, *op. cit.*, I, ii, p. 542; Hughes and Larkin, *op. cit.*, I, p. 274.

61. Strype, *EM* I, ii, p. 402.

62. Gee and Hardy, *op. cit.*, p. 306.

63. Strype, *EM* I, ii, p. 408, 409–10.

64. Foxe, *Acts and Monuments*, V, p. 353, 357. It will be noted that the language used here by Melanchthon was almost identical to that employed by Flacius later in his struggle against the Interim ceremonies.

65. See *CR* 7: 260–64.

66. See Hefele-deClerq, *Histoire des Conciles* X, p. 553.

67. According to the sixteenth-century English chronicler, Charles Wriothesley, there were about three hundred "priests and religious" persons in England who prior to 1539 had presumed to marry (*A Chronicle of England During the Reign of the Tudors*, pp. 102–3.).

68. See J. Ridley, *Cranmer*, pp. 146–48. For Nicholas Harpfield's notorious story of Cranmer having his wife hidden in a chest, see: N. Harpsfield, *A Treatise on the Pretended Divorce between Henry VIII and Catherine of Aragon*, ed. N. Pocock (Westminster, 1878), p. 275, and Ridley's discussion (*Cranmer*, pp. 148–53).

69. See Luther, *De Lib. Christ., WA* 7, 70–71; Melanchthon, *Loci, MW* II/1, p. 160; Zwingli, *Von Erkiesen, SW* I, p. 125; Bullinger, *Decades*, d. III, s. IX, t. II, pp. 317–18; Calvin, *Institutes*, III, XIX, 12; Frith, *A Mirror, WER*, p. 293; Martyr, *Commonplaces*, II, p. 167.

70. Melanchthon, *Loci, MW* II/1, p. 162; Martyr, *Commonplaces* II, p. 167.

71. "An offense is given then, when by thy fault . . . thy brother hath a cause to be offended" and an "offense is not given, but taken . . . not by thy fault, but by the malice or wickedness of another man" (Bullinger, *Decades*, d. III, s. IX, t. II, p. 317). See also Calvin, *Institutes* III, XIX, 11; Hugh Latimer, *Sermons and Remains*, pp. 76–83.

72. R. Bainton, *Here I Stand* (New York, 1950), p. 225. Luther's marriage, it may be noted, came as something of a shock to some of his fellow reformers also (Manschreck, *Melanchthon*, pp. 129–30).

73. On July 16, 1537, the eve of St. Thomas of Canterbury's feast, for example, Cranmer broke the fast by eating meat, an action which, while no longer proscribed by English law (J. Ridley, *Cranmer*, p. 154), was nonetheless, as a chronicler of the age put it, something "never scene before in all the coo [country]" (*Narratives of the Days of the Reformation*, ed. J.G. Nichols [Westminster, 1859], p. 285), and probably therefore more than a little "offensive" to the "pious ears" of such Englishmen as had only the previous year included the "cessation of fasting" in the list of sixty-seven *mala dogmata* they presented to Convocation (Strype, *EM* I, ii, pp. 264–65.).

74. See especially: Melanchthon, *Loci*, *MW* II/1, pp. 62, 160, 162.

75. *De Lib. Christ.*, WA 7, 70.

76. See Luther's 1539 Letter to George Bucholzer as cited *Supra*, III, n. 79.

77. "Ut igitur res necessarias retineamus, sumus in non necessariis minus duri," (*CR* 7, 252).

78. Although mitigated in 1540 (See Foxe, *Acts and Monuments* V, p. 360), the Six Articles Act had originally declared that any priest twice convicted of concubinage would be subject to the death penalty (Gee and Hardy, *op. cit.*, pp. 318–19). According to Jaspar Ridley, "in 1540, Henry would have cut off Cranmer's head—or more probably have burned him—if he could have obtained any advantage by so doing" (*Cranmer*, p. 213).

79. At one point in the Attainder brought against him by the Parliament, Cromwell was charged with having declared publicly that he was "sure" of the king (G. Burnet, *op. cit.*, I, ii, p. 294).

80. Henry apparently learned of Cranmer's secret marriage for the first time in 1543. He chided the Archbishop about it, but did nothing to punish him (See Ridley, *Cranmer*, p. 148).

81. Notwithstanding Hooper's complaint in 1546 that Henry "has destroyed the pope, but not popery" ("Hooper to Bullinger, 1546," *Original Letters* I, p. 36), and Henry's continual efforts to play the political game to his best advantage, and at whatever cost to the Protestant cause (See Ridley, *Cranmer*, p. 247; J. Gairdner, *The English Church in the Sixteenth Century* [London, 1903], pp. 231, 235–36; Foxe, *Acts and Monuments* V, pp. 562–63) there were definite signs during the last four or five years of his life that Henry was becoming increasingly committed to the side of the moderate Protestant reformers. Among such "signs of change" may be noted the exclusion of Gardiner from the Council of regency appointed to govern during Edward VI's minority (Muller, *Gardiner*, pp. 140–42), the appointment of Sir John Cheke to oversee Edward's education (Strype, *Life of Cheke*, p. 22), the growing influence of the Seymour faction at Court (Dickens, *English Reformation*, pp. 195–96), Henry's 1545 commissioning of Cranmer and other bishops "to peruse certain books of service" with an eye toward further reform (Cranmer, *Writings and Letters*, p. 414), Cranmer's need to caution Henry against proceeding too fast with implementation of the same commission's proposals (*Ibid.*, p. 415), Henry's off-hand remark to Cranmer of his intentions to join with the French King in changing the Mass and utterly "extirpating" the Pope (Foxe, *Acts and Monuments* V, p. 564), Parliament's mitigation of the Six Articles Act in 1544 (G. Burnet, *op. cit.*, I, ii, pp. 391–98), its dissolution of the chantries in late 1545 (Scarisbrick, *op. cit.*, pp. 475–78), and finally Henry's calling of Cranmer to his deathbed in 1547 (Foxe, *Acts and Monuments*, V, p. 689). Henry's last speech before Parliament in late 1545, it may be noted, was a studied reassertion of the "indifferent mean" championed earlier by Starkey (See *Ibid.*, pp. 534–35).

82. See Manschreck, *Melanchthon*, pp. 277–92; G.R. Elton, *Reformation Europe, 1517–1559* (New York, 1966), pp. 249–256.

83. Calvin, *Institutes* III, XIX, 9.

84. While the papists destroy Christian freedom by commanding and compelling Christians to do things which God has not commanded or required, Karlstadt and his kind do so, Luther argued, by forbidding and hindering the Christian from doing that which is neither prohibited nor forbidden by God (*Wider die himml. Proph., WA* 18:111). Melanchthon also accused Flacius of trying to impose upon Christians a new tyranny: "Und ist dieses ein neues Papstthum dass solche ungestume Leut alle andre zu ihrer Weis dringen wollen, und wer ihnen nicht folget, denselbigen also greulich verdammen" (*CR* 7, 366).

85. Thus Luther wrote that while he had originally intended to abolish the elevation of the host at Mass, now that Karlstadt has insisted upon its removal as necessary, he (Luther) will not abolish it, so as to defy the "fanatic spirit" (*Wider die himml. Proph., WA* 18, 116). According to Melanchthon, those who command pork to be eaten err no less than those who forbid it (*Loci, MW* II/1, p. 131; see also: *CR* 7:36; 9:23–72, as cited in Manschreck, *Controversy*, p. 174, n. 73). See also: Starkey, *Exhortation*, sig. F, fol. iii(v).

RULE OF CHARITY

AMONG THE MANY EVILS supposedly spawned by the excessive proliferation and estimation of human traditions down through the centuries, one of the worst, according to Erasmus and the reformers, was the fact that in their "superstitious" anxiety over such matters many Christians had either forgotten altogether about the practice of charity or had utterly confused it with some trivial, moralistic scheme of work-righteousness.[1] To restore the primacy of love in the Christian life was, therefore, a major factor in their concern to share their knowledge of adiaphoristic liberty. But such "knowledge" itself could conceivably have become as detrimental to the reign of love as had been the "ignorance" which it was supposed to supplant. And, in fact, no sooner had the sixteenth-century adiaphorists broadcast their adiaphoristic appraisal of certain ceremonies and doctrines than they were being charged with having broken down all the boundaries of love.

To hear Thomas More tell it, for example, one would think that because of his adiaphoristic tendencies, Martin Luther was the very reincarnation of Diogenes of Sinope—the ancient Cynic philosopher who called himself the "Dog" and tried in his every word and action to live up to the name by heaping scorn upon any and every convention of Hellenic society.[2] When Luther suggested, for example, that the times, places, vesture, and ritual of the Eucharistic celebration should be considered adiaphora, More—whose scatological tastes were every bit as bad as Luther's—promptly charged the Wittenberg reformer with being supercilious:

> All things are free for you; nor does it make any difference to you where, when, how you offer the sacrifice, whether by night or by day, whether in the light or in darkness, drunk or sober, clothed or naked, clean or filthy, on the altar or on the toilet, you hang-dog knave.[3]

115

To More, such disdain on Luther's part was symptomatic of a libertine spirit. Thus when Luther wrote that Christians should be free in regard to ceremonial matters, More sarcastically replied:

> Why not? So that while one celebrates Christmas, another may keep Easter, and while religious men fast during Lent, Father Tosspot may celebrate the Bacchanalia with his pot-companions.

Let Luther's views about the "free and indifferent" character of the ceremonies prevail, and before long, More claimed, "the people would neither be ruled by laws nor obey rulers nor listen to doctors, but would be so free and unbridled, with the freedom of the Gospel, of course, that no one would be forced, nor commanded, nor counselled, nor taught anything."[4]

Though less vitriolic than More, Stephen Gardiner raised the same charges against the adiaphorists. Besides encouraging an anarchic contempt of all human law, the adiaphorists, Gardiner contended, were purposely cultivating a spirit of "licentious liberty" so as the more easily to lure others into their camp:

> Ye flatter the world with licentiouse doctrine, and offer them to pull frome theyr neckes all suche yokes as ye thinke dyd at any tyme let or impeche them eyther in thought or dede. Ye promise them libertie of al thing and then to ridde them out of debte ye translate saint Paule thus, that we owe nothynge to no man but love. Ye flatter again the servaunt with pullinge awaye al opinion of faste by abstinence from any meat, either in Lent or otherwise. Ye offer priestes wyves to witte and they can wynne them to you. Ye ridde all of confession and wepyny for synne. Ye take away distinction and difference of apparell, dayes, tymes, and places. Ye take away ceremonies which indede do much let good cheer in assemblyes of good fellows.[5]

"But really," Gardiner concluded elsewhere, "that an Epicurean life should be brought in under pretense of Gospel freedom, is a thing which cannot be suffered."[6]

Such charges were not entirely groundless. As the adiaphorists themselves readily admitted, all too many of their followers had exploited the truth of adiaphoristic liberty as an excuse for an arrogant and unbridled pursuit of freedom[7]—so much so according to Erasmus that toward the end of his career he seemed to have regretted ever having championed the cause of liberty.[8] But what the adiaphorists taught, and how it was sometimes acted upon by others, or even by themselves, were not the same thing. And in theory at least they repeatedly insisted that to be genuine, adiaphoristic liberty must itself be informed by a spirit of charity. For that to be the case, it was assumed in the first place that the "knowledge" of one's liberty in the realm of adiaphora must not become a source of pride.

Like the faith from which it springs, such "knowledge," it was said, is not a work of man's own wisdom, but a "spiritual light bestowed by God on the minds of men." It is a knowledge, therefore, which, far from "puffing up," ought to humble its recipient, giving rise to a spirit of thanksgiving that will make one more, not less, understanding of others. Those who are truly in possession of it, therefore, will not find therein any cause for "judging" those who are not. There is nothing, Jean Colet wrote, that ought to be less practiced among men than "one person's measuring another by the standard of his own power" or "thinking all opinions deserving condemnation which are unlike one's own." Ultimately, only God can judge one's conduct in the realm of adiaphora. Hence, just as the "weak," when they see others venturing on more than they dare themselves, ought not measure such deeds by their own "narrowness and infirmity," so those who are mature in their knowledge of Christian liberty must not abuse their own power by failing to take into account the other's weakness.[9] "For he that knoweth the intent of the law and of words," William Tyndale wrote, "though he observe a thousand ceremonies for his own exercise, he shall never condemn his brother, or break unity with him, in those things which Christ never commanded, but left indifferent."[10] Thus, as the English *Order of Communion* issued by royal proclamation on March 8, 1548, put it, in all such matters as enjoy "no warrant of God's word," Christians are "to follow and keep the rule of charity; and every man to be satisfied with his own conscience, not judging other men's minds or acts."[11]

For one's adiaphoristic liberty to be properly informed by a spirit of charity, it is not enough, however, the adiaphorists said, that one merely refrain from "judging" others. One's actual "election" and "doing" of adiaphora must also be directed by the rule of charity. This, as Peter Martyr expressed it best, was simply another way of saying that things which are adiaphora by definition lose their indifference in the concrete and become either good or evil:

> As touching these things that be indifferent, we must affirme, that onelie (according to their owne kind and nature) they have this indifferencie. But when we come unto election, there is nothing indifferent: for it is of necessitie that the same be either good or evil.[12]

The mainline English adiaphorists understood this conclusion to apply not only to the "election" and "doing" of adiaphora by individual members of the Church, but also to the concrete arrangement or ordering of adiaphoristic matters by Church officials. In contrast to the Puritans,[13] they were not of the opinion that a genuinely edifying church could only be fashioned out of material that was by nature edifying. An edifying order, they felt, could be built out of or upon adiaphoristic matter. But as has been noted in a previous chapter, they did not, unlike the Puritans, conceive of "edification" as a constitutive element in the definition of adiaphora. Still, the Conformists or main-line adiaphorists did insist that any concrete choice of adiaphoristic matter by church officials must be made with an eye toward edification. No less than the Puritans the Conformists rejected any middle ground in the concrete. The concrete arrangement of adiaphora cannot be an indifferent one. It will be either good—i.e., edifying, or bad—i.e., destructive—either in accordance with the Spirit's work of love or contrary to it.[14]

It was to be hoped, of course, that the "election" and "doing" of adiaphora by all Christians, including Church officials, would be good, or in other words, charitable, and edifying. Because "we are not borne to ourselves onelie, but unto Christ, unto the Church, and to our neighbors," Martyr continued, every "election" or "doing" of "meane actions" must follow the "rule of charitie," or the "rule of edifieing."[15] What this meant specifically for Martyr and the other adiaphorists of the early sixteenth century remains now to be seen.

In the first place, it meant that one's "election" and "doing" of adiaphoristic matters must not be of an arrogant, cynical sort that takes no account of the feelings or needs of others. For one thing, special consideration must be shown to the "weak." Care must be taken that they not be "offended." Thus, while it is right to stand up to the "tyrants" and to defy them by doing the very opposite of what they demand, irrespective of any "offense" they might "take", it would be wrong if, in the process, the "weak" were "given" scandal.

Consistent with the Apostle Paul's letter to the Romans (chapter 14), the reformers understood by such an "offense" to the "weak" any sort of action which might provoke them to act against their consciences. It was, of course, part and parcel of the adiaphoristic appraisal of certain matters to suggest that the latter are not binding in conscience. But that precisely was what those "weak" in their faith found it most difficult to accept. Things that the "mature" knew to be of an indifferent nature, the "weak" were inclined to think were "necessary to salvation." Or, to use Paul's example, foods which are known by the "mature" to be "clean" in themselves, the "weak" tend to consider "unclean" (Rom. 14). And because they "think" something is "unclean", Paul added, it becomes for them "unclean" (Rom. 14:14), so that if they go ahead and eat, their action is sinful, and worthy of condemnation (Rom. 14:23).

The high medieval theologians interpreted Paul to have meant thereby that so far at least as indifferent matters are concerned, an "erroneous" conscience is binding.[16] The sixteenth-century reformers embraced the same view, as Peter Martyr, once again, evidenced best. "The conscience hath such a power," Martyr wrote, "as if it be good, it maketh that worke to be good, which in his own nature is [in]different;[17] and on the other side being evill, it maketh it evill."[18] This shows, Martyr pointed out, how important it is that "the conscience be well persuaded about the doing of things."[19] But it also shows, he concluded, that "he sinneth, which attempteth anie thing against his conscience."[20] But if the "weak" sin in going against their "erroneous" consciences, then, Martyr concluded in accordance with Pauline doctrine (1 Cor. 8:9–13), they sin also who by their inconsiderable public exercise of adiaphoristic liberty encourage the "weak" to do what their consciences erroneously forbid them to do:

> And forsomuch as the Lord hath died for such as are weak, they that sinne against them, sinne against Christ; as Paule speaketh to the Corinthians, bicause they do not reverentlie esteeme of his death and blood. The conscience of another man is wounded, when it is ill edified, and is compelled to do those things wereof it judgeth otherwise.[21]

Thus, to avoid incurring the guilt of sin upon themselves, those who are mature in the knowledge of their adiaphoristic liberty may on occasion, the reformers said, have to emulate the example of Paul's circumcision of Timothy (Acts 16:3), and exercise their "election" or "doing" of one or another indifferent matter in a way that will not offend the weak.[22] Such consideration of the weak must be shown, it was said, both in and outside times of tyranny. If, therefore, the laws of "tyrants" touching upon adiaphoristic matters cannot be broken without offense being given to the "weak," one is left with but two alternatives. One would be to submit to the "external" bondage of such laws, knowing all the while that one's freedom before God in this regard remains intact.[23] The second alternative would be to exercise one's freedom only "in secret," keeping the knowledge of it, as the Apostle Paul advised, "between oneself and God" (Rom. 14:22).[24]

Hence, perhaps, another reason why Zwingli, Cranmer, and other sixteenth-century priests chose to keep the fact of their marriages secret over certain periods of time. While convinced of their freedom before God to marry, and ready and willing to avail themselves of that liberty, they also deemed it better to suffer in a spirit of charity the inconveniences of a clandestine marriage—at least until such time as the weak could be afforded a fair chance of understanding the phenomenon of priests marrying and continuing in their ministerial duties. It was not the only charitable course of action open to them, but it was one consistent with their adiaphoristic principles, and it would certainly be wrong to see in it nothing more than an act of duplicity.

This concern not to offend the weak played an important role also in the reformers' determination of which traditional ceremonies were to be retained or rejected outside times of "tyranny." This point was especially emphasized by Luther in 1522 after he returned from the Wartburg for the sake of trying to restore some order out of the havoc created at Wittenberg by Karlstadt's impetuous attempt to purge the church of any and every traditional ceremony.

Karlstadt was wrong, Luther said in the first of his *Invocavit* sermons, not only because he was making a "must" out of what is "free," but also because of the possible "offense" he was thereby giving to the "weak." The day may well come, Luther said, when certain "weaker" individuals will begin to have qualms of conscience about having participated in the overthrow of some one or another traditional ceremony like the abstinence from meat on Friday. And if such qualms develop into a loss of faith, Luther concluded, God will hold Karlstadt and his kind responsible for the damnation of these "weaker" brethren.[25]

The English reformers' sensitivity on this point was evidenced most clearly in the way they handled the traditional practice of auricular confession. As noted earlier, many of the English reformers had come to believe—thanks in large part to Henry VIII's prodding—that auricular confession could not be considered "necessary to salvation." For all that, however, they did not reject the practice. And one reason they did not was precisely their concern for those "weaker" individuals who still felt bound in conscience to confess their sins to the priest.[26]

By thus going out of their way to avoid offending the "weak," the reformers, as noted, were trying to make a charitable allowance for what they considered to be the "mistaken" judgment of the "weak" about the binding force of indifferent matters. The reformers did not, however, conceive of the "weakness" of such individuals as consisting solely in their "erroneous" consciences. For even if the latter could have been brought to recognize that certain matters are indifferent and as such not binding upon consciences, they would still have been considered "weak" by the reformers to the extent that they would remain dependent upon such matters for the maintenance and development of their faith.

Unlike Sebastian Franck and other dualists, the Erasmian and Protestant reformers, as noted earlier, did not consider external ceremonies to be totally useless. Such matters, they said, could serve as "means" toward the higher goals of Christian life. For all that, however, they were also of the view that a genuinely mature faith would in fact have little need for such matters,[27] and on that account were inclined to interpret any dependence upon them as a sign of "weakness". But again, in the context of their concern to keep the exercise of adiaphoristic liberty within the bounds of love, the reformers insisted that this "weakness" must receive the charitable consideration of those who are more mature in their faith.

In the first of his *Invocavit* sermons, Luther encouraged his parishioners—whom Karlstadt had supposedly brought to maturity overnight—to relate to the "weak" as would a mother to her child. Just as a mother first gives the child milk, gruel, and other soft foods until such time as it is able to digest a stronger diet, so the mature should allow the "weak" to have their "milk-food" (1 Peter 2:2) until they too grow strong. The mature must not look only to their own strength, but to that of their brother's also. And so, Luther concluded, if one has been "suckled long enough," one should not on that account deny to another the nourishment of milk, but should rather allow his brother to be suckled just as he himself once was suckled.[28]

Consistent with such advice, the sometimes radical reformer Thomas Müntzer spoke of structuring the Eucharistic Service for his congregation at Munster as for a people who were "like children" to be "fed with milk,"[29] meaning that many ceremonies which he might otherwise have rejected were retained for the edification of the "weak." The generally conservative nature of the Erasmian reform program rested in part upon the same rationale.[30] Luther's defense of the images on the grounds of their assistance to the young and illiterate has already been noted. But his whole reform of the liturgy was, in fact, largely, though not exclusively, controlled by pedagogical concerns,[31] and for that reason, among others, left many of the traditional ceremonies intact, as indeed the Augsburg Confession was so emphatic about pointing out.[32] At Zurich, Basle, Strassburg, and Geneva the quantitative reduction of the traditional ceremonies was far more severe. Perhaps this may be accounted for to some extent by the obsessive fear the reformers of these cities, and especially the Zwinglians, had about heading off any relapse of their parishioners into superstition.[33] But it might also be indicative of a more optimistic view about the general level of maturity among their parishioners. Calvin especially liked to emphasize the emancipation of Christians from the sort of childlike tutelage God had earlier afforded the Jews. But Calvin readily admitted also that a moderate dose of ceremonies could be very useful in the instruction of the "ignorant."[34]

As for the English Reformation, the whole of its initial Henrician stage may be viewed as having been deliberately geared toward an accommodation of the slower pace of the "weak." Early on, Bishop John Fisher had warned the reformers that any wholesale removal of the ceremonies could very well lead to the demise of all divine worship.[35] Thomas Starkey was quick to agree. While insisting upon a qualitative reduction of the ceremonies, he repeatedly castigated those "arrogant" individuals who in the name of Christian liberty would have all the traditional ceremonies thrown out. If such individuals had their way, Starkey wrote, "I think by littell and lytell," all "christen pollices" and "the very doctrine of Christ" would "utterly vanysche away." "Undoubtedly, it should not be longe, before ye shulde se, of very religion the utter ruin and decaye." Why? Because, Starkey said, "the weake vulgare myndes of the people ever have benne after this sorte, that withoute somme exterior and outwarde synes and ceremonies, their simplicitie could never be led to true religion, nor of god to conceyue the divinitie." Thus, just as many of the ceremonies had originally been instituted "to stire the devotion of simple mindes to christen puritie," so many should still be retained as "convenient menes to induce rude and symple myndes, to memory, and to the conceyuyng of the mysteries of our religion."[36]

No less explicit in its concern for the "weak" was the 1535 edition of William Marshall's *Primer*. In an earlier edition, Marshall had eliminated the traditional prayer known as the "litany." The 1535 edition restored it with the remark that "although it be nothing like nor true, as concerning the necessity, that we by the commandment of holy scripture must of necessity pray to our blessed Lady and saints . . . yet . . . for the contentation of such weake mindes, and somewhat to bear their infirmities, I have now at this my second edition . . . caused the litany to be printed."[37]

The English envoy Christopher Mont tried to convince the German princes in early 1539 that Henry's prohibition of clerical marriage rested upon a similar rationale. If priests had been allowed to marry, Mont said, "the common people, as yet weak in the knowledge of the Word, and of other things, might thereby conceive an opinion of concupiscence in them; and by reason thereof condemn their preaching and the word of God." What the king would do afterward "when the people shal wax strong, and able to eat solid meat," Mont admitted that "he could not define nor judge," but had no doubt but that Henry "did nothing without good cause and reason".[38] As the Six Articles Act would reveal shortly thereafter, all this was, of course, so much wishful thinking on the part of Mont so far as it concerned clerical marriage. Still, his remarks were indicative of the sort of rationale often entertained by the Henrician reformers in their retention of one or another traditional ceremony. Much to the chagrin of Turner, Bale, and their like,[39] many ceremonies were retained not only for the sake of avoiding "offense" of the "weak," but also to afford the latter some "means" of instruction and growth in their faith.[40]

During the Edwardine period, not a few of the same ceremonies were pruned away.[41] This need not have meant, however, that the adiaphorists had abandoned their earlier consideration of the "weak."[42] For one thing, not all the changes brought about under Edward VI were inspired by adiaphorists like Cranmer and Ridley. Some resulted rather from pressures exerted by Turner, Bale, Hooper, Knox, and other radicals upon a sometimes reckless and unprincipled Duke of Northumberland.[43] Furthermore, while calling for consideration of the "weak" the adiaphorists had always warned also that care must be taken lest under the pretext of concern for the "weak," certain things would be tolerated which were in fact not indifferent but "blatantly impious."[44] In other words, and as Thomas Müntzer had put it, care would have to be taken that the "milk" offered the "weak" was pure, and not the "milk of dragons."[45]

Already in 1546 the commission of bishops (Cranmer, Heath, and Day) established by Henry VIII "to peruse certain books of service" with an eye toward further reform, had recommended that

> the vigil and ringing of bells all the night long upon Alhallow-day at night, and the covering of images in the church in time of Lent, with the lifting up of the veil that covereth the cross upon Palm-sunday, with the kneeling to the cross the same time, might be abolished and put away, for the superstition and other enormities and abuses of the same.[46]

Henry at first accepted these suggestions, and even added that all kneeling to the cross, and especially the Good Friday ceremony of "creeping to the cross" be halted.[47] But eventually Henry decided not to see the changes through, mainly for fear of jeopardizing a possible alliance with the Emperor Charles V that Gardiner was in the process of trying to seal. The King told Cranmer to "take patience" in the cause of reform, and to "forbear until we may espy a more apt and convenient time for that purpose."[48] Such a time never came until after Henry's death the following year. But it is clear at least that many of the ceremonies abolished under the Protector Somerset—such as the use of ashes, palms, holy bread, holy water, and salt, or "creeping to the cross," and the "elevation" of the Eucharistic host—were such as Cranmer and other adiaphorists had been reluctant to retain in the first place because of the "superstition and other enormities and abuses" with which the same had for so long been associated. In other words, they were matters whose pedagogical value for the "weak" Cranmer and other adiaphorists of a Protestant bent had always considered to have been outweighed by the enticement to superstition they presented, and which should on that account have never been tolerated in the first place, even if they could be reckoned indifferent in themselves.

Finally, while calling for consideration of the "weak," the adiaphorists had always cautioned also that such individuals must not be kept forever on nothing but a diet of "milk."[49] It was to be expected, in other words, that because of the consideration shown them, the "weak" would eventually not only outgrow their vulnerability to "offense," but also become increasingly less dependent upon all external matters of an indifferent sort. It is conceivable, therefore, that Cranmer and other adiaphorists effected the changes they did under Edward VI on the assumption that, after having tolerated the "weak" for some ten years of Henry's reign, they could with every right, and without defaulting the "rule of charity and edification," challenge the "weak" to come a bit more of age and to demonstrate thereby that the earlier consideration shown them had not been altogether futile.[50]

In addition to consideration of the "weak," the "election" and "doing" of adiaphora in accordance with the "rule of charity" also required, the adiaphorists said, a keen regard for the "general welfare" of all members of the Church. By this, the adiaphorists meant in the first place to preclude any exploitation of their doctrine of adiaphoristic freedom as an excuse for the "carnal liberty" of those who would abuse "earthly goods" by using them merely to satisfy their own lusts.

The adiaphorists readily admitted that the libertines were right in contending that the food, drink, money, clothes, leisure, and like matters, which they pursued with such insatiable greed, were in themselves things indifferent, and that it was nothing less than a "doctrine of demons"[51] for the Roman Church to have taught that its laws and ceremonies touching upon such matters were binding in conscience or necessary to salvation. But if such matters are truly indifferent, then the "election" and "doing" of them must also, the adiaphorists said, reveal a certain "indifference".[52] It is hardly convincing, they implied, for the libertines to claim that they look upon their food, money, clothes, and so forth, as being indifferent, while at the same time they pursue, cling, and hoard such matters as if their very salvation depended upon them. The Christian who really and genuinely believes in the indifferent nature of such matters will not evidence such anxiety and avarice in their regard. Rather, following the counsel of the Apostle Paul (I Cor. 7:29–32), he will use food or drink "as if he did not use it," marry "as if he did not marry," buy "as if he did not buy," and so forth.[53]

By thus suggesting that adiaphora should be chosen or used "indifferently," the reformers were obviously employing the latter term rather loosely. For they certainly did not mean thereby that the "election" or "doing" of adiaphora should be undertaken without any reference to the dictates of love. Quite the contrary. The only "indifference" they recognized as genuine in the realm of concrete actions was that which was born of love. A man's treasure being where his heart is, the Christian shows a spirit of "indifference" or "detachment" toward "earthly goods" because, in the first place, he has set his heart upon the promised land of eternal union with God.[54] Furthermore, having cast his lot with God, the Christian has lost all anxiety over what he is to eat or what he is to wear. He believes that in the abundance of earthly goods, God has provided not only for man's necessities, but also for his enjoyment.[55] His reaction to such "goods," therefore, is one of "thanksgiving".[56]

To be genuine, however, this gratitude must express itself in a show of charity toward one's neighbor. God does not bestow his gifts upon us merely for our private use. Whatever he has given us, has been given on the condition that it be applied to the "common good." In other words, God makes us the "stewards" of his gifts, and some day will expect each man to render an account of his stewardship.[57] The only test of this stewardship is the "rule of charity." Each man has his own "calling," and each must humbly accept it and live accordingly. What one man requires by way of "earthly goods" may very well vary from the needs of another.[58] Still, whatever one's station in life, every man must follow the rule of charity, always subordinating his own advantage to the benefit of his neighbor. And, even though this rule of charity cannot be broken down into any hard-fast formulas so far as it pertains to the use of adiaphora, it surely does preclude, the reformers concluded, all unbridled desire, vanity, and immoderate prodigality.[59]

By insisting that a truly charitable "election" and "doing" of adiaphora will evidence a concern for the "general welfare" of the Christian community, the adiaphorists also and especially had in mind to check any danger to the unity and peace of the Church that might come from either the reactionary element on the right, or, as the likes of More and Gardiner were always fretting, from some of those on the left who, under a pretense of liberty, would have the Church drawn down their own antinomian, anarchic ways.

"Peace and concord," Erasmus wrote, pertain to the very essence of true religion.[60] Luther and other of the Continental Protestants may have been inclined to read into such a remark by Erasmus an indication of what they came to suspect was his taste for "tranquility" at any cost. But however that may be, they too considered "peace and unity" in the Christian community to be essential, or at least "far more important than any ceremonies."[61] "To allow ceremonies priority over peace and unity," Luther asserted, would be altogether "unchristian".[62]

Needless, almost, to say, the English adiaphorists agreed. Henry VIII noted in his introduction to the Ten Articles that he counted it among his chief duties "to repress" and "utterly extinguish" any and every "occasion of dissent and discord."[63] His last address to Parliament in 1545 was still preoccupied with the same theme—the need for a "perfect love and concord."[64] The theme runs through almost every major document and theological treatise of the Henrician and Edwardine period,[65] but never so predominantly as in the writings of Thomas Starkey.

After an initial bout with despair over the great "division and discorde" that confronted him upon his return to England in 1534,[66] Starkey wrote to Cromwell that what is to be desired is a "certayn vynte and concord, ye and . . . a certayn bande and knott of charyte, whereby men must knytt themselves togither as members of one body."[67] "To be coupled and kyntte togither" in such a "knott of charity," Starkey later wrote in his *Exhortation,* is what Christ's own word commands "above al other things." Surely, Starkey added, "there is no man so madde and so with out sense," that he would not desire "above all thinge in his harte" to enjoy and embrace the "quietnesse and tranquillitie" of such unity.[68]

It is significant, however, that neither Starkey, nor any of the Continental or English adiaphorists, thought it sufficient to exhort their followers merely to unity. Unity itself could be preserved, they thought, only if the people would also be exhorted to obedience. In the end, therefore, the adiaphorists were brought by their concern for unity back to where they had started, to the whole question, namely, of the legislation of adiaphoristic matters.

NOTES

1. See *Supra,* I, ns. 65, 72.
2. See: Diogenes Laertius, *Lives,* vi, 24.
3. More, *Resp. ad Luth.,* p. 419.

4. *Ibid.*, pp. 429, 259.

5. S. Gardiner, *A Declaration of Such True Articles as George Joye Hath Gone About to Confute As False* (London, 1546), sig. X, fol. ii–ii(v).

6. S. Gardiner, *Contemptum humanae legis, Tracts*, p. 211. It may be noted in passing also that shortly after Robert Barnes' death, John Standish published *A Lyttle Treatise Against the Protestation of Robert Barnes*, in which he accused Barnes of preaching a "carnal liberty" (See Myles Coverdale, *A Confutation of the Treatise of John Standish*, in Coverdale, *Remains*, pp. 336 ff.).

7. See, for example: Luther, *De Lib. Christ.*, WA 7, 69; Calvin, *Institutes* III, XIX, 9; Upon his return from Padua in 1524 Starkey said that he had found in England many "arrogant" individuals who "under the pretense of libertie, covertly purpose to distroye all christen policie, and so in conclusion bringe al to manyfest ruine and utter confusion" (*Exhortation,* sig. G, fol. i).

8. "At one time I wrote in the cause of spiritual liberty; I did so in all sincerity, for I never expected anything like this new generation. I had hoped that the role of ceremonies would have been diminished in favor of true piety. But they have been so brutally rejected that in place of liberty of spirit there has come about a liberty of the flesh." (As cited in L. Bouyer, *Erasmus and His Times*, trans. F.X. Murphy [Westminster, 1959], p. 134). See also, Erasmus' letter to the Strassburg Evangelicals (*EO* X, 1578).

9. J. Colet, *Exposition of Romans*, p. 207, 209–10, 210, 209.

10. Tyndale, *Exposition on Matt., Expositions and Notes*, p. 113.

11. *Two Liturgies*, p. 4. See also the remarks made by Henry VIII in his last address to Parliament about the avoidance of "judgment" (Foxe, *Acts and Monuments* V, pp. 534–35). Henry's remarks, it may be noted, were almost a verbatim repetition of what Starkey had written earlier (*Exhortation,* sig. D, fol. ii–ii[v], sig. G, fol. iii[v], sig. H, fol. iii). See also: Erasmus, *De Amabili Ecclesiae Concordia, EO* V, 504–5; Bullinger, *Decades*, d. V, s. 5, t. 3, p. 195; Martyr, *Commonplaces*, II, pp. 167–68; Calvin, *Institutes* III, XIX, 11.

12. Martyr, *Commonplaces*, II, pp. 164, 165.

13. See J.S. Coolidge, *op. cit.*, pp. 39, 49, 51. Coolidge cites the Elizabethan Puritan Anthony Gilby to the effect that "to know what can edify and build anything, it is necessary to bring things of like [i.e., edifying] substance" (*Ibid.*, p. 49).

14. From these conclusions it should be obvious that this writer finds unacceptable J.S. Coolidge's argument that the English Conformists thought of "edification as subsequent to order" (*op. cit.* p. 49), and its implication that their establishment of an "indifferent mean" was without any immediate direction of the Spirit (*Ibid.*).

15. *Ibid.*, pp. 164, 166. Martyr, it may be noted, like most of the other reformers used these two expressions interchangeably. Whatever may be said of J.S. Coolidge's claim that the Elizabethan Conformists conceived of "edification" as merely a process of "doctrinal instruction" (Coolidge, *op. cit.*, pp. 26, 44, 46), it certainly has no validity so far as the Henrician and Edwardine "conformists" are concerned. The latter, as noted, understood "edification" as that whole process whereby one not only speaks the truth of adiaphoristic liberty but lives it in accordance with the rule of charity.

16. Thomas Aquinas: "Dicunt ergo quod ratio vel conscientia errans circa indifferentia, sive praecipiendo sive prohibendo, obligat; ita quod voluntas discordans a tali ratione errante erit mala et peccatum" (*ST* I–II, 19, 5). See also: O. Lottin, "Problèmes Moraux Relatifs a la Conscience," *PEM* II, pp. 353–417.

17. The text being followed here has only "different," but this was probably a typographical error, as Martyr clearly means to say "indifferent," because if the "work" is "different" from being "good" it must either be "indifferent" or "evil," and Martyr

excludes the latter possibility when he subsequently notes that it "is impossible, that anie worke, which in nature is evill, should by our conscience be made good" (Commonplaces, II, p. 165), and concludes that "the power of the conscience exerciseth her force in those things that be meane or indifferent, and in those actions, which in their owne nature should be good" (Ibid.).

18. Ibid.

19. This "good persuasion" the conscience "cannot have," Martyr added, "otherwise than out of the word of God" (Ibid.).

20. Ibid. See also: Luther, Pred. des Jah. 1522, WA 10ᴵᴵᴵ, 11; Melanchthon, Loci, MW II/1, p. 162; Calvin, Institutes, III, XIX, 11, 16.

21. Martyr, Commonplaces, II, p. 164. For similar assertions to the effect that it would be sinful to "offend" the consciences of the "weak," see: Erasmus, Ichtuophagia, EO I, 799; Luther, De Lib. Christ., WA 7, 71; Pred des Jah. 1522, WA 10ᴵᴵᴵ, 11; Melanchthon, Loci, MW II/1, p. 162; Zwingli, Von Erkiesen, SW I, p. 112; Bullinger, Decades, d. III, s. IX, t. II, p. 315; Bucer, Grund und Ursach, BDS I, pp. 219–54; Calvin, Institutes III, XIX, 11, 16; IV, X, 22; John Frith, A Mirror, WER, p. 293; The Bishops' Book, Lloyd, op. cit., pp. 114–15; Latimer, Sermons, pp. 52–55; Latimer, Sermons and Remains, pp. 76–83; G. Burnet, op. cit., I, ii, pp. 490–91; Coverdale, Remains, pp. 412–13; "Micronius to Bullinger, October 13, 1550," OL p. 571; Hardwick, op. cit., p. 294.

22. Paul's circumcision of Timothy was repeatedly cited in this regard. For a few examples, see: Frith, A Mirror, WER, p. 292; Coverdale, A Confutation of Standish, pp. 412–13; "Micronius to Bullinger, October 13, 1550," OL, p. 571.

23. See, for example, Luther, De Lib. Christ., WA 7, 71; Melanchthon, Loci, MW II/1, p. 162; Zwingli, Von Erkiesen, SW I; Calvin, Institutes III, XIX, 12; IV, X, 22; Martyr, Commonplaces, II, p. 166.

24. Luther: "Quod si uti voles libertate tua, in occulto facito, sicut Paulus dicit Ro. 14" (De Lib. Christ., WA 7, 71); Zwingli: "leer du für und für getrülich, und gebruch dich auch christenlicher fryheit heimlich und by denen, die nitt verletzt werdend" (Von dem touff, SW IV, 256). I have found no explicit assertion of this principle among the English reformers, but it is at least implied in the Bishops' Book (Lloyd, op. cit., p. 115).

25. Pred. des Jah. 1522, WA 10ᴵᴵᴵ, 11, 14.

26. See some of the replies to Cranmer's 1540 questionnaire: G. Burnet, op. cit., I, ii, pp. 361, 362. See also: N. Ridley, Works, p. 338; Latimer, Sermons and Remains, pp. 13, 180; The Order of Communion, Two Liturgies, p. 4.

27. Erasmus was not alone in this view. According to Jaroslav Pelikan, Luther was of the conviction that "the need for ritual was in inverse ratio to the earnestness of Christian faith" (J. Pelikan, Obedient Rebels [New York and Evanston, 1964], p. 93). Zwingli stated that all the ceremonies could be abolished with little detriment to faith (Acta Tiguri, SW I, 49). According to Calvin, it was Christ's intention to impress upon Christians the fact that they no longer stand in need of the "tutelage" God had afforded ancient Israel by way of its "childish" ceremonial rudiments (Institutes IV, X, 14). The rationale provided by the 1549 Prayer Book for why some ceremonies were abolished and some not gave expression to much the same sentiment (Two Liturgies, p. 156).

28. Pred. des Jah. 1522, WA 10ᴵᴵᴵ, 11. See also: Zwingli, Von Erkiesen, SW I, pp. 120, 125, 153; Zwingli, Annot. ad Rom., ZO VI, p. 127; Calvin, Institutes III, XIX, 13; Bucer, Grund und Ursach, BDS I, pp. 218 ff.; Frith, A Mirror, WER, p. 292.

29. As cited in Rupp, Patterns, p. 316.

30. This is obvious from the whole of Erasmus' teaching on the ceremonies, but it was especially brought into focus by the aforementioned emphasis placed upon the allegorical significance of the ceremonies retained.

31. See Vatja, *op. cit.*, pp. 177 ff.

32. Art. XXI; *BEK*, p. 83.

33. See K. McDonnell, *Calvin*, pp. 89–93.

34. *Institutes* IV, X, 14.

35. "Tolle ceremonias ab Ecclesia et apud maximam Christianorum partem Dei cultum statim extingues" (*Assertionis Lutheranae Confutatio, Opera*, p. 587).

36. *Exhortation*, sig. G, fol. iv; sig. V, fol. i; sig. F, fol. iv.

37. *Three Primers*, pp. 123–24.

38. Strype, *EM* I, ii, p. 402. *Ibid.*, pp. 402–3. Cromwell, it may be noted, reported Mont's views to the king in a letter to the latter dated April 24, 1539 (See Merriman, *Cromwell*, II, pp. 220–21).

39. Turner's and Bale's series of tracts against the "Romysche Foxe" do not really pay much attention to the question about consideration of the "weak," but they undoubtedly shared the view of Karlstadt that the efforts of the mainline reformers to slow down the pace of reform for the sake of the "weak" was merely an attempt to compromise on God's word (See Rupp, *Patterns*, pp. 138–39).

40. In addition to the examples already cited, the best indication of this was, as in the case of Erasmus, the great emphasis placed by the English reformers upon the "spiritual" meaning of the ceremonies retained (See *Supra*, IV. ns. 107, 108).

41. For some of the more important changes, see Gee and Hardy, *op. cit.*, pp. 327 f., 366–68; Hughes and Larkin, *op cit.*, I, pp. 416–17; Foxe, *Acts and Monuments*, V, pp. 717–18; Gairdner, *The English Church*, p. 252; *Two Liturgies*, pp. 89 ff., 159 ff., 217, 265, 279, 283, 339, 349; C.W. Dugmore, *The Mass and the English Reformers* (London, 1958), pp. 133–35, 159 f.; C. Hopf, *Bucer*, pp. 48–94; F. Procter and W.H. Frere, *A New History of the Book of Common Prayer* (London, 1951), pp. 73–77, 81–83; G.J. Cuming, *A History of Anglican Liturgy* (New York, 1969), pp. 102–16; F.A. Gasquet and E. Bishop, *Edward VI and the Book of Common Prayer* (London, 1891), pp. 289–99. For the 1551 *Reformatio Legum Ecclesiasticarum* (which was never published until 1571), and a discussion of the same, see: *The Reformation of the Ecclesiastical Laws*, ed. E. Cardwell (Oxford, 1850); Dixon, *op. cit.*, III, pp. 350–82; *The Canon Law of the Church of England*, ed. Archbishop's Commission on Canon Law (London, 1947), pp. 45–63; P. Hughes, *op. cit.*, II, pp. 127–34; Dickens, *English Reformation*, pp. 249–51.

42. Several explicit expressions of such consideration have already been cited. To these may be added Somerset's remarks concerning the pedagogical value of the images (Foxe, *Acts and Monuments* V, pp. 28–29).

43. See the comments about Northumberland in: T.M. Parker, *The English Reformation to 1558* (New York, 1968), pp. 111 f.; Dixon, *op. cit.*, III, pp. 505–6; Dickens, *English Reformation*, pp. 256–57. Hooper, not surprisingly, called Northumberland "the most faithful and intrepid soldier of Christ," "a most holy and fearless instrument of the word of God," "a diligent promoter of the glory of God" (See *OL*, pp. 82, 89, 99). While inaccurate on several details about the Hooper-Ridley vestiarian controversy, John Opie's article on "The Anglicizing of John Hooper" (*Archiv* LIX [1968] pp. 150–77) sheds some light on the relation of Northumberland to Hooper and Cranmer. On Cranmer's not so pleasant relationship to the Duke, see also: C.W. Dugmore, "The First Ten Years, 1549–1559," in *The English Prayer Book, 1549–1662* (London, 1963), pp. 6–30.

44. "Deinde aliud est tolerare infirmos in rebus neutris, sed in manifesto rebus impiis impium est tolerare" ("Luther an den Propst, die Domherren und das Capitel in Wittenberg," *END* IV, p. 4). "At cavendum interim monemus, ne inter media deputentur, ut quidem solent missam et usum imaginum in templo pro mediis reputare, quae revera

non sunt media" (Bullinger, *Helv. Post.*, XXVII, Schaff, *op. cit.*, p. 303). See also: Calvin, *Institutes* III, XIX, 13; Martyr, *Commonplaces*, II, p. 164. An interesting note may be added at this point about William Tyndale's position on the question of Henry VIII's divorce from Katherine of Aragon. The question, it will be recalled, centered rightly or wrongly (See Scarisbrick, *op. cit.*, pp. 187–97) upon whether, in view of the law laid down in Leviticus 18:16 ("you shall not uncover the nakedness of your brother's wife"), Henry had done rightly in marrying Katherine who had been the wife of his older brother Arthur. After noting that in Deuteronomy 25:5 ff. Moses had commanded "that if a man die without issue, his brother must marry his wife," Tyndale states that it would be absurd to argue first that the Leviticus regulation renders any marriage of a brother's wife filthy and unnatural, and then insist that the Deuteronomy precept is only a ceremony (Tyndale, *Exposition*, pp. 324–27). The only way out of this dilemma—i.e., two texts seemingly forbidding and commanding the same thing—is to conclude that in the Leviticus text "Moses forbiddeth a man to take his brother's wife as long as he liveth." (*Ibid.*, p. 328). Therefore, "at the uttermost," Tyndale concludes, it is an "indifferent thing" for a man to marry his brother's wife if the brother dies after having had issue by her, and if his brother die childless, it is now lawful, though no commandment, for the man to take his brother's wife (*Ibid.*, p. 329). In brief, Tyndale concludes that Henry's marriage to Katherine was not against the natural law, but that in itself it was indifferent, and therefore, once contracted, valid, while his divorce from her was not indifferent, but impious (*Ibid.*, pp. 329, 332).

45. Rupp, *Patterns*, p. 314. Calvin wrote much the same: "For milk is not poison. They are therefore lying when they claim to be feeding those whom they are cruelly killing under the guise of blandishments" (*Institutes* III, XIX, 13).

46. Cranmer, *Writings and Letters*, p. 414.

47. *Ibid.*

48. See Foxe, *Acts and Monuments* V, pp. 562, 563.

49. The "weak," Martyr wrote, "must be borne withall for a time, and not continualie, unlesse they will alwaies be learning, and never come to the knowledge of the truth" (*Commonplaces*, II, p. 173).

50. If the weak "never grow up sufficiently to be able to bear even some light food at least," Calvin wrote, "it is certain that they were never brought up on milk" (*Institutes* III, XIX, 13).

51. For a few examples of the Reformers' application of this Pauline passage to the Romans' ceremonial legislation, see: Luther, *I Tim.*, WA 26, 67–75; *Unterricht der Visitatoren*, WA 26, 228; *Von Menschenlehre zu meiden*, WA 10^{II}, 77; Melanchthon, *Loci*, MW II, 1, p. 160; *Aug. Konf.*, BEK, p. 88; *Apologia*, BEK, p. 386; Zwingli, *Von Erkiesen*, SW I, pp. 91–98; Calvin, *Institutes* IV, IX, 14; Martyr, *Commonplaces*, II, p. 168.

52. See especially Calvin, *Institutes* III, XIX, 9, and Colet, *Exposition of Romans*, pp. 210, 214. Their remarks in this connection bear a close resemblance to Clement of Alexandria's comments about eating and drinking (See *Stromata* VI, 12: PG 9, 322; *Paedagogus*, II, 2: PG 8, 410–32).

53. See Melanchthon, *Apologia: BEK*, p. 341; Calvin, *Institutes*, III, X, 4; Bullinger, *Decades*, d. III, s. II, t. II, p. 53.

54. "For riches are indifferent, and are not evil of themselves: but they are made evil, when our heart is set upon them, and that we put hope in them" (H. Latimer, *Sermons and Remains*, p. 202; also: *Ibid.*, p. 214). "We must not settle our minds upon nor be in love with [riches] ... Heaven is the goal whereat we run ... set not your hearts upon [riches])" (Bullinger, *Decades*, d. III, s. II, t. II, p. 53). For other such assertions, see: Luther, *Grosser Katechismus*, BEK, p. 674; Bucer, *De Regno Christi*, MB, pp. 356–57;

Calvin, *Institutes* III, IX, 3–5; Calvin, *Gospel according to St. John 11–21 and the First Ep. of John*, trans. T.M. Parker (Edinburgh, 1961), pp. 37 f., 125, 253; W. Tyndale, *Exposition of Matt.*, *Expositions and Notes*, pp. 106, 111; *The Bishops'* and *King's Book*, Lloyd, *op. cit.*, pp. 188, 192, 344; S. Gardiner, *Contemptum Humanae Legis*, *Tracts*, p. 195; M. Coverdale, *The Catechism*, p. 389.

55. See: Luther, *Grosser Katechismus, BEK*, pp. 674, 680–82; Bucer, *De Regno Christi, MB*, pp. 306, 303; Calvin, *Institutes*, III, X, 2, 3, 5; Calvin, *Commentary on II Cor., Tim., Titus, and Philemon*, trans. T.A. Smail (Edinburgh, 1964), pp. 108, 110, 282; Bullinger, *Decades*, d. III, s. II, t. II, pp. 53–55; Tyndale, *Expositions and Notes*, pp. 16, 101, 106–7; Latimer, *Sermons*, pp. 397–98; Latimer, *Sermons and Remains*, pp. 116, 202; *Bishops'* and *King's Book*, Lloyd, *op. cit.*, pp. 191, 343–44; Coverdale, *The Catechism*, pp. 387, 389, 390; Coverdale, *A Treatise of Fasting*, in *The Catechism*, p. 538.

56. See: Luther, *I Tim., WA* 26, 74; Bucer, *De Regno Christi, MB*, p. 354; Calvin, *Institutes* III, X, 3; Bullinger, *Decades*, d. III, s. II, t. II, p. 54; *Bishops' Book*, Lloyd, *op. cit.*, p. 191; Latimer, *Sermons and Remains*, p. 116; Coverdale, *The Catechism*, p. 390.

57. See: Luther, *Unterricht der Visitatoren, WA* 26, 225; Bucer, *De Regno Christi, MB*, pp. 354–57; Calvin, *Institutes* III, X, 5; III, VII, 5; Calvin, *Commentary on II Cor. (etc.)*, pp. 108, 110, 114; Calvin, *Gospel according to John 1–10*, trans. T.H.L. Parker (Edinburgh, 1959), pp. 147, 148; Calvin, *Epistle of Paul to Galatians, Ephesians, Philipians, and Colossians*, trans. T.H.L. Parker (Edinburgh, 1965), p. 193; Calvin, *Epistles of Paul to Romans and Thessalonians*, trans. Ross MacKenzie (Edinburgh, 1960), pp. 418–20; Bullinger, *Decades*, d. III, s. II, t. II, pp. 59–64; Tyndale, *Expositions and Notes*, p. 106; Latimer, *Sermons*, pp. 398–400, 406–8; *Bishops' Book*, Lloyd, *op. cit.*, p. 188; Coverdale, *A Treatise of Fasting*, in *The Catechism*, p. 538; Coverdale, *The Catechism*, pp. 389–90.

58. See: Luther, *WA* $10^{1,2}$, 308–9; *WA* 40^{III}, 299; *WA* $10^{1,1}$, 307–9 as cited in Althaus, *Ethics of Luther*, pp. 36–42; see also bibliographical references in same; Bucer, *De Regno Christi, MB*, p. 356; Calvin, *Institutes* III, X, 6, and the bibliography provided by editor in n. 8; Bullinger, *Decades*, d. III, s. II, t. II, p. 55; Tyndale, *Expositions and Notes*, p. 106; Latimer, *Sermons*, pp. 214, 402–3; Latimer, *Sermons and Remains*, pp. 37–39, 214, 215; *Bishops'* and *King's Book*, Lloyd, *op. cit.*, pp. 190, 342, 343; Coverdale, *A Confutation of Standish, Remains*, p. 339; Coverdale, *The Catechism*, p. 399.

59. See: Luther, *De Lib. Christ., WA* 7, 69; Bucer, *De Regno Christi, MB*, pp. 303, 354–57; Calvin, *Institutes* III, XIX, 9; III, X, 3; Bullinger, *Decades*, d. III, s. II, t. II, pp. 53, 57; Tyndale, *Exposition and Notes*, pp. 94 f.; Latimer, *Sermons and Remains*, pp. 15, 19, 108, 202; *The King's Book*, Lloyd, *op. cit.*, pp. 215, 219; Hughes and Larkin, *op. cit.*, I, pp. 260–61; Martyr, *Commonplaces*, II, pp. 164–65, 167; Coverdale, *A confutation, Remains*, p. 339; Coverdale, *The Catechism*, pp. 399, 400.

60. Letter to Carondelet, *EE* V, p. 177.

61. *Der 82. Psalm ausgelegt, WA* 31^{1}, 210.

62. *Ibid.*; see also: *Eyne Christliche Vormahnung, WA* 18, 417–21.

63. Lloyd, *op. cit.*, p. xv.

64. Foxe, *Acts and Monuments* V, pp. 534–35.

65. See, for some examples: Colet, *Corinthians*, p. 191; Colet, *Romans*, pp. 210, 211; Lloyd, *op. cit.*, p. xvi; G. Burnet, *op. cit.*, pp. 490–91; *OL* pp. 624–25; Coverdale, *Remains*, p. 338; Gardiner, *Tracts*, pp. 179–81; Cranmer, *Letters and Writings*, pp. 512–13, 516; *Two Liturgies*, pp. 156–57.

66. See *Exhortation*, sig. D, fol. iii(v); sig. H, fol. iv(v); also: Herrtage, *Starkey's Life and Letters*, pp. lxi–lxii, lii.

67. Herrtage, *Starkey's Life and Letters*, p. xliii.

68. *Exhortation*, sig. C, fol. ivff; sig. H, fols. ii–iv; sig. Z, fols. ii–iii; sig. D, fol. i(v).

CHAPTER 7

UNITY SPIRITUAL AND UNITY POLITICAL

A CENTURY OR SO after Thomas Starkey had written his *Exhortation to Unity and Obedience,* John Milton, siding with the Puritans in their struggle against the Elizabethan Settlement, would ask by what right the Conformists had changed the nature of adiaphora by submitting them to legislation.[1] Milton, obviously, was of the opinion that adiaphora are by nature beyond legislation. And he was, of course, entitled to his own conception of adiaphora. But his was also an opinion which few, if any, earlier adiaphorists had shared. In previous centuries, adiaphorists like the Apostle Paul, Augustine, Aquinas, and Jan Hus had indeed protested frequently against the excessive number and obligation of laws touching upon adiaphoristic matters. But it had never been their intention to suggest thereby that the legislation of adiphora must be precluded by definition.

For all his talk of Christian liberty, the Apostle Paul had himself laid down a few rules concerning such "indifferent" matters as the headdress of women (1 Cor. 11:1–16) and their silence at liturgical gatherings (1 Cor. 14:34–35). In the same respect could be cited the Council of Jerusalem's prohibition of "strangled" meats (Acts 15:20, 28–29).

That Augustine had no objection to the legislation as such of adiaphora is clear from the authority over such matters he afforded to bishops and from the fact that to his view matters which at one time have been indifferent become "essential" when legislated by a Plenary Council.[2]

Thomas Aquinas spoke of adiaphora being left to "man's own decision," but also qualified this statement to mean that while adiaphora are sometimes left to the decision of the individual, at other times, when the common good is at stake, to the decision of the temporal or spiritual superiors.[3] And, as has been seen, most high medieval theologians were of the view that on the whole the subject never has the right to oppose his own will to the commands of his superiors

132

regarding adiaphoristic matters.[4] Even such late medieval, reform-minded theologians as John Wyclif, Jan Hus, and Wessel Gansfort did not question as such the right of church officials to legislate in the realm of adiaphora.[5]

C.L. Manschreck has written that Melanchthon would have "agreed with Milton that requiring adiaphora is a denial of liberty."[6] But that is hardly accurate. For Melanchthon, in fact, saw no more contradiction in the legislation of adiaphora than did Erasmus[7] or the other mainline Continental and English reformers of the sixteenth century. Some legislation of such matters as the times and places of assembly, the shape of the liturgy, and so forth, is not only legitimate, it was said, but indispensable to the survival of the church.[8] Why? Because, as Calvin put it, "such diversity exists in the customs of men, such variety in their minds, such conflicts in their judgments and dispositions," that "no organization is sufficiently strong unless constituted with definite laws," and no "procedure" can be maintained "without some set form." When, therefore, churches are deprived of such "laws" or "forms," Calvin concluded, "their very sinews disintegrate and they are wholly deformed and scattered."[9]

If, therefore, the security of the church is to be provided for, close attention, Calvin and all the mainline reformers said, must be given to the Apostle Paul's command that "all things be done decently and in order" (1 Cor. 14:40). But this requirement of "decorum and order" cannot possibly be met unless certain definite laws and observances be established.[10] Thus, just as Paul himself made many such ordinances, so, the 1539 English *Manual of Prayers* asserted, "such may be made among us."[11] While differing with Stephen Gardiner's tendency to equate the obligation of divine and human laws, most mainline Continental and English reformers had no real argument with his assertion that "God's apt scholars will not be those who . . . bear it so grudingly that laws should be made for all men on things indifferent."[12]

It was one thing, however, to allow for the legislation of adiaphora, and quite another to determine whose prerogative it was to make such legislation. In its broadest ramifications, the latter question concerned the relation of one local church to another or to the church as a whole, and the diversity which might or might not be allowed to play within such relationships.

During the earliest of Christian centuries, the local churches had for the most part been allowed to go their own way in the determination of certain non-essential matters, however much diversity resulted therefrom. Most revealing in this regard was the so-called Easter Controversy of the second century. As reported by Eusebius of Caesaria, both the churches of Asia Minor and the churches of Rome, Palestine, Gaul, and Greece claimed an apostolic origin for their respective and differing observance of the date of Easter. But, in the end, both sides also came to recognize that conformity in such a matter was not essential, and not even desirable if it would mean the loss of that which was essential. Thus, although Pope Anicetus (d.166) and Polycarp could not agree on the date of Easter, they nevertheless "communed with each other . . . and separated from each other in peace." Pope Victor I (d.199) was at first inclined to take a less irenic course. He threatened to excommunicate the Quartodecimans. But other bishops objected and promptly urged Victor to contemplate that course which would promote peace, unity, and love of one another. In a letter to Victor, Irenaeus wrote that the "very difference in our fasting establishes the unanimity in our faith."[13]

Similar in some respects to the settlement of the Easter Controversy was the solution offered by Cyprian and Firmilian to such problems as the re-admission of repentent adulterers to the Christian community, and the rebaptizing of heretics. With these two early Church Fathers, however, it was a question of reconciling diversity not so much with the existence of an unwritten apostolic tradition, as with what they referred to as the Evangelical Law of Scripture.

For all their emphasis upon Scriptural authority, Cyprian and Firmilian were also of the opinion that on administrative matters each bishop is free to decide for himself which course of action will best fulfill his responsibility to God, and that local traditions, therefore, may be respected without jeopardizing the bond of concord between the various Christian communities. Thus Cyprian noted approvingly that while some of his predecessors refused to re-admit adulterers to the Christian community, they were not so obstinate as to break communion with those fellow bishops who followed a different course of action. And on the question of rebaptizing heretics, Cyprian said that although he thought Scripture was on his side, he had no intention of trying to force his own decision upon other bishops. For his part, Firmilian bitterly rebuked Pope Stephen for having broken the peace with other bishops over the matter of rebaptizing heretics. He suggested that the Pope's action was all the more despicable in that while at Rome itself the original traditions have not always been respected, and while as much diversity has obtained there as elsewhere on such matters as the celebration of Easter, no cause had been found therein for a disruption of the peace and unity of the Church.[14]

Given its generally less than positive attitude toward the society and culture of this world, one might expect the leaders of the early Church to have held its members to a tight and uniform discipline regarding the various civil laws under which Christians found themselves. And, to be sure, the early Fathers insisted that there were limits to the obedience which Christians could afford the civil laws. While continuing to ascribe a divine origin to civil government,[15] they argued that the latter could be obeyed only to the extent that its statutes did not contradict divine positive or natural law.[16] Thus, not surprisingly, Christians were often accused of civil disobedience.[17]

On the other hand, however, early Christians were advised by the likes of Origen, and in explicitly adiaphoristic terms, not to become disturbed over civil laws and customs which do not contradict the law of God. Thus, for example, when Celsus presented Origen with a citation from Herodotus about the case of Amman forbidding people of the cities of Marea and Apis to eat cows, Origen simply concluded that the eating of cows is an indifferent matter and typical of the sort of things over which Christians would do best not to contend.[18] And as the author of the so-called *Letter to Diognetus* was quick to point out, Christians were, as a matter of fact, for the most part conforming to the customs of the country in which they lived.[19]

In the fourth century, Augustine, Socrates, and Sozomen all attested to the great variety of Christian observances obtaining in their time from one place to another, and saw therein a further indication of the adiaphoristic nature of the observances involved.[20] As a practical rule of conduct, Augustine encouraged Januarius and Casulanus to follow the happy advice he had himself received from Ambrose, namely, that "when in Rome, one should do as the Romans do."[21] Augustine especially castigated those who by their "contentious obstinacy" or "superstitious timidity" were continually agitating these questions as if all were wrong except what they themselves do.[22] Unless mutual respect is shown toward local differences in adiaphoristic matters, he said, the result will be endless contention over questions that admit of no definitive answer.[23] Sozomen referred to the decision by Anicetus and Polycarp not to break communion with each other over the non-essential matter of dating the Easter celebration as a very wise one, and implied that all the other various customs listed ought to be handled similarly.[24]

Notwithstanding its aforementioned overall thrust toward uniformity, the medieval church continued to witness considerable diversity, and not always with reluctance. In advising Augustine of Canterbury about the shape of the Anglo-Saxon church, Pope Gregory the Great suggested that Augustine select from the Roman, Gaulish, or any other church, whatever customs would best serve the Christian development of the English people. The Pope added that the pagan temples need not be destroyed and that one or another tribal ceremony or festival might be introduced into Christian practice, assuming that it had been purified of its earlier pagan significance.[25] It was Gregory's opinion that "so long as the Church preserves one faith, there is nothing inconsistent about a divergence of customs."[26] Although Augustine himself seems to have taken little advantage of Gregory's generous attitude,[27] the rise and growth of such a variety of liturgies like the Roman-African, Gallican, Celtic, Mozarabic, and Milanese[28]—to mention only those of the West—during the centuries following the barbarian invasions, suggests in itself that the Gregorian dictum was not altogether overlooked.

Furthermore, despite the generally hostile mood that had come to characterize relations between the Eastern and Western branches of Christianity, and the tendency on the part of some like Charlemagne, Cerularius, or the Studite monk Nicetas, to make conformity in ceremonial matters a condition of the *jus communionis*, there were also many individuals throughout the eleventh and twelfth centuries, in both the East and West, who were of the view that divergence in such matters was no reason to break the communion in faith between the two branches of Christendom. Cardinal Humbert, for example, wrote to Cerularius that Rome was well aware "that customs which differ by virtue of time and place in no way impede the salvation of believers while the one faith, informed by charity, commends all to the one God."[29] Two of the most learned men of the eleventh century, Anselm of Canterbury and Archbishop Theolphylact of Ochrida, voiced a similar opinion,[30] as did also Bishop Anselm of Havelberg and Archbishop Nicetas of Nicomedia during their famous dialogue at Constantinople in 1136.[31]

Many late medieval theologians, while recognizing the dangers inherent to any play of diversity, and emphasizing, therefore, the need for unity in essentials, nonetheless objected strongly to the canonists' rather successful attempt to impose upon the Church a burdensome uniformity based upon papal or episcopal *fiat*. Jean Gerson, for example, embraced wholeheartedly Augustine's dictum that in non-essentials local custom should be respected, and saw therein the key for establishing concord between the Western and Eastern churches, and for the reformation of the Gallican church without undermining its freedom.[32] Gerson's concern for the liberties of the Gallican church was matched by Wyclif's for the *ecclesia Anglicana*, Hus' for the Bohemian church, and was at least akin to the sort of respect for the local church that had always been part and parcel of Eastern ecclesiology.[33]

Another late medieval thinker, Nicholas of Cusa (d.1464), went still further, and called for toleration of diversity in rites and ceremonies not only among local or national Christian churches, but among all religions in general. Written against the background of the fall of Constantinople in 1453, Cusa's *De Pace Fidei* represented a rather fanciful appeal for an end to religious intolerance by way of applying his doctrine of the coincidence of opposites to the cosmos of religions.

Like the physical world,[34] the cosmos of religions, Cusa implied, *coram Deo* is homogeneous. All religions are equally near and far from God—equally far, because the God of all religions is the utterly transcendent One; equally near, because all religions are ultimately grounded in the same faith in Christ. Once this fundamental point is granted, Cusa concluded, the diversity of rites and customs among the various religions need be no cause of dissension, for all such things are merely sensible signs of the truth of faith, and, unlike faith itself, subject to change. To seek to impose exact conformity in everything pertaining to the sacraments, therefore, would only serve to disturb the peace, Cusa said. Church authorities would do much better to respect local conditions, by tolerating a diversity of rites. Similarly, in regard to matters like Fasting, Abstinence, the forms of prayer, and so forth, the various nations should be permitted their own devotions and ceremonies. Such diversity would enhance devotion by way of the spirit of competition it would generate.[35]

Cusa's humanist colleague, Marsilio Ficino, added that "it is even possible that such a variety [in rites] through God's own disposition gives birth to a certain beauty in the universe."[36] Though less appreciative of the "pagan" religions, Erasmus of Rotterdam would also speak of the "many churches" arising out of the "distinction of persons and places," and generally showed himself willing and ready to accept the fact of diversity in adiaphoristic matters introduced by the Protestants in the sixteenth century.[37]

Confronted with the latter, even the most conservative papalists of the sixteenth century, it should be noted, agreed that in "indifferent things" variety does not destroy the unity of faith.[38] If, therefore, the reformers have in mind "special" or "particular" rites, the papalists said, "they are to be praised" for not regarding a variety of rites as breaking the bond of faith. It was such "special" rites to which Gregory the Great and Augustine of Hippo were referring when they upheld diversity, the papalists argued. But "universal" church rites are not "indifferent" matters, they said, and the reformers, therefore, are wrong in not observing them and thereby place themselves in diametrical opposition to Augustine's advice to Januarius that "what has been universally delivered by the church must be universally observed."[39]

The papalists had a point. Augustine had indeed linked his adiaphoristic appraisal of certain ceremonies with their "particularity." He did not conceive of their adiaphoristic nature as something fixed once and for all time. On the contrary, what by virtue of its "particularity" was once considered "indifferent," might at a later point become "essential" when decreed, for example, by a General Council or some other representative of the "universal" church.[40] In one sense, therefore, Roman authorities were acting in accordance with Augustine's views when during the Middle Ages they concluded that many ceremonies which before had been of a purely local, and, therefore, adiaphoristic nature, were now, since their imposition upon the universal church, no longer to be considered indifferent. On the other hand, however, one would also have to ask whether Augustine would ever have sanctioned such an imposition of "particular" ceremonies upon the whole church, to the loss of their once adiaphoristic nature. Given his "fundamental principle" that the burden of Christian obedience must be light and easy, it seems very unlikely that he would have. To that extent, the reformers might well have argued that fidelity to Augustine's thought would have dictated that the local traditions of the Roman or any other local church should never have been imposed upon the whole of the Western church in the first place, and on that account remained indifferent notwithstanding the actual fact of their having been so imposed.

In any event, the mainline Continental reformers were certainly of the view that the adiaphoristic nature of ceremonial matters had not been altered by their having been embraced by the universal church in a previous age, and that diversity in their regard was, therefore, no less legitimate in the sixteenth century than it had been in Augustine's time.

It is not necessary, they said, for all ecclesiastical rites and ceremonies to be everywhere alike.[41] In the words of Martin Bucer, "the unity of the Church does not consist in garments, ceremonies, and the like, but in the unity of the spirit, of charity, of the word of God, of Christ, of the sacraments, and in the communion of gifts."[42] Thus, for example, every local church is free to decide for itself in what external form it might best celebrate the Eucharist. So long as the essence of the sacrament as instituted by Christ is respected, diversity in other matters makes no difference.[43] Thomas Müntzer declared that no one should be surprised at the German Mass he had developed for his congregation at Allstedt. "We are not the only ones to use another fashion than Rome," Müntzer noted. The Milanese, the Croats, the Armenians, the Bohemians, the Mozarabs, and the Russians, Müntzer added, have their own special ceremonies and observances. "Why, then, should not we use our opportunities? For we at Allstedt are Germans and not foreigners."[44] In support of their own diverse ceremonies, other of the Continental reformers appealed to the aforementioned settlement of the first Easter controversy, cited the incidence of diversity in the early Church as reported in the *Tripartite History,* and quoted dicta of Pope Gregory I and Augustine to the effect that diversity does not violate the unity of the Church, and that the unity of the Church does not consist in external human ordinances.[45]

The English reformers agreed, and argued in the first place that a clear distinction must always be made between "the vnyte spiritual and vnyte polytycal." While the former builds upon the "essentials" of faith, the latter, Thomas Starkey wrote, has to do with the indifferent matters of "worldly policie." Spiritual unity can remain, Starkey concluded, even "though there be neuer so moche diuersitie of worldly policie." Had Pole and the Charterhouse monks kept this distinction between spiritual and political unity in mind, Starkey added, they would not have been so quick to conclude that the English Church would "run to ruyne" by breaking with the "political" traditions of Rome.[46]

The unity of the "one, catholic church is a mere spiritual unity," the *Bishops'* and *King's Book* declared, consisting in "the unity which is in one God, one faith, one doctrine of Christ and his sacraments."[47] Such unity cannot "be anything hurted, impeached, or infringed in any point" by the "divers using and observation of such outward rites, ceremonies, traditions and ordinances, as be instituted by [local authorities]."[48] Just as the "church of Corinth and of Ephese were one church in God . . . though also in traditions, opinions and policies there was some diversity among them," so, the *King's Book* concluded, "the church of England, Spain, Italy, and Poole be not separate from the unity, but be one church in God, notwithstanding that among them there is great distance of place, diversity of traditions, not in all things unity of opinions, alteration in rites, ceremonies, and ordinances, or estimation of the same."[49] To this appeal to the example of the New Testament churches, Thomas Cranmer and Nicholas Ridley added references to the second century Easter controversy in order to prove "that no part of the church ought to be cut off" or have their "unity in faith" broken on account of variety in ceremonial matters.[50]

Consistent with this view that "divers realms, may order such things diversly, as they shall seem convenient, after the disposition of the people there,"[51] and without jeopardizing the "spiritual" unity of the church thereby, the Dispensations Act of 1534 had declared that while the English king and his subjects in no way intended "to decline or vary from the congregation of Christ's Church in any things concerning the very articles of the Catholic faith of Christendom, or in other things declared, by Holy Scripture and the Word of God, necessary for your and their salvations," they would henceforth feel themselves bound only to such human laws "as have been devised, made, and ordained within this realm."[52] Such an assertion was not understood by the English reformers to mean that all past papal and conciliar laws touching upon adiaphoristic matters were henceforth to be disregarded. But it certainly was intended to limit or remove altogether any authority papal or conciliar canons concerning adiaphora may previously have enjoyed in themselves.[53]

Starkey's adiaphoristic appraisal of papal authority has already been noted, and it would serve little purpose to cite the flood of other propaganda pieces supporting Henry VIII's rejection of the pope's authority over the English church. By trying to support Henry's actions by appealing to the superiority of the General Councils, however, some of these propaganda pieces had left open the possibility that conciliar decisions touching upon adiaphoristic matters might be deemed superior to those of local authorities.[54]

Against such a possibility, Starkey argued that while General Councils are good for giving "instruction and brotherly exhortation," and can help in the avoidance of heresy and schism, they are "not necessary to the conservation of Christian faith and doctrine," and enjoy "no power of commandment in things indifferent." In all such things as are indifferent, Starkey noted, "respect should be had of the nature of the people and country in every state and cominaltie." But the latter "cannot be so wel juged" by "general counsel," and the first councils, Starkey pointedly added, had not meddled in things indifferent, but had stuck to "the interpretation of Scripture and thynges pertaynyng by necessitie to man's salvation."[55]

According to Gilbert Burnet, Thomas Cranmer also "had much doubting in himself as to general councils; and he thought that only the word of God was the rule of faith, which ought to take place in all controversies of religion."[56] The speech apparently delivered by the Archbishop in 1535 before the House of Lords would seem to bear out Burnet's conclusion. In the past, Cranmer asserted, the General Councils' authority extended only to the declaration of points of faith and the condemnation of heretics, and their decrees were not considered laws until they had been enacted by princes. Enlarging upon this historical evidence, Cranmer stated that should a Council proceed against a king, its sentence would be of no force, "as being without [its] sphere." What a Council determines "ought to be well considered and examined by the scripture, and in matters indifferent men ought to be left to their freedom."[57]

Not all the English bishops shared Cranmer's views in this regard, as was evidenced especially by a remark in a draft of the 1543 *King's Book* to the effect that all must "humbly submit to the judgment of the whole Church."[58] Henry VIII, however, refused to approve the latter remark,[59] and generally favored the position of Starkey and Cranmer, at least to the extent that so far as adiaphora were concerned, the Council had no authority. In late 1535 an English delegation headed by Edward Fox had succeeded in eliciting from the Protestant princes of Germany a formal petition asking Henry VIII to become the "protector and defender of their league." Among the conditions laid down by the princes for Henry's admission to their league was one to the effect that if the pending General Council would be "just, catholic, and free," the king and the confederates would defend the conciliar decrees concerning doctrine and ceremonies.[60] Henry replied that he would submit to doctrinal decisions of the Council, "but as touching the ceremonies, there may be different rites, and such dyuersite used in dyuers domynyons, *fere per totum mundum,* that it will be hard to conclude anye certentie in them," and on that account their "order and limitation should be left to the arbitrees of the governours of euerye domynyon, supposing that euery of them can tell what is most comodious for his owne domynyons."[61]

In the end, therefore, the question about whose prerogative it was to legislate adiaphora came down to a choice between ecclesiastical or civil local authorities. Even the most adamant defenders of papal authority in the Middle Ages had, at least in theory, afforded civil rulers control over adiaphora of a purely secular nature.[62] Not until Marsilius of Padua wrote his *Defensor Pacis,* however, had anyone seriously argued that civil rulers also enjoyed authority over ecclesiastical adiaphora. Marsilius himself did not, as noted earlier, employ an explicitly adiaphoristic terminology, but had all the same centered his defense of the prince's right upon the quasi-adiaphoristic conclusion that Evangelical Law has left entirely "uncovered," and therefore in the hands of the princes, the government of man's external affairs.[63]

Among the sixteenth-century Continental reformers, Zwingli came closest to embracing the Marsilian view, possibly through his ties with

Erasmus whose own thought shows certain Marsilian influences. The city of Zurich had a long history of civil control of external ecclesiastical matters prior to Zwingli's arrival there in late December of 1518. Instead of trying to check such an exercise of civil authority, Zwingli actually extended it, and built upon it his own Gelasian-like conception of the relation of the *regnum* and *sacerdotium* within the *corpus christianum*. He reserved control over the preaching and interpretation of the Scriptures to the pastors, whose authority he had early on convinced the city magistrates to accept over that of Rome. But once assured of the magistrates' submission to pastoral authority in that respect, he left them, much to the chagrin of the Anabaptists, a broad prerogative to direct the external, adiaphoristic affairs of the church.[64]

Martin Bucer also was inclined to afford civil authorities considerable control over external ecclesiastical affairs.[65] The other major Continental reformers did so, however, only very reluctantly.

Luther eventually found it necessary to seek the help of the German princes in the organization of the evangelical churches, and naturally called upon his followers to heed the decrees of the princes regarding ecclesiastical adiaphora. But while this may have obscured somewhat his earlier distinction of the temporal and spiritual realms, it hardly indicated any radical shift in his thinking about the respective roles of church and civil authorities. His distrust of the princes was visceral, and what control he did allow them over ecclesiastical adiaphora resulted more from political expediency than from any conviction that they enjoyed some special right thereto.[66]

Melanchthon's submission to secular control of ecclesiastical adiaphora was equally reluctant. According to Manschreck, Melanchthon "might have accepted such control as a 'harsh servitude' but not gladly and humbly as Starkey advocated."[67] That may be an exaggeration, being based too much on Melanchthon's attitude toward Charles V's imposition of the Interims. But Melanchthon's misgivings about the Protestant princes were real enough. At one point he even went so far as to announce his readiness to accept papal rule on a *jure humano* basis in order, Manschreck says, to devise some means "for keeping Church polity independent of the state."[68]

Although the situation was such at Geneva that during most of his life Calvin had to submit to one form or another of civil control over ecclesiastical matters of an indifferent nature, he certainly did so with less than enthusiasm. A persistent champion of the Church's independence, he repeatedly let it be known that in his view the establishment of the ecclesiastical order should be left in the hands of the pastors. His most dramatic demonstration of this point came in 1538 when he and Farel chose to depart from Geneva rather than submit to the ceremonies which the civil officials of Bern were trying to impose upon the Genevan Church. At a subsequent synod in Zurich, Calvin made it perfectly clear that it was not the ceremonies themselves to which he objected, "but the imposition of these by act of the magistracy."[69]

A.G. Dickens has noted that during the early stages of the Henrician revolution "theory tended to remain in the storehouse until the political situation demanded its production and its use as propaganda."[70] The theory of adiaphorism was no exception. Familiarity with the adiaphoristic writings of Erasmus, Luther, or Tyndale and Frith, may have made it easier for a "conscientious" Henry VIII to have assumed control over external ecclesiastical affairs. But even when the propaganda began to flow, the theory of adiaphorism was relatively late in being exploited in Henry's favor. Most of the earlier Henrician propaganda pieces make no explicit mention of the adiaphoristic nature of those matters over which Henry had assumed control.

Probably the first explicit attempt to link up the theory of adiaphorism with the Royal Supremacy may be found in William Marshall's *Goodly Prymer in English*. The Primer stated that "among good works, the chief are, to be obedient in all things unto kings, princes, judges, and such other officers, as far as they command civil things; that is to say, such things as are indifferent, and not contrary unto the commandments of God."[71] This passage from *Marshall's Primer* is all the more significant in that by the time of its appearance its author was already "glossing" Marsilius of Padua's *Defensor Pacis* in preparation for the English translation of the latter which he would publish, with Cromwell's financial assistance, in 1535.[72] It may very well have been Marshall who most immediately inspired Thomas Starkey to have centered his *Exhortation to Unity and Obedience* upon a correlation of Marsilian views with the theory of adiaphorism.

Starkey readily admitted his debt to Marsilius. Underlying his *Exhortation* was the conclusion that Christ "never taught one point of worldly policie."[73] In an earlier letter sent by Starkey to Reginald Pole along with a copy of Marshall's translation of the *Defensor Pacis,* Starkey frankly admitted having derived this conclusion from Marsilius' *Defensor Pacis*, and suggested that Pole too would be convinced of its truth "by the readyng of Marsilius."[74]

On the assumption that Christ had had no intention of settling man's earthly affairs, Marsilius, as noted, had concluded that all such matters must be left to control of the prince. Starkey reached the same conclusion, and like Marshall before him, linked it up explicitly with the theory of adiaphorism. It pertains to their very definition, Starkey said, that adiaphora have been left by God "to worldly policie," or to "them which in every countrey or nation be in hie authoritie," which in England is the "princely power and comon counsell."[75]

Whatever may have been the English clergy's initial feelings on this matter, from about 1529 on they were left with little choice but to submit to secular control of ecclesiastical affairs. In October of 1529, Henry had dropped the ominous remark to the imperial ambassador that the clergy enjoyed no other power over the laity than to absolve them of sin. Then, a month later, and with Henry's *fiat,* had come Wolsey's fall from power and the anti-clerical attacks from Parliament. Another six months and the whole of the English clergy found itself charged under *Praemunire* on the grounds of "having exercised the jurisdiction of the Courts Christian within the realm." The bishops had hardly "bought" themselves out of that predicament before Henry had them in another, this time, February, 1531, by demanding that he be recognized as the "Protector and Supreme Head of the English Church and Clergy." This the bishops said they would grant only "so far as the law of Christ allows." Next came the Supplication of the Commons against the Ordinaries (1532) wherein, among other things, complaints were filed against the power of Convocation to fashion laws without royal assent or the consent of the laity, against the excessive number of holy days, and against the heresy trials at which the or-dinaries were said to have put the laity to "such subtle interrogatories, concerning the high mysteries of our faith, as are able quickly to trap a simple, unlearned, or yet a well-witted layman without learning, and bring them by such sinister introduction soon to his own confusion." Inspired by Stephen Gardiner, Convocation attempted an answer to the Supplication, but after the king encouraged Commons to carry on their attack and himself proceeded to charge the bishops with "double allegiance," Convocation retreated and on May 15, 1532, submitted to the royal demands.[76]

The 1537 *Bishops' Book* still argued that priests and bishops enjoy by "the authority of God's law" the jurisdiction "to make and ordain certain rules or canons" regarding indifferent ecclesiastical matters, and seemed to imply that "kings and princes" could restrain only that clerical jurisdiction which had been assigned to the clergy by the "kings and princes, and not by the authority of God and his gospel."[77] But, as noted earlier, Henry's corrections of the *Bishops' Book* removed any doubt the latter had cast over his supremacy, and in the revised, official 1543 *King's Book,* the earlier section on clerical jurisdiction was simply omitted, and in its stead was inserted yet another apology for the royal supremacy.[78] The clergy continued to exercise considerable control over ecclesiastical adiaphora, but always with a sense of their subservience to Parliament and especially to the king. Like most other Englishmen, the majority of bishops embraced the view that "all jurisdiction, both ecclesiastical and secular, derives from the [king] as from the one same source," and added their own to the long chorus of appeals for obedience to the king in matters indifferent that could be heard from the beginning to the end of the Henrician and Edwardine period of reform in England.[79]

Time and again, therefore, Englishmen were reminded that private innovation in the realm of adiaphora was not to be tolerated. Thomas Cromwell's 1538 Injunctions, for example, stated among other things, that

> no person shall from henceforth alter or change the order and manner of any fasting day that is commanded and indicted by the Church, nor of any prayer or divine service, otherwise than is specified in the said injunctions, until such time as the same shall be so ordered and transposed by the king's highness's authority.[80]

The Protector Somerset could later chide Stephen Gardiner for fretting so much about any and every innovation,[81] but the innovations to which Somerset referred were offically sanctioned, and the 1547 Edwardine Injunctions were in fact no less insistent than Cromwell's that no alteration in "the order and manner of any fasting-day" or in the Divine Service be made without royal sanction.[82] Similarly, a royal proclamation of February 6, 1548, criticized those who

> do rashly attempt of their own and singular wit and mind, in some parish churches and otherwise, not only to persuade the people from the old and accustomed rules and ceremonies but also themself bringeth in new and strange orders, every one in their church, according to their fantasies.[83]

In May of the same year, Somerset wrote a letter to all licensed preachers, reasserting that

> it is not a private man's duty to alter ceremonies, to innovate orders in the church; nor yet it is not a preacher's part to bring that into contempt and hatred, which the prince doth either allow, or is content to suffer.[84]

All preachers were urged to conform their teaching to the king's will, and "not to intermeddle further to the disturbance of a realm, the disquieting of the king's people, the troubling of men's consciences, and disorder of the king's subjects."[85] The Acts of Uniformity preceding publication of the 1549 and 1552 Prayer Books emphasized the same point, as did also the Ordinal and the Prayer Books themselves. The appointment of a "seemly and due order," it was said, pertains "not to private men," but only to those who "be lawfully called and authorized thereunto."[86] The thirty-third of the 1553 Forty-Two Articles added that "whosoever through his private judgment willingle, and purposelie doeth openlie breake the tradicions and ceremonies of the Churche, which bee not repugnaunte to the worde of God, and bee ordeined, and approued by common aucthoritie, ought to be rebuked openlie (that other maie feare to doe the like)."[87]

This appeal for an effective punishment of innovators was all the more intelligible if, as we have noted earlier, the specific laws touching upon adiaphoristic matters of an ecclesiastical sort were not considered binding in conscience by most English reformers. For if one can no longer encourage obedience to such laws by appealing to their obligation in conscience, it obviously becomes all the more imperative that an effective police force and penal system be developed to assure adherence to the law. Indeed, as with Marsilius of Padua, "coercion" becomes so constitutive an element of the law that law and punishment, policy and police, lawmaker and policeman, become almost identical. This need not mean that one should expect to find a Thomas Cromwell playing the role of a tyrant, which in fact he did not. But it would lead one to expect that those who, like Cromwell, shared the responsibility of executing legislation touching upon ecclesiastical adiaphora would, assuming the union of church and state, take their policing responsibilities far more seriously than they would were the laws they were asked to enforce considered binding in conscience. In brief, one would expect to find in a Cromwell as tough a policeman as indeed he was, according to G.R. Elton's latest reckoning.[88]

The suppression of private innovation, it should be noted, did not in itself require an absolute uniformity among inhabitants of England in the external exercise of their adiaphoristic liberty. It implied only that all should conform to the will of the "princely power and common counsell." And although the latter clearly had in mind as a general aim to establish a uniform order throughout the realm of England, they could conceivably, and in fact did, tolerate some diversity in adiaphoristic matters.

When the Prayer Book was published in 1549, an assertion was included to the effect that in establishing the liturgical order contained therein, English church officials meant "to condemn no other nation, nor prescribe anything, but to our own people only."[89] Thanks to the

Emperor Charles V and France's King Henry II, however, England by this time had seen a considerable influx of Protestant refugees from the Continent. Were all these foreigners to be made to conform to the established Church of England, or were they to be allowed to follow the Protestant traditions of their own countries? An argument for conformity could perhaps have been reconciled with the adiaphoristic principles which had by now become a traditional part of the English Church. Those favoring conformity might, for example, have appealed to Ambrose's advice to Augustine that "when in Rome, one should do as the Romans do." But a no less cogent argument could have been drawn from those same adiaphoristic principles for allowing the foreigners a degree of diversity in their worship. For as we have just seen, it was also said that national differences regarding adiaphora must be respected, and must not be thought to jeopardize the unity of Christ's Church. Eventually, the latter argument prevailed, but not without a struggle.

Already in 1548, thanks largely to Cranmer, some French Protestants had been allowed to form their own congregations at Lambeth and in London. And when à Lasco returned to England on May 13, 1550, the Flemish and German refugees were spurred on to seek a similar arrangement. On July 24, the latter were afforded a church building, the right to congregate under the supervision of à Lasco, and the license to use and exercise their own rites and ceremonies and their own peculiar ecclesiastical discipline, notwithstanding their disagreement with the rites and ceremonies used in England. Cranmer supported this project, but other of the bishops, and most notably Nicholas Ridley, were opposed to it. Repair of the church which had been assigned to the foreigners was deliberately delayed, and when à Lasco complained about the same to Paulet, the lord treasurer, he was asked why the foreigners chose to have ceremonies "different from the English, since the English ones are not repugnant to the word of God." After much discussion, the treasurer "concluded by stating, that foreigners must either adopt the English ceremonies or disprove them by the word of God." He also refused à Lasco's request for a key to the church, on the grounds that "the church was the king's gift, and could not therefore be given up . . . until it had been handsomely decorated." Later in the year, the foreigners succeeded in securing another church building, but it was not until the autumn of 1551 that they won the right to administer the sacraments, and still in 1552 some of them were being arrested for not attending their parish churches. On November 4, the Council ordered Ridley and à Lasco to confer for the sake of clarifying the situation, and it was finally resolved that no foreigner would be "eligible to the rights of an English citizen, without having previously made a confession of his faith to the ministers of the foreign churches." Micronius reported to Bullinger that by this point the Foreigners' Church was "in a flourishing condition."[90]

As the resolution reached by Ridley and à Lasco suggests, the Foreigners' Church was used by the English authorities as something of a check on the influx of a more radical—i.e., Anabaptist—element. But that need not mean that it was not also projected on the basis of a genuinely adiaphoristic respect for national differences.

To allow a group of foreigners the right to construct a diverse order after the fashion of their own national tastes and needs, did not, of course, imply any license for diversity among native Englishmen. And throughout the Henrician and Edwardine periods church officials clearly entertained a general policy of holding the latter to a uniform "indifferent mean." Still, in their efforts at establishing such uniformity, the emphasis was far more upon obedience than upon uniformity as such. *The Bishops' Book,* it will be recalled, had explicitly stated that for "some good and reasonable cause," individuals could "lawfully omit or do otherwise than is prescribed by the said laws and commandments of the priests and bishops," so long as such divergence was not undertaken out of "contempt," and did not cause "offense."[91] And, although the *King's Book* dropped this passage, church officials continued up to at least 1549 to overlook or connive at non-contemptuous divergence in adiaphoristic matters, such as those which occurred in 1548 during liturgical services held at the Royal Chapel, London's St. Paul's Church, and elsewhere.[92] The Uniformity Act of 1549 noted that those responsible for such diversity had not been punished because "they did it of good zeal."[93] Furthermore, although the Uniformity Acts of 1549 and 1552 were certainly intended to enforce a stricter uniformity than had theretofore obtained, some exceptions to the rule of uniformity were still allowed thereafter, and not only to foreigners.

It has been seen earlier that the English adiaphorists shared the view that in the external exercise of adiaphoristic liberty care must be taken not to offend the "erroneous" consciences of the "weak," and on that account had purposely refrained from initiating certain changes which might otherwise have been desirable. But however slow was the pace of reform, for some it would always be too fast. Furthermore, by trying to slow down the pace of reform out of consideration for the "weak," many things were retained which some Englishmen on the left felt they could not in conscience accept. Whatever "indifferent mean" was settled upon, in other words, there were always some on either the right or left who found their consciences in conflict with the law of the land.

Confronted with the dilemma created thereby, it might have been argued that the obligation of obedience overrides the dictates of conscience. But, as noted earlier, the English adiaphorists themselves were of the view that it is always sinful to go against one's conscience, even if it is in error—a view which at least implied the conclusion drawn several centuries earlier by Thomas Aquinas to the effect that so long as it "endures" an "erroneous" conscience binds more than a superior's "command."[94] If such a conclusion did not mean that superiors had to suspend all their laws touching upon adiaphora until such time as those with "erroneous" consciences could be better instructed, it did at the very least imply that the authorities would have to show some respect for such consciences. And there is considerable evidence to suggest that church officials of the Henrician and Edwardine periods did.

Among the conservatives on the right there were, to be sure, some, like Bonner and Gardiner, whose reluctance to adhere to the established ceremonial order contributed to their deprivation and imprisonment. But this was due largely to the fact that their opposition was rightly or wrongly judged to be of a "seditious" sort.[95] Furthermore, the toleration shown some conservatives was sometimes so politically motivated—as in the case of the future Queen Mary—that it has little bearing upon the question at hand. But there were cases also when the "erroneous" consciences of the "weak" were treated with genuine respect—so much so in fact that Archbishop Cranmer became notorious for the leniency he showed toward the conservatives, on the grounds that they should not be deterred by harshness from embracing the truth of the Gospel which they had not yet fully grasped.[96]

Toward those on the left Cranmer was, again by his own admission, far more severe in punishing non-conformity.[97] But both he and other church officials could also show considerable sensitivity to those on the left whose consciences balked at total conformity. In 1548, for example, Cranmer joined bishops Ridley and Henry Holbeach in consecrating Robert Ferrar bishop of St. David's, even though the latter voiced certain objections to the appointed vestments, and as a matter of fact refused to wear the episcopal cap after his consecration.[98] Two years later, in the summer of 1550, Cranmer and Ridley took it upon themselves to ordain Thomas Sampson a priest without his wearing the vestments to which he conscientiously objected.[99] And there is every reason to suppose that John Hooper could have received similar consideration had he shown a bit more diplomacy.

According to Hooper himself, the king "understood" his objections to the vestments (and the oath), and that at the May 15, 1550, Council meeting the question was settled to his "satisfaction."[100] Notwithstanding John Stumphius' dubious report on the latter meeting,[101] the Council apparently had given Hooper some indication that he could expect a personal dispensation from wearing the vestments and taking the oath.[102]

According to Micronius, Hooper was again before the king and Council on July 20, and convinced the king himself to erase the objectionable reference to the saints and evangelists from the oath prescribed in the Ordinal.[103] Three days later, on July 23, Warwick sent Cranmer a letter instructing him not to make Hooper take the oath in its objectionable form.[104] After this there seems to have been no more controversy over the oath.[105] But the vestments dispute lingered on.

On August 5, and at Hooper's urging, the king and Council sent Cranmer a second letter, this time assuring him that his supposed fears about becoming subject to *Praemunire* charges should he consecrate Hooper without adhering to the ceremonial rubrics of the Ordinal approved by Parliament, were groundless.[106] But, as Micronius later reported to Bullinger, Hooper "gained nothing by this, as he was referred from the archbishop of Canterbury to the bishop of London (Ridley) who refused to use any other form of consecration than that which had been prescribed by parliament."[107]

Shortly thereafter, Ridley was informed by the king and Council that he was free to consecrate Hooper in the manner desired by the latter. But Ridley then went to the Council in person, and so won over its members that henceforth they became reluctant even to listen to Hooper's self-defense.[108]

Apparently, Ridley succeeded in convincing the Council members that the dispensation they had granted Hooper at the May 15 meeting might well be construed to mean that official policy prohibiting private innovation in the realm of adiaphora was being reversed. Hence their prompt and unequivocal action to set the record straight. The Council allowed Hooper to present a written apology of his position, but also asked Ridley to present a rebuttal.[109] Upon reception of Hooper's *Notes*, the Earl of Warwick wrote back to the bishop-elect, saying that "the king must be obeyed in matters of indifference."[110] Hooper tried to rally support from the foreign theologians living in England, but with little success. In December of 1550 Hooper was put under house arrest and forbidden to preach or lecture. On January 13 of the following year, the Council consigned Hooper to Cranmer's custody, either to be reformed or to be further punished. Two weeks later, after

Cranmer reported him as being hopelessly adamant in his position, Hooper was sent to the Fleet, where he remained, until on February 15 he wrote Cranmer a sufficiently submissive letter, asserting that he now agreed with the opinion of Bucer and Martyr that neither the vestments, nor their use, were impious in themselves, but only their abuse, and that he was now prepared to subject himself to Cranmer's judgment. On March 8, attired in the traditional vestments, Hooper was consecrated by Cranmer and Ridley.[111]

In his analysis of this sequence of events, John Primus has tried to differentiate Hooper and Ridley respectively as the champion and foe of freedom of conscience.[112] But the facts will hardly bear such an interpretation. That Ridley, or for that matter all the Conformists, considered "freedom [of conscience] as a threat to the authority of the church" was undoubtedly true to some extent, and it is hard to see how they might have felt otherwise so long as they entertained, as they did, the notion of a "decent and orderly" organization of a community whose ecclesiastical and civil dimensions merged into one. One could, of course, question the wisdom of entertaining such a notion in the first place. But given the fact of its existence, the consideration shown Hooper seems, if anything, rather delicate, or at least more delicate than Hooper and his kind would probably have shown their opponents had they gained control of the Edwardine church. As noted, if Hooper had not given the impression that he was of a "seditious" bent, the dispensation which apparently he was initially granted would in all likelihood have stood. In any event, Ridley's and Cranmer's actions on other occasions suggest beyond a doubt that they had no insurmountable objections to the toleration as such of some diversity for the sake of respecting "erroneous" consciences. When it came to a question of sedition, however, they, like the majority of sixteenth-century Englishmen who knew anything of England's bloody past, quickly sided with Thomas Starkey's view that anyone, on either the right or left, who would "sediciously" undermine the "indifferent mean," is "not worthy to lyue in that common pollycy, nor to be a membyr thereof."[113]

NOTES

1. See, R.H. Bainton, *The Travail of Religious Liberty*, pp. 179–207.
2. *Ep.* XXXVI, 32, LIV, 1: *PL* 33, 151, 200.
3. *ST* I–II, 108, 2; *ST* I–II, 99, 2. See also: *ST* I–II, 108, 1, 2; II–II, 101, 4.
4. See *Supra*, III, ns. 48–50.

5. See Wyclif, *De Mandatis Divinis* VIII, p. 68; Hus, *De Ecclesia*, pp. 186–87; 199, 201; Gansfort, *De Dign. et Pot. Eccl., Opera*, p. 755.

6. Manschreck, *Controversy*, p. 181.

7. On Erasmus, see *Supra*, III, pp. 48 f.

8. Luther, *Von den Konz. und Kir., WA* 50, 614; Melanchthon, *Com. ad Rom., MW* V, p. 331; *Augs. Konf., BEK*, pp. 130–31; Zwingli, *Von dem touff, SW* 4, pp. 254–56; Bullinger, *Helv. Post.*, XXII, XXIV, Schaff, *op. cit.*, pp. 296–98; Bucer, *De Regno Christi, MB*, pp. 248–56; Calvin, *Institutes*, IV, X, 27; for the English reformers, see especially: *The Bishops' Book*, Lloyd, *op. cit.*, pp. 110–13; Gardiner, *A Detection*, sig. P, fol. viii–viii(v); *Manual of Prayers*, in *Three Primers*, pp. 427–28; Martyr, *Commonplaces*, II, p. 172; *Prayer Book*, in *Two Liturgies*, pp. 156–57.

9. *Institutes* IV, X, 27.

10. *Ibid*. See also: *Unterricht der Visitatoren, WA* 26, 222, 228; Melanchthon, *Apologia*, XV, 20–21: *BEK*, p. 301; Bullinger, *Helv. Post.* XXII; Schaff, *op. cit.*, p. 296; Bucer, *De Regno Christi, MB*, p. 256; *Ten Articles* and *Bishops Book*; Lloyd, *op. cit.*, pp. xvi, 110; *Three Primers*, p. 428; Burnet, *op. cit.*, I, ii, pp. 339, 490–91; Becon, *Catechism*, p. 300; J. Bale, *Yet a Course*, sig. K, fol. vi(v); Gardiner, *A Detection*, sig. P, fol. viii(v); Hooper, *Christ and His Office, Early Writings*, p. 85; *Two Liturgies*, pp. 155, 156.

11. *Three Primers*, p. 428.

12. *Contemptum Humanae Legis, Tracts*, p. 209.

13. *Historiae Ecclesiasticae* V, xxiii, 1: V, xxiv, 2–7; V, xxv; V, xxiv: *PG* 20, 489–508; 491–510; 406–508.

14. See *Epistolae* LII, LXXII, LXXV, LXXV, in *Collectio Selecta SS. Ecclesiae Patrum XIV, S. Cyprianus*, ed. D.A.B. Caillou (Paris, 1829), pp. 148, 259, 301, 289.

15. See for example, *I Clement* 61, 1: C. Kirch, *Enchiridion Fontium Historiae Ecclesiasticae Antiquae* (Friburgi Brisgoviae, 1923), p. 15.

16. See: Origen, *Contra Celsum* V, 37: *PG* 11, 1238; Bardaison of Edessa, *The Book of the Laws of Countries*, trans. J.J.W. Drijvers (Assen, 1964), p. 61.

17. J. Pelikan, *The Emergence of the Catholic Tradition (100-600)* (Chicago and London, 1971), p. 28.

18. *Contra Celsum* V, 34 and 36: *PG* 11, 1231, 1235.

19. *Ep. ad Diognetum* 5: Kirch, *op. cit.*, p. 89.

20. Augustine, *Ep.* LIV, 2: *PL* 33, 200; Socrates, *HE* V, xxii, *PG* 67, 627–46; Sozomen, *HE* VII, XIX, *PG* 67, 1473–80.

21. *Ep.* XXXVI, 32: *PL* 33, 151; *Ep.* LIV, 3: *PL* 33, 200–201.

22. *Ep.* LIV, 3: *PL* 33, 201.

23. *Ep.* XXXVI, 2: *PL* 33, 136–37.

24. *HE* VII, XIX: *PG* 67, 1475.

25. Bede *EH*, pp. 80–82; 108.

26. As quoted in Jungmann, *op. cit.*, p. 74.

27. See *Supra*, I, pp. 7–8; and W.H. Hunt, *The English Church from its Foundation to the Norman Conquest (597–1066)* (London, 1907), p. 28. The missionary Ceolfrith did admit, it may be noted, that "a difference in tonsure is not hurtful to those whose faith in God is untainted and their love for their neighbor sincere" (Bede, *EH*, p. 547).

28. See Jungmann, *op. cit.*, pp. 33–37.

29. *PG* 143, 764.

30. See Anselm, *De Azymo et Fermentato: PL* 158, 541; Theophylact, *De Iis Quorum Latini Incusantur, PG* 126, 246.

31. See D'Achery, *op. cit.*, especially pp. 164–66, 170.

32. *Sermo coram Rege, Opera* II, 148.

33. See: E.C. Tatnall, "John Wyclif and *Ecclesia Anglicana,*" *JEH* 20(1969), pp. 19–43; Denys Hays, "The Church of England in the late Middle Ages," *History* 53(1968), pp. 35–50; M. Spinka, *Hus' Concept of the Church,* p. 240; Y. Congar, "Ecclesiological Awareness in the East and in the West from the Sixth to the Eleventh Century," *The Unity of the Churches of God,* trans. Polycarp Sherwood (Baltimore, 1963), pp. 127, 138–40.

34. See E. Cassirer, *The Individual and the Cosmos in Renaissance Philosophy,* trans. M. Domandi (New York, 1963), pp. 28, 17, 18, 20.

35. *De Pace Fidei, Opera Omnia,* pp. 51–52; 61, 62.

36. As cited in J. Lecler, *op. cit.,* I, p. 11.

37. *De Amabili Ecclesiae Concordia, EO* V, 475; *Inquisitio de Fide, EO* I, 732.

38. *Conf. Pont.,* Reu, *op. cit.,* p. 376.

39. *Ibid.,* pp. 353–54, 357, 376–77.

40. See Augustine, *Ep.* LIV, 1: *PL* 33, 200.

41. *Augs. Konf.,* VII, 3: *BEK,* p. 61; Torgau Arts., Reu, *op. cit.,* p. 81; *Variata,* Reu, *op. cit.,* pp. 404–6; Bullinger, *Helv. Post.,* XXVII, Schaff, *op. cit.,* p. 302; Bucer, *De Regno Christi, MB,* p. 256; Calvin, *Institutes* IV, X, 32.

42. As cited in Trinterud, *op. cit.,* p. 90.

43. See Bucer, *De Regno Christi, MB* pp. 255–56; and Muller, *op. cit.,* p. 159.

44. As cited in Rupp, *Patterns,* p. 319.

45. *Augs. Konf.* XXVI, 42–45; *BEK,* pp. 106–7; Torgau Arts., Reu, *op. cit.,* p. 81; Bullinger, *Helv. Post.* XXIII; Schaff, *op. cit.,* p. 297; XXVII, pp. 302–3; Calvin, *Institutes,* IV, XII, 20.

46. See Starkey, *Exhortation,* sig. R, fol. iv(v); S, iv; Herrtage, *Starkey's Life and Letters,* p. xx.

47. Lloyd, *op. cit.,* pp. 56, 247.

48. *Ibid.,* pp. 56, 246. For almost identical assertions see the Wittenberg and Thirteen Articles (Tjernagel, *op. cit.,* pp. 273, 290–91, 300–301).

49. Lloyd, *op. cit.,* pp. 56, 247.

50. Cranmer, *Writings and Letters,* p. 77; *Writings of Bradford,* p. 389.

51. Cranmer, *Writings and Letters,* p. 516. See also: *Prayer Book, Two Liturgies,* p. 157; and Somerset's letter of June 4, 1549, to Reginald Pole (*Troubles Connected with the Prayer Book of 1549,* ed. N. Pocock [Westminster, 1884], p. xiii).

52. Gee and Hardy, *op. cit.,* pp. 210, 225.

53. In an August 26, 1536, letter to the king, Cranmer, for example, noted that he himself was preaching that some of the papal laws were "good and laudable," and that while these have no power to remit sin, still, since they have been "received as laws" of your realm," they are not to be "condemned or despised," but observed "until such time as others should be made" (*Writings and Letters,* p. 326).

54. See, for example, *A Glasse of the Truthe* (N. Pocock, *Records of the Reformation* [Oxford, 1870], II, p. 407); the *Articles devised by the Holle consent of the King's Council* (Pocock, *op. cit.,* p. 527); *A Litel Treatise against the mutterynge of some papists in corners* (Pocock, *op. cit.,* p. 546). See also: Scarisbrick, *op. cit.,* pp. 391, 397–98; Baumer, *op. cit.,* pp. 51 ff.

55. *Exhortation,* sig. T, fol. ii–ii(v); Sig. C, fol. i; sig. U, fol. ii; sig. C, fol. i(v)–ii.

56. Cranmer, *Writings and Letters,* p. 77.

57. *Ibid.,* pp. 77, 463–64; Baumer, *op. cit.,* pp. 54–55.

58. See Scarisbrick, *op. cit.,* p. 391.

59. *Ibid.*

60. *Strype, EM,* I, ii, pp. 234, 235.

61. G. Burnet, *op. cit.*, III, ii, pp. 145–46. See also S. Gardiner's similar remark in Muller, *Gardiner's Letters*, p. 72.

62. See W. Ullmann, *op. cit.*, p. 42.

63. See *Def. Pacis*, II, ix, 3.

64. See R. Walton, *Zwingli's Theocracy* (Toronto, 1967), pp. 21–29; 3–16; 5; 225–26; 221, 225; 159–75, 221, 225; also: Lecler, *op. cit.*, I, p. 316. Bullinger, it may be noted, offered no major alteration in this fundamental Zwinglian position (See *Decades*, II, vii, pp. 323 ff.), and no doubt was largely responsible for its embrace by his one-time pupil Thomas Luber (Erastus) (O. Chadwick, *The Reformation*, p. 150).

65. See W. Pauck, *The Heritage of the Reformation* (New York, 1966), pp. 78–79.

66. *Ibid.*, p. 72; R. Bainton, *Here I Stand*, pp. 244–46; G. Rupp, *The Righteousness of God* (London, 1963), pp. 289 ff.; *Unterr. der Vis.*, WA 26, 223; Rupp, *Righteousness*, p. 287.

67. Manschreck, *Controversy*, p. 181 n.

68. Manschreck, *Melanchthon*, p. 251.

69. See McNeill, *Calvinism*, pp. 163 ff., 143; O. Chadwick, *The Reformation*, pp. 83 ff.; Williston Walker, *John Calvin* (London and New York, 1906), pp. 208–15.

70. Dickens, *English Reformation*, p. 85.

71. *Three Primers*, p. 72.

72. See Elton, *Policy and Police*, p. 186, n. 2; Elton, *Reform and Renewal* (Cambridge, 1973), pp. 26, 62; McConica, *op cit.*, p. 136; Dickens, *English Reformation*, pp. 110, 170; Dickens, *Cromwell*, p. 83.

73. *Exhortation*, sig. N, fol. iii(v).

74. Herrtage, *Starkey's Life and Letters*, pp. xxiv–xxv. See also: Zeeveld, *op. cit.*, pp. 133–35; F. le von Baumer, "Thomas Starkey and Marsilius of Padua," *Politica* II (1936–37), pp. 188–205; Harry S. Stout, "Marsilius of Padua and the Henrician Reformation," *Church History* (September, 1974), pp. 308–18.

75. "Thinges indifferent, I calle all suche thinges, which by goddis worde are nether prohibyted nor commanded, but lefte to worldly polycie, whereof they take their ful authority" (*Exhortation*, sig. B, fol. ii[v]; see also: Sig. T, fol. i[v]; sig. C, fol. i[v]).

76. See Scarisbrick, *op. cit.*, p. 246, 274, 275–78; Dickens, *English Reformation*, p. 103, 115; C.W. Ferguson, *Naked to Mine Enemies* (New York, 1965), II, pp. 223–43; Gee and Hardy, *op. cit.*, pp. 146, 150, 151–52, 154–78, 195–200; J.R. Muller, *Stephen Gardiner and the Tudor Reaction* (New York, 1926), pp. 46–48.

77. Lloyd, *op. cit.*, pp. 110, 114.

78. *Ibid.*, pp. 277–89.

79. *Reformatio Legum Ecclesiasticarum*, in *The Reformation of the Ecclesiastical Laws*, p. 200; See, for other examples: Barnes, *Supplication* (1534), sig. B, fol. ii ff.; *Marshall's Primer, Three Primers*, p. 72; Starkey, *Exhortation*, sig. B, fol. iv(v); sig. T, fol. ii; *Bishops'* and *King's Book*, Lloyd, *op. cit.*, pp. 121, 287; Thirteen Articles, Tjernagel, *op. cit.*, pp. 291–92; *Manual of Prayers, Three Primers*, pp. 430, 432–33; Hughes and Larkin, *op. cit.*, I, pp. 273–75; Gardiner, *Contemptum, Tracts*, pp. 175–81, 187–89, 207–9; Foxe, *Acts and Monuments* V, Appendix, n. XVI; V, 734, 745–46; VI, p. 67; *Rationale of Ceremonial*, pp. 3–4, 43; Hooper, *Christ and His Office, Early Writing*, p. 85; *A Short Instruction*, p. 40; Martyr, *Commonplaces*, II, pp. 167, 172; *Two Liturgies*, p. 155; Cranmer, *Writings and Letters*, pp. 164–67, 186, 188–202; *Prayer Book Troubles*, pp. 144–48, 178–79, 191–93; Micronius to Bullinger, October 13, 1550, *OL* p. 571; Forty-Two Articles, Hardwick, *op. cit.*, p. 294.

80. Gee and Hardy, *op. cit.*, p. 280.

81. Foxe, *Acts and Monuments*, VI, pp. 28–30.

82. *Articles and Injunctions*, p. 122.

83. Hughes and Larkin, *op. cit.*, I, p. 416.

84. Cranmer, *Writings and Letters*, p. 512.

85. *Ibid.*, p. 516.

86. Gee and Hardy, *op. cit.*, pp. 358 ff., 372; *Two Liturgies*, pp. 1-2, 4; 155, 156-57, 197-99.

87. Hardwick, *op. cit.*, p. 294.

88. In addition to Elton's recent work *Policy and Police*, see also: Elton, "The Rule of Law in 16th c. England," in A.J. Slavin, *Tudor Men and Institutions* (Baton Rouge, 1972), pp. 267-94.

89. *Two Liturgies*, p. 157.

90. See Strype, *Memorials of Cranmer*, pp. 1034-35; F. de Schickler, *Les Eglises du refuge en Angleterre* (Paris, 1892), I, pp. 25-26, 30, 33, 35-36; Micronius to Bullinger, May 20, 1550, *OL*, p. 560; Burnet, *op. cit.*, II, ii, pp. 291, 288-92; Micronius to Bullinger, August 28, 1550, *OL*, pp. 567-68; 568, 569, 570; Utenhovius to Bullinger, April 9, 1551, *OL*, pp. 586-87; Micronius to Bullinger, August 14, 1551, *Ibid.*, p. 575; Micronius to Bullinger, February 18, 1553, *OL*, p. 581. For a description of the actual organization and form of worship and discipline adopted by à Lasco's congregation, see de Schickler, *op. cit.*, I, pp. 36-55; Knappen, *Tudor Puritanism*, pp. 92-95; Dugmore, *op. cit.*, pp. 164-68; Procter and Frere, *op. cit.*, pp. 89-90. It should be noted that in 1551 a similar "foreigners'" church was established at Glastonbury for some French and Dutch immigrants, under the supervision of Valerian Poullain (See Dixon, *op. cit.*, III, pp. 326-27; de Schickler, *op. cit.*, I, pp. 59-67; Dugmore, *The Mass and The English Reformers*, pp. 168-70; Procter and Frere, *op. cit.*, pp. 86-89.

91. Lloyd, *op. cit.*, p. 115.

92. See C. Wriothesley, *Chronicle* II, p. 2; Knappen, *Tudor Puritanism*, p. 86; Foxe, *Acts and Monuments*, V, p. 720.

93. Gee and Hardy, *op. cit.*, p. 359.

94. See *De Veritate*, q. XVII, a. 5.

95. See Muller, *Gardiner*, pp. 181 ff.; and Ridley, *Cranmer*, pp. 297 ff., 315 f.

96. See, for example, the "Autobiography of Edward Underhill, *Narratives of the Reformation*," p. 157; "Morice's Anecdotes of Archbishop Cranmer," *Ibid.*, pp. 246-47.

97. See *Ibid.*, p. 247.

98. Knappen, *Tudor Puritanism*, p. 86.

99. See Strype, *Mem. of Cranmer*, p. 273; Ridley, *Cranmer*, p. 310; Knappen, *Tudor Puritanism*, p. 86.

100. "Hooper to Bullinger, June 29, 1550," *OL*, p. 87. Apparently, Somerset, who by now was back on the Council, had stood up for Hooper's cause (See "Ab Ulmis to Bullinger, May 28, 1550," *OL* p. 410).

101. To hear Stumphius tell it, it was Hooper who at last brought the bishops "to confess that these things (the vestments) were merely matters of indifference" (Stumphius to Bullinger, June 1, 1550, *OL*, pp. 466-67). Primus seems to accept Stumphius' report without question (*op. cit.*, pp. 10-11).

102. See Micronius to Bullinger, August 28, 1550, and Ab Ulmis to Bullinger, August 22, 1550, *OL*, pp. 566-67, 415-16.

103. See Micronius to Bullinger, August 28, 1550, and Ab Ulmis to Bullinger, August 22, 1550, *OL*, pp. 566-67, 415-16.

104. Foxe, *Acts and Monuments*, VI, p. 641.

105. The 1552 Prayer Book eliminated the reference in the oath to the saints and evangelists (See *Two Liturgies*, p. 349).

106. Foxe, *Acts and Monuments*, VI, p. 640.

107. Micronius to Bullinger, August 28, 1550, *OL*, p. 567.

108. *Ibid.*

109. *Ibid; APC*, October, 1550; for Ridley's *Reply* see *Writings of Bradford*, pp. 375–95.

110. Micronius to Bullinger, October 13, 1550, *OL*, p. 571.

111. See Hooper, *Later Writings*, p. xv; xv–xvi; *APC*, January 13, 1551; January 27, 1551; *Writings of Bradford*, p. 374; Ridley, *Cranmer*, p. 314. Shortly thereafter, Hooper preached before the king, and according to Foxe, was attired in "a long scarlet chimere . . . a white linen rochet . . . (and) upon his head he had a geometrical, that is, a four-squared cap, albeit that his head was round" (*Acts and Monuments* VI, p. 641).

112. Whereas Hooper "showed considerable regard for the conscience of the individual," his chief opponent in the Vestment controversy, Nicholas Ridley, Primus claimed, "saw such freedom as a threat to the authority of the church" (Primus, *op. cit.*, p. 24). "In permitting the Church to retain the role of making judgments for the individual conscience," Ridley, Primus adds, "was conservatively clinging to a medievalism which Hooper, better versed in Reformation theory as well as practice, could not accept." (*Ibid.*).

113. Herrtage, *Starkey's Life and Letters*, p. lxxii.

CHAPTER 8

CONCLUSION:
THE INDIFFERENT MEAN

THE ADIAPHORISTIC SETTLEMENT reached during the Henrician and Edwardine stages of the English Reformation was conceived by those who fashioned it as a movement along the lines of a middle way. In the words of Thomas Starkey, it was meant to be an "indifferent mean."[1]

Some who had read an early draft of Starkey's *Exhortation* had criticized it precisely on the grounds that it inclined neither to the one side, nor to the other.[2] To Thomas Cromwell's view, however, the median position of Starkey's draft should have received more, not less, emphasis.[3] Starkey himself was naturally inclined to agree with Cromwell. What others had "notyed for a grete faute" was in his own opinion, he later wrote to Cromwell, the book's "chefe vertue."[4] In the final version of his *Exhortation,* therefore, Starkey tried to follow Cromwell's advice and bring into still clearer focus the medial implications of his adiaphoristic position.

Starkey admitted that "to stryke upon and wysely to touch" such an "indifferent mean" was no easy task.[5] But "I will not cesse to pray," he wrote to Cromwell, that the same God who had inspired Henry VIII to alter policy in the first place would also grace him with the wisdom to "fynd out the most convenyent mean [and] to set hyt forward wyth a common quyetness."[6] Apparently, Starkey thought his prayers answered, for, like Cromwell,[7] he frequently praised the king for having "set forth the indyfferent mean."[8] And, as was best exemplified in his last speech before Parliament late in 1545, Henry VIII himself was convinced that his reform program amounted to a *via media.*[9] After Henry's death, the Protector Somerset gave expression to much the same conclusion,[10] and it was his views, not Northumberland's, which were shared by the majority of those Englishmen who, like the Archbishop Thomas Cranmer, were most responsible during the Edwardine period for plotting the future course of the English Church.

157

As viewed by Starkey, this "indifferent mean" was a course that ran between the extremes of "blind superstition" and "arrogant blindness."[11] Cromwell located it between the "inveterate superstition and stiffness" of those on the right, and the "rashness and licentiousness" of those on the left.[12] These lines of demarcation roughly paralleled those drawn by Luther when he described his own adiaphoristic *via media* as a path running between those who clung to the ceremonies as if their salvation depended on them and those who thought they could prove themselves Christian and free simply by neglecting and despising the traditional ceremonies.[13] In a more general way, Henry VIII referred to the "indifferent mean" as a path between those who "be too stiff in their *mumpsimus*," and those who "be too busy and curious in their new *sumpsimus*."[14] Somerset spoke merely of a mean between those who wanted no reform at all and those who wanted to overthrow everything.[15]

As far as they went, such descriptions were not inaccurate. But they were also either too narrow or too broad to convey adequately all the many intricate and complex moves which the English adiaphorists have been seen in previous chapters to have made in the pursuit of their "indifferent mean." To avoid a final over-simplification of the latter, therefore, it will be well, by way of a summary, to recall in the remaining few pages some of the more salient points at which the moderate adiaphorists have been seen to have parted ways from those on their right and left.

The point of departure, it will be recalled, was the reiteration of that age-old complaint against the intolerable burden of ceremonies and like matters which was supposedly oppressing the Christian community. Like their colleagues across the Channel, the English adiaphorists repeatedly bewailed the confusion of values resulting therefrom. Given the almost endless proliferation of ceremonies, their "meaning," it was said, had frequently been lost, and with the spread of this ignorance or "blindness," the craving for more and more ceremonies had simply doubled—hence that vicious circle of superstition which, according to some of the English adiaphorists, had been exploited or even set up by officials of the Roman Church to satisfy their lust for power. While God's own law and other essentials of Christian life were neglected or even scorned, ceremonial matters were elevated to the first rank, with the result that many Christians found themselves trapped in a dismal morass of scrupulosity, or a condition of spiritual slavery worse than that of the ancient Jews from which the "light yoke" and "easy burden" of Christ was supposed to have been a relief.

To escape this situation, the adiaphorists might have placed priority upon a quantitative reduction of the ceremonies, in the hope that just as the proliferation of the latter had helped to spawn their excessive evaluation, so their reduction in number might bring their relative insignificance back into focus. But so long as the ceremonies were as highly valued as they were, any chance of reducing their number would have been rather slim. Not surprisingly, therefore, the adiaphorists proceeded contrarywise. Their first emphasis was upon a qualitative reduction of the ceremonies.

This project was undertaken within the context of a renewed emphasis during the late middle ages and the early sixteenth century upon faith, interiority, Scripture, and antiquity by advocates of the *devotio moderna,* humanism, and the doctrines of solafideism and *sola Scriptura.* And for not a few sixteenth-century reform-minded Christians the only escape from the supposed superstition of the Roman Church seemed to lie in either a full retreat to a "pure" Church of primitive, New Testament times, or in a total withdrawal by one or another route into the realm of pure "spirituality." For most of these individuals, therefore, the concern for reducing qualitatively the traditional ceremonies eventually developed into a blatant reductionism of either a biblical or spiritualistic sort. While such reductionism amounted for all practical purposes to an attempt simply to strip the Church of all the traditional ceremonies, its underlying rationale was the conviction that for one or another reason all such matters must be considered evil and forbidden. While emphasizing, therefore, that the traditional ceremonies were not so commendable as the Roman Church, with its history of monastic idealism, its sacral and semi-Pelagian proclivities, and above all its passion for uniformity, had made them out to be, the adiaphorists also had to insist that ceremonial matters and the like were not so detestable as some of the radicals on the left were wont to suppose.

Expressed in the philosophically adiaphoristic terms of the Erasmian appraisal of the ceremonies, this conclusion translated into the assertion that the latter in themselves were neither good, nor evil, but indifferent. The ancient Cynic philosophers, it will be recalled, had drawn a similar conclusion about the conventions of Greek society within the context of their more general conviction that outside the human intention, or the interior disposition of "wisdom," all things and actions are in themselves equally indifferent or neutral. By designating the Greek conventions indifferent, therefore, the Cynics had had in mind to suggest that such matters were by nature absolutely lacking in value or disvalue. The Stoics modified this radical Cynic view by suggesting that not all externals are equally indifferent. Some, they said, are absolutely indifferent, in that in themselves they incline neither toward nor against a life in accordance with nature. But others do so incline and on that account should be classified as either "preferred" or "rejected" adiaphora. Notwithstanding these distinctions, however, the Stoics still considered the interior disposition to be in the final analysis the sole criterion of the good or evil, right or wrong, of exterior things and actions.

A few Christian thinkers, like Abelard, were inclined to embrace this Stoic version of adiaphorism without qualification, arguing that outside the human intention, all external actions are in themselves, and notwithstanding the intrinsic inclination of one or another such action toward good or evil, indifferent. But most Christian theologians concluded otherwise. Not a few of those things or actions which the Stoics had classified as "preferred" or "rejected" adiaphora were said by the majority of Christian adiaphorists of the early and medieval Church to be of such goodness or evil in themselves as to be altogether essential to, or incompatible with, a life of Christian virtue. Within the limits of such a qualification, however, Stoic adiaphorism had, from at least the third century on, received a warm welcome in even the most orthodox circles of Christian thought. Consequently, there evolved a Christian tradition of philosophical adiaphorism which, if not as expansive as the Stoic version, was nonetheless closely akin to it in its definition and understanding of the term adiaphoron. Certain things or actions were said to be indifferent in themselves, in the sense that by definition their value or disvalue was not of such degree as to be decisive factors in the determination of their moral quality, so that whether they were ultimately to be deemed good or evil in the concrete would depend upon the direction they were given by the human intention. It was primarily in such a moderate philosophical sense that the term adiaphoron was appropriated by Erasmus and his sixteenth-century Continental and English followers, and put to work in their critique of the traditional ceremonies of the Roman Church.

Consistent with his humanist and mystic tendencies, Erasmus insisted time and again that the height of Christian perfection lies within, in the heart, in the interior disposition of love—not in the performance of some one or another external ceremony. Certain external actions, he admitted, are by nature of such decisive moral value or disvalue that whatever the human intention in their regard they remain good or evil. But most of the traditional ceremonies, he noted. do not fall into that category. They cannot in any ultimate sense be said to be good or evil in themselves. Whatever ultimate value or disvalue they come to enjoy can only be derived from their reference beyond themselves to some higher or lower goal by the interior disposition of love or hatred. While, therefore, the Roman party is wrong in treating its traditional ceremonies as ends in themselves, those radicals also are in the wrong, it was said, who do not recognize that all such matters could, notwithstanding their material nature or previous abuse, still be treated as the "goods," the "stuff," the "intermediate goals," or the "means" by which either charitable or uncharitable intentions can be expedited in the concrete.

Drawn along theologically adiaphoristic lines, the conclusion that the traditional ceremonies were neither so commendable, nor so detestable as certain parties on the right and left claimed, found expression in the assertion that such matters are in themselves neither commanded, nor forbidden, but permitted. For most of the mainline Continental reformers and their English sympathizers, like Tyndale, Frith, Barnes, Latimer, and Cranmer, this theological conclusion was closely linked, as it had been in the thinking of earlier adiaphorists like Pupper, Ruckrat, and Gansfort, with the doctrine of solafideism. It presupposed, in other words, that those matters designated things permitted were not to be considered sources of justification. Contrary to the suspicions of John Eck, the Tridentine Fathers, and some modern scholars, however, neither the Continental nor the English reformers who subscribed to the doctrine of solafideism conceived of the latter as the constitutive element in their definition of things permitted. To be sure, some early Christians who were mostly of a Gnostic bent, had interpreted the Pauline doctrine of solafideism to mean that outside faith, everything is indifferent or permitted. And perhaps, As C.C.E. Schmid long ago suggested,[16] there may have been some "careless followers" of the mainline reformers who embraced such a radical view. But the latter had been rejected already by most early and medieval Christian theologians on the grounds that the Christian remains bound to the external moral commands and prohibitions of the divine positive law revealed in Scripture. Luther and other Continental and English solafideists objected to the legalism that had sometimes been implicit to this earlier position of Christian theologians toward the biblical moral commands and prohibitions. But for all their insistence upon the Christian's radical emancipation from the "curse" of the written law, they could and did argue that a genuinely Christian interior disposition of faith and love will "necessarily" coincide concretely with the biblical commands and prohibitions. That the latter were not to be considered sources of justification did not mean, therefore, that they were also to be treated as things indifferent or permitted. And in fact, like those many English reformers who did not subscribe to the doctrine of solafideism, most advocates of the latter limited their application of the term adiaphoron to only such matters as had been neither commanded nor forbidden in Scripture, and understood the term in accordance with these limitations. By failing to recognize this point, or by choosing to ignore it, the Tridentine Fathers and others in the Roman party distorted the reformers' position and thereby reduced still further any chance of reconciliation.

The key issue underlying the rise and development of the English reformers' theological adiaphorism was not, therefore, so much the question of "justification" as it was a question about the relation of Scripture and Tradition. On the eve of her reformation, the English Church could claim some of the most conservative thinkers on this issue in the persons of Thomas More, John Fisher, and Henry VIII, according to whom Tradition, with its backbone of the ecclesiastical Magisterium, was thought to enjoy an authority equal to Scripture's. Henry, of course, came to reverse his opinion in this regard, and saw to it that More and Fisher were no longer around. But there would remain many others, like Reginald Pole, John Stokesley, Richard Smith, and to some extent Stephen Gardiner, who readily picked up where the "defenders of the faith" had left off and continued to champion the necessity to salvation and obligation in conscience of the "unwritten traditions" and many other matters which over the centuries had won the sanction of canon law or universal custom.

Against such Roman claims, the English adiaphorists appealed to the sufficiency of Scripture for the ultimate determination of all that is essential to the final goal of Christian life. What Scripture has commanded, the Christian must do; what Scripture has forbidden, the Christian must omit. But what Scripture has neither commanded, nor forbidden, must be considered indifferent, permitted, free, voluntary—in the sense that so far as man's relation to God is concerned, all such matters make no difference in themselves. Lacking any essential connection with the Spirit's work of love in the man of faith, they cannot be considered necessary to salvation, or binding in conscience. For Christians to think otherwise is the epitome of superstition, and for Church officials to have cultivated such thought was the height of tyranny.

Many of those on the left would readily have concurred in these conclusions so far as they pertained to matters of a genuinely adiaphoristic sort. But they seriously questioned whether many of the ceremonies designated adiaphora by the mainline reformers could in fact so qualify. Their misgivings in this regard are far more significant to an understanding of their respective positions than historians have heretofore recognized. This is especially true of the Puritans and main-line reformers in England. Subscription or non-subscription to an adiaphoristic appraisal of one or another ceremony was a major factor in their conflict, and it is only when the same is taken into adequate account that the differentiation of their respective positions can be properly appreciated.

In attempting to demonstrate that many of the traditional cere-monies could not properly be designated adiaphora, those on the left frequently pointed to the superstitious abuse or the tyrannical imposi-tion suffered by such matters in previous ages, or to their supposedly inextricable ties with Judaism and "popery."

Underlying such arguments by some of those on the left, like Sebas-tian Franck, was a spiritualistic dualism of a sort that inclined them to conceive of all externals as the "dregs of Satan." Most, however, based their arguments upon a peculiar attitude toward the doctrine of *sola Scriptura*. Not a few of the Anabaptists, Lollards, and other radicals were biblical reductionists in the strict sense of believing that only those matters could qualify as adiaphora which were explicitly "per-mitted" in the Scriptural text. Whatever Scripture has not clearly per-mitted, they said, must be considered "forbidden." The early, pre-Elizabethan Puritans, did not go that far. They were not, strictly speak-ing, biblical reductionists. But neither were they willing to accept the Conformists' position that for one or another matter to qualify as an adiaphoron it is sufficient that it be "not repugnant" to Scripture. To their view, things can qualify as genuine adiaphora only to the extent that they are in "positive accord" with Scripture. Thus, positive Scrip-tural principles, like the rule of edification, which the Conformists were inclined to apply to external matters only after the latter had already been designated adiaphora, or, in other words, to their concrete use, the Puritans looked upon as criteria for the qualification of one or another matter as an adiaphoron. In the final analysis, therefore, the Puritans actually recognized no wider a realm of adiaphora than did the strict biblical reductionists, and like the latter were inclined to consider evil and forbidden many of the traditional ceremonies which had been designated indifferent and permitted by the Conformists.

In the first place, therefore, the adiaphoristic course pursued by the English reformers may be viewed as a middle way between the posi-tion of those on the right who, because of their excessive estimation of the ceremonies, were "inveterately stiff" in their adherence to such matters, and the position of those on the left who, because they deemed the traditional ceremonies for one or another reason to be evil and forbidden, thought their rejection absolutely essential to the purification of the Church. Against both these extremes, the adiaphorists insisted that the ceremonies and like matters were things which in themselves are neither good nor evil, neither commanded nor forbidden, but indifferent and permitted, and which as such should be neither clung to nor despised in such wise as would suggest that either their retention or their abolition had in itself any essential bearing upon the Spirit's work of love in the Christian community.

But England's "indifferent mean" cannot be demarcated solely along such lines. For in the position on the left of the mainline reformers were also many individuals who did not conceive of the traditional ceremonies, or at least not all of them, as being evil and forbidden, and who, as a matter of fact, were inclined to concur in the adiaphoristic appraisal of the same. Their opposition to the mean position, therefore, must be sought along other lines. It is to be found in a conception of adiaphoristic liberty which advocates of the mean position found unacceptable.

In the first place, there were some on the left who were inclined to think that because certain traditional ceremonies were indifferent and permitted the Christian was left with no choice but to reject them so as to demonstrate his liberty in their regard. Karlstadt was apparently of such a view, as were also some of the Puritans in regard to those few matters which they actually deemed adiaphoristic. On occasion, and much to the confusion of everyone involved, it was even used to prove that one or another ceremony could not be considered a genuine adiaphoron. Also on the left were some who, upon hearing that the traditional ceremonies and like matters were indifferent and permitted, immediately saw therein an excuse for licentiousness or "carnal" liberty.

It was these individuals who misconstrued the notion of adiaphoristic liberty that the mainline Continental and English reformers most immediately had in mind when they themselves sought to describe the position of those on their left. Theirs was the position to which Starkey and Cromwell were principally referring when they spoke of the "arrogant blindness" or the "rashness and licentiousness" of the radicals.

In reviewing their response to this "arrogant blindness," it should first of all be recalled that the advocates of the mean position were not of the opinion that the truth of adiaphoristic liberty should be "hid under a bushel." Although they did extend the theory of adiaphorism to include the designation of certain doctrinal matters as adiaphora also, they apparently did not conceive of the truth of adiaphoristic liberty itself as being of such sort. Thus, and notwithstanding the misgivings of some Englishmen like Stephen Gardiner, they deemed it imperative that their fellow Christians, and especially those who were "weak" in their faith, be instructed in the truth of adiaphoristic liberty. Those "stubborn" or "hypocritical" individuals who, for fear of losing their "tyrannical" grip on Christian consciences, refused to accept the truth could simply be "let go"—at least so far as they themselves were concerned. But to the extent that their tyrannical views threatened to ensnare others they were to be boldly confronted and stood up to. On occasion, this need to instruct the "weak" or to stand up to the "tyrants" could, the mainline adiaphorists admitted, make it important for the Christian to openly declare his freedom before men, even to the point of defiantly doing the exact opposite of what the "tyrants" were demanding. Unlike Karlstadt, Flacius Illyricus, and others, however, the mainline adiaphorists refused to admit that this was the only way by which a genuine witness to the truth of adiaphoristic liberty could be given. In other words, they refused to tie such a witness down, even during times of "tyranny," to any one or another particular mode of external conduct in the realm of adiaphora. A Christian, they said, could, for example, continue to observe the traditional ceremony of abstaining from meat on every Friday throughout his life and still be true to his adiaphoristic freedom in the choice of foods.

Underlying this position of the mainline adiaphorists was their conception of adiaphoristic liberty as something altogether "spiritual," whose whole force lies in calming men's consciences before God about the use or non-use of things indifferent. To their view, therefore, adiaphoristic liberty was first and last an affair between man and God, consisting above all in the "knowledge" that in themselves matters of an indifferent sort make no difference to God. Those who share in this "knowledge" are, it was said, by that very fact adiaphoristically free, whether others witness it in an external form or not. This explains why the mainline English adiaphorists considered "instruction" about the adiaphoristic nature of the traditional ceremonies far more important than any quantitative reduction of the latter.

It was also fundamental to their rejection of any "carnal" interpretation of adiaphoristic liberty. Because the latter is first and last an affair between man and God, it adds nothing, they said, in men's sight. Thus, just as the adiaphoristic appraisal of ceremonial and like matters does not in itself require of the Christian subscription to any one or another particular mode of external conduct, so neither, it was said, does it afford the Christian any license to deal with such matters in any or every manner whatever that might please his private selfish interests. To be genuine, adiaphoristic liberty must rather be informed by a spirit of charity.

This meant in the first place that the "knowledge" of one's liberty before God in the realm of adiaphora should not become "puffed up," and that Christians should refrain, therefore, from "judging" or condemning one another over such matters. So far as the actual choice and use of adiaphora was concerned, it was simply another way of saying that such matters lose their indifference in the concrete and become either good or evil—charitable or uncharitable. In the actual "election" or "doing" of adiaphora, Christians (including those church officials responsible for the concrete arrangement of adiaphoristic matters,) must first of all, therefore, show consideration for their "weaker" brethren. Care must be taken not to "offend" them. While, therefore, it may be proper to stand up to the "tyrants" by doing the very opposite of what they demand, irrespective of any "offense" they might "take" thereat, it would be wrong, if in the process, the "weak" were "given" offense. If the "weak" sin in acting contrary to their "erroneous consciences," so too do they who by their inconsiderate exercise of adiaphoristic liberty encourage the "weak" to do what their consciences "erroneously" forbid them to do. To avoid incurring the guilt of sin upon themselves, therefore, those who are mature in the knowledge of their adiaphoristic liberty may, on occasion, have to exercise their "election" or "doing" of adiaphora "in secret," or even by submitting to the external bondage of certain "tyrannical" laws. Furthermore, even after the "weak" have outgrown the vulnerability to "offense," their non-scrupulous dependence upon external ceremonies for the maintenance and development of their faith would also have to be taken into charitable account by those who, because of their maturity, can do without such pedagogical means. The mature must not look only to their own strength, but to that of their brothers also and allow the latter to be "suckled" just as they themselves had earlier been suckled.

Much to the chagrin of some of the radicals on the left, therefore, the mainline English adiaphorists retained many of the traditional ceremonies not only for the sake of avoiding "offense" to the "weak," but also to afford the latter some means of instruction and growth in their faith. In this regard, however, the mainline adiaphorists were also concerned lest the "weak" always be kept on a diet of "milk," or that the milk given them would be less than "pure," and on that account proceeded to remove those ceremonies which they considered to be, not indifferent, but "blatantly impious," or even, as during especially the Edwardine period, some ceremonies which were genuinely indifferent, on the assumption that having been given special consideration over so long a time, the "weak" could be expected to have come a bit more of age and less dependent upon adiaphora.

In addition to consideration of the "weak," the "election" and "doing" of adiaphora in accordance with the rule of charity or edification also required, it was said, a keen regard for the general welfare of all members of the Church. Such concern will preclude, it was said, all unbridled desire, vanity, or immoderation. The Christian who really believes in the indifferent nature of food, money, clothes, and like matters, will not be anxious or avaricious in their regard, but having cast his lot with the Lord, and recognizing the latter's Providence, he will accept all such things in a spirit of thanksgiving, and exercise in their regard a charitable stewardship that is in accordance with his station in life.

A charitable concern for the general welfare of the Christian community will also mean, it was said, that one's "election" and "doing" of adiaphora will not be of a dissentious, anarchic sort, but will instead contribute to the edification of the Church in such wise that quietness and tranquility will prevail, and all Christians will find themselves in a "bande and knott of charity." Toward this end, the Christian must strive to keep the public exercise of his adiaphoristic liberty within the bounds of policy established by the proper officials. Unlike the Puritans and other radicals, the mainline adiaphorists had no objection to the legislation as such of adiaphora. Given the variety and conflict of human opinions, some such legislation, they said, was indispensible to the Church's survival. In this regard, however, it was emphasized that neither the pope nor the Councils enjoy any prerogative to dictate universal policy in the realm of adiaphora. Every local (i.e., national) church must be left free to decide its own policy. If one bears in mind a proper distinction between spiritual and political unity, the diversity in adiaphoristic matters resulting therefrom will not be thought to jeopardize the Christian community's "unity in faith." Just as the incidence of diversity in the early Church on a variety of adiaphoristic matters like the dating of Easter was not viewed as a threat to the "spiritual" unity of the various local churches, so the Church of England could establish a policy in adiaphoristic matters to suit the needs and tastes of its own people and not thereby break its ties with the one Church of God, even though that policy be ever so different from that of the churches of Spain, Italy, Germany, and so forth. The English adiaphorists did not take this to mean that all past Roman, papal, or conciliar laws touching upon adiaphoristic matters must be abrogated.

But they did certainly mean to say that all such laws would continue to carry force in England only to the extent and so long as they enjoyed the sanction of local authorities.

On the question about which local officials—ecclesiastical or civil—enjoyed ultimate authority over ecclesiastical adiaphora, the English adiaphorists decidedly favored the latter. Among the first Englishmen to champion this point of view within a specifically adiaphoristic frame of reference were William Marshall and Thomas Starkey, both of whom were greatly indebted to Marsilius of Padua's *Defensor Pacis*. On the assumption that Christ had "never taught one point of worldly policie," Marsilius had concluded that all earthly affairs must be left to the control of the prince. Like Marshall before him, Starkey explicitly linked this conclusion up with the theory of adiaphorism, and concluded that all adiaphora, civil and ecclesiastical alike, have been left by God "to worldly policie," or to "them which in every country or nation be in hie authority," which in England is the "princely power and common counsell." Although the bishops continued to defend their own share of jurisdictional authority over ecclesiastical adiaphora, they also did not proffer any serious challenge to the princely prerogatives championed by Starkey and so readily appropriated by Henry VIII and his successors, and sooner or later they added their own to the long chorus of appeals for obedience of the king in matters indifferent that could be heard from the beginning to the end of the Henrician and Edwardine periods of reform. All Englishmen, it was said, must conform their conduct in the realm of adiaphora to the "seemly and due order" appointed by the king and Parliament, and those who do not will be subjected to open rebuke, lest others lose their fear of doing likewise—a threat which was all the more meaningful in that, unlike Starkey, most of the English adiaphorists were of the view that the specific laws touching upon ecclesiastical adiaphora were not to be considered binding in conscience, and to that extent were largely dependent for their enforcement upon the penalty attached to their disobedience.

For all their emphasis upon obedience and conformity, however, church officials could and did tolerate some diversity within the English realm on adiaphoristic matters. The "foreigners" who had settled in England found the greatest license in this regard. But non-contemptious and non-offensive divergence on the part of native Englishmen was also occasionally tolerated, or, as in the 1537 *Bishops' Book,* even encouraged. Even after the Uniformity Acts of 1549 and 1552, exceptions to the rule of uniformity were allowed, especially when the conscience of one or another individual was found to be "erroneously" in conflict with existing laws. John Hooper could probably have won a similar dispensation, except that, rightly or wrongly, his opposition to the appointed vestments came to be viewed as being of a seditious sort.

As a result of having developed along the lines of this indifferent mean, the early English reformation became to no small extent a "hidden" one. In fact, so far as its external ceremonies were concerned, the English Church continued throughout the reigns of Henry VIII and Edward VI to look very much as it had prior to the inception of its reformation. A casual observer might easily receive the impression thereby that nothing of significance had occurred in the interim. But such an impression would be false, missing the very point that the adiaphorists were most intent upon establishing—the point, namely, that their freedom over against adiaphoristic matters was of a primarily spiritual sort, which, as such, could not be tied down to any one or another particular mode of external conduct.

By basing their reform program upon such a conception of adiaphoristic liberty, the English reformers came to be far more concerned about changes of an intentional or attitudinal kind than about whether one or another traditional ceremony was retained or rejected. What mattered to them most was whether, for having been taken down the route of an indifferent mean, members of the English Church were better instructed, more knowledgeable, less superstitious, less scrupulous, less judgmental, and more tolerant and charitable in their attitude toward ceremonial matters, more attentive to God's own word and law, less inhibited in their relation to the material goods of this world, and more relaxed in the pursuit of their mundane affairs. Evidence of such attitudinal changes—of which there is much— would suggest that even if nothing at all had been altered in the external realm of ceremonies, the early stages of the English reformation would still have represented real progress.

That is not to say, however, that by subscribing to the theory of adiaphorism the English reformers became altogether unconcerned about the external arrangement of their church. Quite the contrary. Part and parcel of their adiaphoristic approval of ceremonies and the like was their conviction that such matters in themselves make no difference to God. But they did not conceive of this "divine indifference" as that of some *deus otiosus* who, having tired of human affairs, abandons man to himself and withdraws disinterestedly to the sky. They believed rather than God's providence was comprehensive. That God, in the person of Christ, had abrogated the old, Judaic ceremonial and judicial codes, without supplying any new, specific directives for the arrangement of matters previously covered thereby, was not therefore, considered by the English adiaphorists indicative of a total lack of concern about such matters on God's part. If God is "indifferent" toward such matters, his "indifference," they implied, is of a calculated sort. It is like the indifference of the parent or teacher who at the proper moment withdraws a certain distance from the child or pupil so as the better to afford the latter room to grow. In his providence, the adiaphorists implied, God has provided Christians with adequate guidance at all essential points. But also in his providence, he has refrained from treating Christians like infants. Like the good parent or teacher he has refused to pass judgment on a wide variety of less essential matters so as to encourage his "children" or "pupils" thereby to assume greater responsibility over their own lives.

Far from being a show of total lack of interst, or for that matter a mere act of "indulgence" or "dispensation," therefore, God's "permissive" or "indifferent" attitude toward ceremonial matters was conceived by the English adiaphorists as constituting a positive invitation to man to come of age and share in God's creative activity in a way that presupposed and symbolized, but was not simply co-terminous with, the Christian's more radical lordship over all externals.

In their awareness of God's "indifference," or in the knowledge of their adiaphoristic freedom, the English reformers, therefore, did not see any excuse for lapsing into some quietistic, cynical, or irresponsible mood in the realm of adiaphora. They experienced their adiaphoristic liberty rather as a gift that must be received in a spirit of thanksgiving and translated concretely into a sense of stewardship, responsibility, and creativity of such broad dimensions as neither the Roman party, with its tendency to confuse papal *"fiat"* and divine will, nor the Puritans, Lollards, and Anabaptists, with their excessive dependence upon the Bible as the sole "creator" of ecclesiastical polity, could ever accept.

Within the context of such a conception of adiaphoristic liberty, adiaphora themselves came to be viewed as enjoying the potentiality of becoming something more than mere "dead and beggarly elements" (Gal. 4:9). For it implied that although such matters cannot in themselves contribute anything essential to the building up of the Christian community, they remain nonetheless the "goods," the "stuff," the "raw material" which might, when impressed with man's creative intentions, contribute significantly to the enhancement of God's "living temple."

In pursuing their adaiphoristic *via media*, therefore, the mainline English reformers found themselves falling back upon their own resources. For one thing, and consistent with the earlier and later views expressed by Reginald Pecock and Richard Hooker, they were forced to rely more upon reason. Hounded by one or another party on their right or left to explain their rejection or retention of this or that ceremony, the adiaphorists could in the end very often appeal to nothing else but the "reasonableness" of their action.

This concern for a rational arrangement of the external affairs of their church in turn naturally inclined the English reformers also to fall back repeatedly upon the creative instrumentality of law. To no small extent, in fact, the English reformers simply turned the whole realm of adiaphora over to the civil authorities. In the process, the English people could well have found their adiaphoristic freedom sold out from under them. Had their "indifferent mean" developed solely along the lines of its conception by Thomas Starkey, they could well have found themselves struggling under a new "pope"—Henry VIII—and the same old "intolerable burden." But Starkey's opinion that things indifferent change their nature and become necessary to salvation when legislated by the "princely and common authority" was not shared by the majority of English adiaphorists, and did not, so far at least as ecclesiastical adiaphora were concerned, find a place in the "official" Henrician and Edwardine version of the indifferent mean. That it did not, gave rise to an increased emphasis upon policing activities by the likes of Thomas Cromwell. But the refusal to allow any intrusion upon man's conscience in the realm of ecclesiastical adiaphora also brought into clearer focus the priority afforded by the English adiaphorists to the creative potential of Christian love. For it was, in one sense, simply another way of saying that rational concepts and man-made laws can never infallibly inculcate the dictates of Christian love, and must on that account always remain subservient to the latter as they are discerned in the light of Christian faith.

To have given so much play to the principle of love was all the more remarkable in view of the dangers to which the English Church was then exposed. The fears expressed by Reginald Pole and other papalists that England would "run to ruin" once severed from Rome were not entirely unwarranted. An undercurrent of social unrest, the rising tide of anticlericalism, and the polarization of public opinion that inevitably results during periods of dramatic change, could easily have combined to have thrown England and its church into a state of turmoil. In the face of such a threat it would hardly have been surprising to have found the English reformers severing their ties with Rome only to scramble all the more desperately for some other "unshakable ground," like the biblical text or royal decree, upon which to build a decent and orderly church. For all their respect for the Bible, and for all the authority they afforded the king and Parliament, however, those English reformers of an adiaphoristic bent did not in the end succumb to such temptations. Just as they rejected biblical reductionism, so they also refused to absolutize human law. In the final analysis, their indifferent mean was not nearly so much the work of rational legislation as it was the work of love—a "bande and knott of charity."

It would be folly, of course, to think that the Anglican Church was born of none but the noblest motives. A general weariness over the exigencies of reform no doubt occasionally dulled the English reformers' adiaphoristically inspired spirit of creativity—much to the delight, perhaps, of Stephen Gardiner and his kind, who because of their desire to preserve the *status quo,* would have been only too happy had the theory of adiaphorism proven soporiferous. But on the whole both the Continental and English adiaphorists pursued their "lordship" with such passion and imagination that Gardiner himself—betraying his lack of genuine understanding of the theory of adiaphorism—charged them with having contradicted themselves by expending so much time and energy on matters which they themselves had deemed indifferent.[17]

One may also doubt whether the English adiaphorists always used the opportunities for love which they had set for themselves in their indifferent mean. All too often, probably, the chance for individuals to relate to one another in terms of true charity and mutual respect, or for church authorities to fashion an external order genuinely conducive to the edification of all because it could take into serious account the contingencies of time and place, was exploited to camouflage a variety of fears and ambitions. It is certainly not out of the question, for example, that Henry VIII's and Cromwell's initial enthusiasm for the "indifferent mean" betrayed something of a Machiavellian appreciation for the quick and easy route it might afford them in the execution of their Erastian designs upon the English Church, or that they at first saw in the theory of adiaphorism little more than a weapon for propagandizing the English people into support of their king's rejection of papal supremacy. Be that as it may, however, the fact that the English reformers would have set for themselves such opportunities for charity in the first place remains no less admirable for all their inability to have seen them perfectly through. Furthermore, even if such opportunities were on occasion exploited in the interest of goals less noble than charity, on many other occasions they were not.

In many ways, the actual, concrete arrangement of ceremonial and similar matters during the Henrician and Edwardine period does reflect a conscious concern for charity. The very fact that out of consideration for the "weak" so few of the traditional ceremonies were rejected, and that on that account also the early English reformation remained so "hidden," was itself a reflection of such a concern. But some changes were made in the realm of ceremonies, and more often than not precisely out of a charitable concern for respecting the tastes and needs of an English people caught up in a more nationalistic, more spiritual, and more mature disposition than had theretofore been the case.

Finally, in concluding this study, it should be emphasized that only the very first phase of what in fact became a long and complex history of English adiaphorism has been covered. With the accession of Mary to the throne in 1553, English Protestants found themselves in a situation not entirely unlike that faced by the Lutherans in Germany after the promulgation of the Augsburg and Leipzig Interims. Mary proved less willing than Charles V had in yielding "essential" ground to the Protestants, and that was a crucial difference. Still, in both cases, the question arose as to whether one should or should not submit to "popish tyranny" in the realm of adiaphora. In Germany, as has been seen, such a crisis precipitated a bitter controversy among the Protestants themselves. Whether a similar controversy ensued among the English Protestants under Mary needs to be studied more closely, and that in the context of examining the actual policy toward adiaphora followed by Marian officials like Pole and Gardiner. Gardiner, it will be recalled, had been brought to an explicit embrace of adiaphoristic principles at one point during Edward's reign, and it would be important to see how the same fared in his thought and action under Mary. If he needed any goad to start him writing again, Turner was still around to provide it. Even before the Papal Legate, Pole, had had time to set foot on English soil again, Turner, now again in exile on the Continent, had fired off yet another of his diatribes against the pope.[18] And Turner's was only one in the steady stream of anti-Marian propaganda pieces that came from the Marian exiles, all of which, together with the response of the Marian officials, warrant further study from an adiaphoristic point of view.

Considerable significance for the future development of English adiaphorism lay also in the controversies which arose among the Marian exiles themselves. The "troubles at Frankfort," which pitted Richard Cox, John Jewel, and others against the likes of William Whittingham and John Knox in a battle over the *Prayer Book,* clearly involved a discussion of adiaphoristic principles, and needs to be reexamined in the light of the same as something of a preview of similar debates that would follow in the reigns of Elizabeth I, James I, and beyond. Furthermore, a closer look at the actual shape of the exile-churches established at other cities than Frankfurt—and especially at the one set up at Geneva under Calvin's eye—would be important for an understanding of the future course of English adiaphorism.

As for the adiaphoristic thrust of the Elizabethan Settlement and the development of English adiaphorism up to the time of the Oxford Movement, when the Tractarians would bring the theory once again to the fore—these, obviously, are subjects upon which much further study can and should be made. Until such a re-examination can be made, and the full picture of English adiaphorism uncovered, the conclusions drawn about that part of the picture surveyed in this study must of necessity remain relatively tentative. But if the Henrician-Edwardine "indifferent mean" outlined above is anywhere approximate to accuracy, it may rightly be afforded a piece of the praise heaped by T.S. Eliot upon the Elizabethan Settlement—to the effect, namely, that because of its "determination to stick to essentials... awareness of the needs of the time, the desire for clarity and precision on matters of importance, and the indifference to matters indifferent,"[19] it "became something representative of the finest spirit of England of the time."[20]

NOTES

1. See, for example, Herrtage, *Starkey's Life and Letters,* pp. lx–lxi.
2. *Ibid.,* p. lxxi.
3. Zeeveld, *op. cit.,* p. 147.
4. Herrtage, *Starkey's Life and Letters,* p. lxxi.
5. *Ibid.*
6. *Ibid.,* p. lxxii.
7. See Burnet, *op. cit.,* I, p. 549.
8. See Herrtage, *Starkey's Life and Letters,* pp. lx–lxi.
9. See Foxe, *Acts and Monuments* V, pp. 534–35.
10. See *Ibid.,* VI, pp. 28–30, 34–36.
11. See Starkey, *Exhortation,* sig. J, fol. iii(v); F, iii.
12. Burnet, *op. cit.,* I, p. 549.
13. See Luther, *De Lib. Christ.,* WA 7, 70; *Wider die himml. Proph.,* WA 18, 112; *Pred. des Jah. 1522,* WA 10[III], 14.
14. See Foxe, *Acts and Monuments,* V, pp. 534–35.
15. See *Ibid.,* VI, pp. 28–30.
16. Schmid, *op. cit.,* p. 617.

17. See Gardiner, *Tracts*, p. 195.

18. W. Turner, *The Huntyng of the Romyshe Wolfe* (London, 1554).

19. T.S. Eliot, *For Lancelot Andrewes: Essays on Styles and Order* (London, 1928), p. 17.

20. *Ibid.*, p. 15.

BIBLIOGRAPHY

I. PRIMARY SOURCES

A. Collections of Documents

Brewer, J.S., and Gairdner, J., eds. *Letters and Papers, Foreign and Domestic of the Reign of Henry VIII.* 21 vols. London: 1862–1910.

Bruns, H. *Canones Apostorum et Conciliorum Veterum Selecti.* Torino: 1959.

D'Achery, L. *Spicilegium sive Collectio veterum Aliquot Scriptorum.* Paris: 1723.

Dasent, J.R., ed. *Acts of the Privy Council.* 32 vols. London: 1890–1907.

Die Bekenntnisschriften der evangelisch-lutherischen Kirche. Göttingen: 1967.

Ehses, S., ed. *Concilii Tridentini Actorum.* 6 vols. Friburgi Brisgoviae: 1911.

Frere, W.H., and Kennedy, W.M., eds. *Visitation Articles and Injunctions.* London: 1910.

Gee, H., and Hardy, W.J. *Documents Illustrative of English Church History.* New York: 1896.

Haddon, A.W., and Stubbs, W. *Poenitentiale Theodori, Councils and Ecclesiastical Documents relating to Great Britain and Ireland.* Oxford: 1871.

Hughes, P.L., and Larkin, J.F. *Tudor Royal Proclamations.* New Haven: 1964.

Ketley, J., ed. *The Two Liturgies, A.D. 1549 and A.D. 1552, With Other Documents set forth by Authority in the Reign of King Edward VI.* Cambridge: 1844.

Kirch, C. *Enchiridion Fontium Historiae Ecclesiasticae Antiquae.* Friburgi Brisgoviae: 1923.

Lloyd, C. *Formularies of Faith.* Oxford: 1825.

Mentz, G. *Die Wittenberger Artikel von 1536.* Vol. II of *Quellenschriften zur Geschichte des Protestantismus.* Edited by C. Stange. Leipzig: 1905.

Pocock, N. *Records of the Reformation.* 2 vols. Oxford: 1870.

———. ed. *Troubles Connected With The Prayer Book of 1549.* Westminster: 1884.

Reu, J.M. *The Augsburg Confession, A Collection of Sources.* St. Louis: 1966.
Schaff, P. *The Creeds of Christendom.* 3 vols. New York, 1919.
Strype, J. *Ecclesiastical Memorials.* 2 vols. Oxford: 1822.
———. *Memorials of Thomas Cranmer,* 2 vols. Oxford: 1840.
Whitelock, D. *English Historical Documents, c. 500–1042.* London: 1955.

B. *Collections of Letters*

Allen, P.S., ed. *Opus Epistolarum D. Erasmi.* 12 vols. Oxford: 1906–1958.
Burnet, J. *Letters of John Calvin.* Philadelphia: 1858.
Currie, M.A., ed. *Letters of Martin Luther.* London: 1908.
Emerton, E. *The Letters of Boniface.* New York: 1940.
Enders, E.L., ed. *Dr. Martin Luthers Briefwechsel.* 14 vols. Stuttgart and Leipzig: 1884–1912.
Herrtage, S. *England in the Reign of Henry VIII: Starkey's Life and Letters.* E.E.T.S., extra series no. xxxii. London: 1878.
Merriman, R.B. *Life and Letters of Thomas Cromwell.* 2 vols. Oxford: 1902.
Muller, J.R. *The Letters of Stephen Gardiner.* New York: 1933.
Robinson, H., ed. *Original Letters Relative to the English Reformation.* 2 vols. Cambridge: 1847.
———. *The Zurich Letters.* Cambridge: 1842.
Smith, P. *The Life and Letters of Martin Luther.* New York: 1911.
Wright, T., ed. *Three Chapters of Letters Relating to the Suppression of Monasteries.* London: 1843.

C. *Works*

Alesius, A. *Of the Authorite of the Word of God agaynst the Bishop of London.* London: 1538.
Aquinas, T. *Opera Omnia.* 25 vols. Parmae: 1852–1873; New York: 1948.
———. *Summa Theologiae.* 5 vols. Ottawa: 1953.
Arnim, H.F.A. von, ed. *Stoicorum Veterum Fragmenta.* 4 vols. Lipsiae: 1921.
Bale, J. *Select Works.* Edited by H. Christmas. Cambridge: 1849.
———. *Yet a Course at the Romyshe Foxe.* Zurich: 1543.
Bardaison of Edessa. *The Book of the Laws of Countries.* Translated by J.J.W. Drijvers. Assen: 1964.
Barnes, R. *A Supplication.* n.p., 1531.
———. *A Supplycatyon.* n.p., 1534.
Becon, T. *The Catechism, With Other Pieces.* Edited by J. Ayre. Cambridge: 1844.
———. *Early Works.* Edited by J. Ayre. Cambridge: 1843.
———. *The Fortress of the Faithful.* London: 1550.
———. *Prayers and Other Pieces.* Edited by J. Ayre. Cambridge: 1844.
Bede's Ecclesiastical History of the English People. Edited by B. Colgrave and R.A.B. Mynors. Oxford: 1972.

Biel, G. *Canonis Misse Expositio*. Edited by H. Oberman and W.J. Courtenay. Wiesbaden: 1963.

──. *Defensorium Obedientiae Apostolicae et Alia Documenta*. Edited and translated by H. Oberman, D.E. Zerfoss, and W.J. Courtenay. Cambridge, Massachusetts: 1968.

Bradford, J. *Writings*. Edited by A. Townsend. Cambridge: 1853.

Bucer, M. *Deutsche Schriften*. Edited by R. Stupperich. 7 vols. Gütersloh: 1960.

──. *Scripta Anglicana*. Basle: 1577.

Bullinger, H. *Decades*. Edited by T. Harding. 4 vols. Cambridge: 1850.

──. *Leben und Ausgewählte Schriften*. Edited by C. Pestalozzi. Elberfeld: 1858.

──. *A Treatise or Sermon . . . concernynge magistrates and obedience of subjects*. London: 1549.

Calvin, J. *Commentary on II Cor., Tim., Titus, and Philemon*. Translated by T.A. Smail. Edinburgh: 1964.

──. *Gospel according to John 1-10*. Translated by T.H.L. Parker. Edinburgh: 1959.

──. *Gospel according to St. John 11-21 and the First Ep. of John*. Translated by T.M. Parker. Edinburgh: 1961.

──. *Epistles of Paul to Galatians, Ephesians, Philippians, and Colossians*. Translated by T.H.L. Parker. Edinburgh: 1965.

──. *Epistles of Paul to Romans and Thessalonians*. Translated by Ross MacKenzie. Edinburgh: 1960.

──. *Institutes of the Christian Religion*. Edited by J.T. McNeill, translated by F.L. Battles. 2 vols. Philadelphia: 1967.

──. *Opera quae supersunt omnia*. Edited by J.W. Baum *et al*. 59 vols. Brunswick and Berlin: 1863-1900. Vols. XXIX–LXXXVII of *CR*.

Cicero. *De Legibus*. Translated by C.W. Keyes. London: 1961.

──. *De Natura Deorum*. Translated by H. Rackham. London: 1961.

──. *De Officiis*. Translated by W. Miller. London: 1961.

Clichtove, J. *Compendium veritatum*. Paris: 1529.

Cochlaeus, J. *De authoritate ecclesiae et Scripturae*. n.p., 1524.

──. *Drei Schriften gegen Luthers Schmalkaldische Artikel*. Edited by P.H. Volz. Münster: 1932.

Colet, J. *An Exposition of St. Paul's Epistle to Romans*. Translated by J.H. Lupton. London: 1873; Republished, Ridgewood, New Jersey: 1965.

──. *En Exposition of St. Paul's First Epistle to the Corinthians*. Translated by J.H. Lupton. London: 1874; Republished, Ridgewood: 1965.

──. *Two Treatises on the Hierarchies of Dionysius*. Translated by J.H. Lupton. London: 1869; Republished, Ridgewood: 1966.

Coverdale, M. *Remains*. Edited by G. Pearson. Cambridge: 1846.

Cranmer, T. *Cranmer's Liturgical Projects*. Edited by J.W. Legg. London: 1915.

──. *Miscellaneous Writings and Letters*. Edited by J.E. Cox. Cambridge: 1846.

Cusa, Nicholas of. *De Pace Fidei*. Edited by R. Klibansky and H. Bascour. Vol. VII of *Opera Omnia*. Hamburg: 1959.

Cyprian. *Collectio Selecta SS. Ecclesiae Patrum XIV*. Edited by D.A.B. Caillou. Paris: 1829.

Eck, J. *Defensio contra Amarulentes D. Andreae Bodenstein Carolstatim invectiones*. Edited by J. Greving. Münster: 1919.

———. *Enchiridion locorum communium adversus Lutherum et alios hostes Ecclesiae*. Paris: 1559.

Erasmus, D. *The Essential Erasmus*. Edited by J.P. Dolan. New York: 1964.

———. *Opera Omnia*. Edited by J. Clericus. 10 vols. Leiden: 1703–06.

Fisher, J. *English Works*. Edited by J.E.B. Mayor. E.E.T.S., extra series no. xxvii. London: 1876.

———. *Opera Omnia*. Würzburg: 1597.

Fox, Edward. *The true dyfferens betwen the regall power and the Ecclesiastical power*. London: 1548.

Foxe, J. *Acts and Monuments*. Edited by G. Townsend. 8 vols. London, 1843–49.

Gansfort, W. *Life and Writings*. Edited by E. Waite Miller, translated by J.W. Scudder. 2 vols. New York: 1917.

———. *Opera*. Groningen: 1614.

Gardiner, S. *A Declaration of Such True Articles as Georg Joye Hath Gone About To Confute As False*. London: 1546.

———. *A Detection of the Devil's Sophistry wherewith he robbeth the unlearned people of the true byleef in the most blessed Sacrament of the Aulter*. London: 1546.

———. *Obedience in Church and State: Three Political Tracts*. Edited by P. Janelle. New York: 1968.

Gerson, J. *Opera Omnia*. Edited by E. du Pin. 5 vols. Antwerp: 1706.

Harpsfield, N. *A Treatise on the Pretended Divorce between Henry VIII and Catherine of Aragon*. Edited by N. Pocock. Westminster: 1878.

Henry VIII. *Assertio Septem Sacramentorum*. Edited by L. O'Donovan. New York: 1908.

Hooper, J. *Early Writings*. Edited by S. Carr. Cambridge: 1843.

———. *Later Writings*. Edited by C. Nevinson. Cambridge: 1852.

Hus, J. *Super IV Sententiarum*. Edited by V.W. Fljshaus and M. Kominkova. Osnabruck: 1966.

———. *Tractatus De Ecclesia*. Edited by S.H. Thomson. Cambridge: 1956.

Illyricus, Matthias Flacius. *Omnia Latina scripta hactenus sparsim contra Adiaphoricas*. n.p., 1550.

Joye, G. *George Joye Confuteth Winchesters False Articles*. Wesill in Cliefe Lande: 1543.

———. *The Refutation of the Bishop of Winchesters derke declaration of his false articles*. London: 1546.

Kant, I. *Die Religion innerhalb der Grenzen der blossen Vernunft*. Edited by K. Vorländer, Hamburg: 1956.

Knox, J. *Works*. Edited by D. Laing. 6 vols. Edinburgh: 1846.

Laertius, Diogenes. *Lives of Eminent Philosophers*. Translated by R.D. Hicks. New York: 1931.

Latimer, H. *Sermons*. Edited by G.E. Carrie. Cambridge: 1844.

――――. *Sermons and Remains*. Edited by G.E. Carrie. Cambridge: 1845.

Latomus, B. *Zwei Streitschriften gegen M. Bucer*. Edited by L. Keil. Münster: 1924.

Luther, M. *Werke, Kritische Gesamtausgabe*. 58 vols. Weimar: 1883-1948.

――――. *Works*. 55 vols. Philadelphia and St. Louis: 1955 ff.

Marsilius of Padua. *Defensor-Pacis*. Edited by C.W. Previte-Orton. Cambridge: 1928.

――――. *The Defender of Peace*. Translated by A. Gewirth. New York: 1956.

Melanchthon, P. *Werke in Auswahl*. Edited by R. Stupperich, H. Engelland, *et al.* 5 vols. Gütersloh: 1952.

Melanchthon and Bucer. Edited by W. Pauck. Philadelphia: 1969.

More, T. *Complete Works*. Edited J.M. Headley. 5 vols. New Haven and London: 1969.

――――. *The Dialogue Concerning Tyndale*. Edited by W.E. Campbell. London: 1927.

――――. *The Utopia*. Edited by M. Campbell. New York: 1947.

Migne, J.P. *Patrologiae cursus completus. Ser. Latina*. 221 vols. Paris: 1844-1904.

――――. *Patrologiae cursus completus. Ser. Graeca*. 217 vols. Paris: 1857-66.

Müntzer, T. *Schriften und Briefe*. Edited by G. Frantz. Gütersloh: 1968.

Oecolampadius, J., and Myconius, O. *J. Oekolampad und Oswald Myconius, Leben und ausgewählte Schriften*. Edited by K.R. Hagenback. Elberfeld: 1859.

Origen. *First Principles*. Translated and edited by G.W. Butterworth, with an Introduction by H. de Lubac. New York: 1966.

Pecock, Reginald. *Repressor of OverMuch Blaming of the Clergy*. Edited by C. Babington. Vol. 19 of Public Record Office Publications. London: 1860.

Pole, Reginald. *Defense of the Unity of the Church*. Translated by J.G. Dwyer. Westminster, Maryland: 1965.

Rationale of Ceremonial, The. Edited by C.S. Cobb. London: 1910.

Reformation of the Ecclesiastical Laws, The. Edited by E. Cardwell. Oxford: 1850.

Ridley, N. *Works*. Edited by H. Christmas. Cambridge: 1843.

Schatzgeyer, Kaspar. *Scrutinium Divinae Scripturae*. Münster: 1922.

Schleiermacher, F.D.E. *Werke*. Leipzig: 1910.

Sentences of Sextus. Edited by H. Chadwick. Cambridge: 1959.

Short Instruction into Christian Religion, A. Edited by E. Burton. Oxford: 1829.

Spiritual and Anabaptist Writers. Edited by G.H. Williams. London: 1957.

Starkey, T. *An Exhortation to the People, Instructynge them to Unite and Obedience*. London: 1535.

Three Primers Put Forth in the Reign of Henry VIII. Oxford: 1848.

Turner, W. *The Huntyng and Fyndyng out of the Romishe Fox*. Basel: 1543.

————. *The Rescuynge of the Romishe Fox, The Seconde Course of the Hunter at the Romish Fox and Hys Advocate*. Zurich: 1545.

————. *The Huntynge of the Romyshe Wolfe*. London: 1554.

Tyndale, W. *An Answer to Sir Thomas More's Dialogue*. Edited by H. Alter. Cambridge: 1850.

————. *Doctrinal Treatises*. Edited by H. Walter. Cambridge: 1848.

Tyndale, W. *Expositions and Notes*. Edited by H. Walter. Cambridge: 1849.

————, Frith, J. *The Works of the English Reformers: William Tyndale and John Frith*. Edited by T. Russell. 3 vols. London: 1831.

————, Frith, J., Barnes, R. *Writings of Tindal, Frith, and Barnes*. Edited by The Religious Tract Society. London: n.d.

Vermigli, Pietro Martire. *The Commonplaces . . . with a large addition of manie theologicall and necessarie discourses*. Translated by A. Marten. 2 vols. London: 1583.

Whether it be mortall sinne to transgress civil laws. N.p.:n.d.

Wyclif, J. *De Ecclesia*. Edited by J. Loserth. London: 1886.

————. *De Mandatis Divinis*. Edited by J. Loserth and F.D. Matthew. London: 1922.

————. *De Veritate Sacrae Scripturae*. Edited by R. Buddensieg. London: 1905–07.

————. *Tracts and Treatises*. Edited by R. Vaughan. London: 1845.

Zwingli, H. *Latin Works*. Translated by S.M. Jackson. Philadelphia: 1922.

————. *Opera*. Edited by M. Schulero. Turici: 1838.

————. *Sämtliche Werke*. Edited by E. Egli and G. Finsler. 16 vols. Berlin and Zurich: 1905 ff. Vols. LXXXVIII–CIV of *CR*.

————, Bullinger, H. *Zwingli and Bullinger*. Edited by G.W. Bromiley. Philadelphia: 1953.

D. *Chronicles*

Chronicle of the Greyfriars of London. Edited by J.G. Nichols. London: 1852.

Hall, E. *Chronicle*. London: 1809.

Narratives of the Days of the Reformation. Edited by J.G. Nichols. Westminster: 1859.

Wriothesley, C. *A Chronicle of England*. Edited by W.D. Hamilton. Westminster: 1875.

II. SECONDARY SOURCES

A. *Narratives and General Histories*.

Blunt, J.H. *The Reformation of the Church of England*. London: 1882.

Burnet, G. *The History of the Reformation of the Church of England*. 3 vols. Oxford: 1829.

Capes, W.W. *The English Church in the Fourteenth and Fifteenth Centuries.* London: 1903.

Chadwick, O. *The Reformation.* Baltimore: 1968.

Collier, J. *Ecclesiastical History of Great Britain.* 2 vols, folio edition. London: 1708.

Collinson, P. *The Elizabethan Puritan Movement.* Berkeley: 1967.

Copleston, F. *A History of Philosophy.* 7 vols. Garden City: 1962.

Cuming, G.J. *A History of Anglican Liturgy.* New York: 1969.

Dickens, A.G. *The English Reformation.* New York: 1964.

Dixon, R.W. *History of the Church of England.* London: 1878.

Elton, G.R. *Reformation Europe. 1517–1559.* New York: 1966.

————. ed. *The Reformation, 1520–1559. The New Cambridge Modern History.* Vol. II. Cambridge: 1958.

Gairdner, J. *The English Church in the Sixteenth Century from the Accession of Henry VIII to the Death of Mary.* London: 1903.

————. *Lollardy and the Reformation in England.* 2 vols. London: 1908–1913.

Harnack, A. von. *History of Dogma.* Translated by N. Buchanan. 7 vols. Boston, 1898–1903.

Hefele, C.J., and de Clerq, C. *Histoire des Conciles.* 11 vols. Paris: 1907.

Hughes, P. *The Reformation in England.* 2 vols. New York: 1963.

Hunt, W.H. *The English Church from its Foundation to the Normal Conquest (597–1066).* London: 1907.

Jedin, H. *A History of the Council of Trent.* Translated by E. Graf. Edinburgh: 1957.

McNeill, J.T. *The History and Character of Calvinism.* New York: 1967.

Parker, T.M. *The English Reformation to 1558.* Oxford: 1968.

Procter, F., and Frere, W.H. *A History of The Book of Common Prayer.* London: 1951.

Rouse, R. and Neill, S.C. *A History of the Ecumenical Movement, 1517–1948.* London: 1954.

Ullmann, W. *A History of Political Thought: The Middle Ages.* Baltimore: 1968.

Williams, G.H. *The Radical Reformation.* Philadelphia: 1962.

B. Biographies

Bainton, R. *Erasmus of Christendom.* New York: 1969.

————. *Here I Stand.* New York: 1950.

Bender, H.S. *Conrad Grebel. 1498–1526. Founder of the Swiss Brethren.* Scottsdale: 1950.

Bouyer, L. *Erasmus and His Times.* Translated by F.X. Murphy. Westminster, Maryland: 1959.

Chambers, R.W. *Thomas More.* Ann Arbor: 1968.

Dickens, A.G. *Thomas Cromwell and the English Reformation.* New York: 1964.

Ferguson, C.W. *Naked to Mine Enemies*. 2 vols. New York: 1965.

Huizinga, J. *Erasmus and the Age of Reformation*. Translated by F. Hopman. New York: 1957.

Lorimer, P. *John Knox and the Church of England*. London: 1875.

——. *Patrick Hamilton*. Vol. I of *Precursors of Knox*. Edinburgh: 1857.

Lupton, J.H. *Life of John Colet*. London: 1887.

Manschreck, C.L. *Melanchthon, The Quiet Reformer*. New York and Nashville: 1958.

Mozley, J.F. *William Tyndale*. London: 1937.

Muller, J.R. *Stephen Gardiner and the Tudor Reaction*. New York: 1926.

Pollard, A.F. *Thomas Cranmer and the English Reformation*. New York and London: 1904.

Preger, W. *Mathias Flacius Illyricus und Seine Zeit*. 2 vols. Munich: 1861.

Ridley, J. *Thomas Cranmer*, Oxford: 1962.

——. *John Knox*. New York and Oxford: 1968.

Rilliet, J. *Zwingli, Third Man of the Reformation*. Translated by H. Knight. Philadelphia: 1964.

Scarisbrick, J.J. *Henry VIII*. Berkeley and Los Angeles: 1969.

Smith, P. *Erasmus, A Study of His Life, Ideals and Place in History*. New York: 1962.

Strype, J. *The Life of Sir John Cheke*. Oxford: 1821.

Walker, W. *John Calvin*. New York and London: 1906.

Williams, C.H. *William Tyndale*. London: 1969.

C. *Special Studies*

Adam, K. *Christ Our Brother*. Translated by J. McCain. New York: 1962.

Alexander, P.J. *The Patriarch Nicephorus of Constantinople*. Oxford: 1958.

Althaus, P. *The Ethics of Martin Luther*. Translated by R.C. Schultz. Philadelphia: 1972.

——. *Grundriss der Ethik*. Gütersloh: 1953.

——. *The Theology of Martin Luther*. Translated by R.C. Schultz. Philadelphia: 1966.

Arnold, E.V. *Roman Stoicism*. London: 1958.

Audet, J.P. *Structures of Christian Priesthood*. Translated by R. Sheed. New York: 1968.

Bainton, R. *Concerning Heretics*. New York: 1935.

——. *Studies on the Reformation*. Boston: 1966.

——. *The Travail of Religious Liberty*. Philadelphia: 1951.

Baumer, F. le von. *The Early Tudor Theory of Kingship*. New Haven: 1940.

Bayne, D.C. *Conscience, Obligation and the Law*. Chicago: 1966.

Benrath, G.A. *Reformtheologen des 15. Jahrhunderts*. Gütersloh: 1968.

Bente, F. *Historical Introductions to the Book of Concord*. St. Louis: 1965.

Biechler, J.E. *Law for Liberty*. Baltimore: 1967.

Blunt, J.H. *Dictionary of Sects, Heresies, Ecclesiastical Parties and Schools of Religious Thought*. London: 1892.

Böckle, F. *Law and Conscience.* Translated by M.J. Donnelly. New York: 1966.
Boehlens, M. *Die Klerikerehe in der Gesetzgebung der Kirche.* Paderborn: 1968.
Bonhoeffer, D. *Ethics.* Translated by N.H. Smith. New York: 1967.
Bouquillon, T.J. *Theologia Moralis Fundamentalis.* Brugis: 1903.
Brezzi, P. *The Papacy.* Translated by J.J. Yannone. Westminster: 1958.
Brightman, F.E. *The English Rite.* 2 vols. London: 1915.
Butterworth, C.C. *The English Primers 1529-1545.* Philadelphia: 1953.
Canon Law of the Church of England, The. Edited by Archbishops' Commission on Canon Law. London: 1947.
Cassirer, E. *The Individual and the Cosmos in Renaissance Philosophy.* Translated by M. Domandi. New York: 1963.
Clebsch, W.A. *England's Earliest Protestants.* New Haven and London: 1964.
Congar, I. *Tradition and Traditions.* Translated by M. Naseby and T. Rainborough. New York: 1967.
Coolidge, J.S. *The Pauline Renaissance in England, Puritanism and the Bible.* Oxford: 1970.
Cranz, F.E. *An Essay on the Development of Luther's Thought on Justice, Law and Society.* Cambridge: 1959.
Crump, C.G. and Jacob, E.F. *The Legacy of the Middle Ages.* Oxford: 1926.
Cullmann, O. *The Earliest Christian Confessions.* Translated by J.K.S. Reid. London: 1949.
Darlington, R.R., and Chadwick, O., *et al. The English Church and the Continent.* London: 1956.
Davies, H. *Worship and Theology in England From Cranmer to Hooker, 1534-1603.* Princeton: 1970.
Davies, W.D., and Daube, D. *The Background of The New Testament and its Eschatology.* Cambridge: 1956.
Dickens, A.G. *Lollards and Protestants in the Diocese of York, 1509-1558.* Oxford: 1959.
Dodd, C.H. *The Apostolic Preaching.* New York: 1962.
Doernberg, E. *Henry VIII and Luther.* Stanford: 1961.
Dolan, J.P. *The Influence of Erasmus, Witzel and Cassander in the Church Ordinances and Reform Proposals of the United Duchees of Cleve During the Middle Decades of the Sixteenth Century.* Münster: 1957.
Dugmore, C.W. *The Mass and the English Reformers.* London: 1958.
———, *et al. The English Prayer Book, 1549-1662.* London: 1963.
Elert, W. *Law and Gospel.* Translated by E.H. Schroeder. Philadelphia: 1967.
Eliot, T.S. *For Lancelot Andrewes: Essays on Styles and Order.* London: 1928.
Elton, E.R. *Policy and Police: The Enforcement of the Reformation in the Age of Thomas Cromwell.* Cambridge: 1972.
———. *Reform and Renewal.* Cambridge: 1972.
Etienne, J. *Spiritualisme Erasmien et Théologiens Louvainistes.* Louvain: 1956.
Fagerberg, J. *A New Look at the Lutheran Confessions.* Translated by C.J. Lund. St. Louis: 1972.

Garside, C., Jr. *Zwingli and the Arts.* New Haven and London: 1966.

Gasquet, F.A., and Bishop, E. *Edward VI and the Book of Common Prayer.* London: 1891.

Geiselmann, J.R. *Die Heilige Schrift und die Tradition.* Freiburg: 1962.

Gestrich, C. *Zwingli als Theologe.* Stuttgart: 1967.

Hanson, R.P.C. *Tradition in the Early Church.* London: 1962.

Hardwick, C. *A History of the Articles of Religion.* London: 1852.

Herron, M. *The Binding Force of Civil Laws.* Paterson: 1958.

Hopf, C. *Martin Bucer and the English Reformation.* Oxford: 1946.

Huizinga, J. *The Waning of the Middle Ages.* Garden City: 1954.

Huschke, Rolf B. *Melanchthons Lehre vom Ordo politicus.* Gütersloh: 1968.

Iserloh, E. *Gnade und Eucharistie in der Philosophischen Theologie des Wilhelm von Ockham.* Wiesbaden: 1956.

Joest, W. *Gesetz und Freiheit.* Göttingen: 1968.

Jungmann, J. *The Mass of the Roman Rite.* Translated by F.A. Brunner and C.K. Riepe. New York: 1959.

Kadai, H.O. *et al. Accents in Luther's Theology.* St. Louis: 1967.

Kantzenbach, F.W. *Das Ringen um die Einheit der Kirche im Jahrhundert der Reformation.* Stuttgart: 1957.

King, N.C. *The Emperor Theodosius and the Establishment of Christianity.* London: 1961.

Kisch, Guido. *Erasmus und die Jurisprudenz seiner Zeit.* Basel: 1960.

Klomps, H. *Kirche, Freiheit und Gesetz bei dem Franziskaner Theologen Kaspar Schatzgeyer.* Münster: 1959.

Knappen, M.M. *Tudor Puritanism.* Chicago: 1939.

Lang, A. *Puritanismus und Pietismus.* Darmstadt: 1972.

Lecler, J. *Toleration and the Reformation.* Translated by T.L. Westow. 2 vols. London: 1960.

Locher, G.W. *H. Zwingli in Neuer Sicht.* Stuttgart: 1969.

Lottin, O. *Psychologie et morale aux XIIe et XIIIe siècles, problèmes de morales.* 3 vols. Louvain: 1948.

Mausbach, J. *Die Ethik des hl. Augustin.* 2 vols. Freiburg: 1909.

McConica, J.K. *English Humanists and Reformation Politics.* Oxford: 1965.

McDonnell, K. *John Calvin, the Church and the Eucharist.* Princeton: 1967.

McSorley, H. *Luther: Right or Wrong?* Glen Rock and Minneapolis: 1969.

Morrall, J.B. *Gerson and the Great Schism.* Manchester: 1960.

Müller, J. *M. Bucers Hermeneutik.* Gütersloh: 1965.

Müller, K. *Die Forderung der Ehelosigkeit für alle Getauften in der alten Kirche.* Tubingen: 1927.

New, J.N. *Anglican and Puritan: The Basis of their Opposition. 1558–1640.* London: 1964.

Niebuhr, H.R. *Christ and Culture.* New York: 1956.

Oberman, H. *Forerunners of the Reformation.* New York: 1966.

———. *The Harvest of Medieval Theology.* Cambridge: 1963.

Ozment, S.E. *Mysticism and Dissent: Religious Ideology and Social Protest in the Sixteenth Century.* New Haven: 1973.

Pascoe, L.B. *Jean Gerson, Principles of Church Reform.* Leiden: 1973.

Pauck, W. *The Heritage of the Reformation.* New York: 1966.

Pelikan, J. *Obedient Rebels.* New York and Evanston: 1964.

———. *The Emergence of the Catholic Tradition (100-600).* Chicago and London: 1971.

Pohlenz, M. *Die Stoa, Geschichte einer geistigen Bewegung.* 2 vols. Göttingen: 1948.

Porter, J.C. *Puritanism in Tudor England.* Columbia: 1971.

Primus, J.H. *The Vestments Controversy.* Kampen: 1960.

Ratzinger, J. and Fries, H. *Einsicht und Glaube.* Freiburg im Breisgau: 1962.

Rist, J.M. *Stoic Philosophy.* Cambridge: 1969.

Rogge, J. *Zwingli und Erasmus.* Stuttgart: 1962.

Rordorf, W. *Sunday, The History of the Day of Rest and Worship in the Earliest Centuries of the Christian Church.* Translated by A.A.K. Graham. Philadelphia: 1968.

Rose-Troup, F. *The Western Rebellion of 1549.* London: 1913.

Runciman, Steven. *The Eastern Schism.* Oxford: 1956.

Rupp, E.G. *The English Protestant Tradition.* Cambridge: 1949.

———. *Patterns of Reformation.* Philadelphia: 1969.

———. *The Righteousness of God.* London: 1963.

Schickler, F. de. *Les Eglises du refuge en Angleterre.* 2 vols. Paris: 1892.

Schmid, C.C.E. *Adiaphora, wissenschaftlich und historisch untersucht.* Leipzig: 1809.

———. *Controversia de Adiaphoris.* Jena: 1807.

Schlink, E. *Theology of the Lutheran Confessions.* Translated by P. Koehneke and J. Bouman. Philadelphia: 1961.

Sherwood, P., ed. *The Unity of the Churches of God.* Baltimore: 1963.

Slavin, A.J. *Tudor Men and Institutions.* Baton Rouge: 1972.

Smith, L.B. *Tudor Prelates and Politics.* Princeton: 1953.

Søe, N.H. *Christliche Ethik.* München: 1965.

Southern, R.W. *Western Society and the Church in the Middle Ages.* Harmondsworth: 1970.

Spinka, M. *Advocates of Reform.* Philadelphia: 1953.

———. *John Hus' Concept of the Church.* Princeton: 1966.

Stacey, J. *John Wyclif and Reform.* Philadelphia: 1964.

Surtz, E. *The Works and Days of John Fisher.* Cambridge: 1967.

Tavard, G. *Holy Writ or Holy Church.* New York: 1959.

Taylor, H.O. *The English Mind.* New York: 1962.

Thomas, K. *Religion and the Decline of Magic.* New York: 1971.

Thomson, J.A.F. *The Later Lollards. 1414-1520.* Oxford: 1965.

Tjernagel, N.S. *Henry VIII and the Lutherans.* St. Louis: 1965.

Trillhaas, W. *Ethik.* Berlin: 1959.

Trinterud, L.J. *Elizabethan Puritanism.* New York: 1971.

Ullmann, C. *Reformers Before the Reformation.* Translated by R. Menzies. 2 vols. Edinburgh: 1863.

Vajta, V. *Luther on Worship.* Translated by U.S. Leupold. Philadelphia: 1958.

Valeske, U. *Hierarchia Veritatum*. Munich: 1968.
Vööbus, A. *Celibacy: A Requirement for Admission to Baptism in the Early Syrian Church*. Stockholm: 1951.
Vooght, P. de. *Hussiana*. Louvain: 1960.
————. *Les Sources de la doctrine Chrétienne*. Paris: 1954.
Walton, R.C. *Zwingli's Theocracy*. Toronto: 1967.
Wendel, F. *Calvin, The Origins and Development of His Religious Thought*. Translated by P. Mairet. New York and Evanston: 1963.
Whitaker, W.B. *Sunday in Tudor and Stuart Times*. London: 1933.
Wolf, G., ed. *Luther und die Obrigkeit*. Darmstadt: 1972.
Zeeveld, W.G. *Foundations of Tudor Policy*. Cambridge: 1948.

III. ARTICLES

Bainton, R. "The Development and Consistency of Luther's Attitude to Religious Liberty." *Harvard Theological Review* XXII(1929), 107–149.
————"The Struggle for Religious Liberty." *Church History* 10(1941), 95–124.
Barmann, L.F. "Reform Ideology in the *Dialogi* of Anselm of Havelburg." *Church History* 30 (Dec., 1961), pp. 379–95.
Baudrillart, A. "Adiaphorites." *DTC* Vol. I.
Baumer, F. le von. "Thomas Starkey and Marsilius of Padua." *Politica* II (1936–37), 188–205.
Brown, Peter, "A Dark-Age Crisis: Aspects of the Iconoclastic Controversy." *EHR* 347(1973), 1–34.
Chenu, M.D. "Contribution à L'Histoire Du Traité De La Foi." *Melanges Thomistes* III, 123–40.
Dunn, E. "In Defense of the Penal Law." *TS* 18(1947), 41–50.
Dvornick, F. "National Churches and the Church Universal." *Eastern Churches Quarterly* 5(1942–44), 172–219.
Fitzmyer, J.A. "Saint Paul and the Law." *Jurist* 27(1967), 18–36.
Gottschick, J. "Adiaphora, and the Adiaphoristic Controversies." *The New Schaff-Herzog Religious Encyclopedia*, Vol. I.
Hays, D. "The Church of England in the Late Middle Ages." *History* 53(1968), 35–50.
Headley, J.M. "Thomas More and Luther's Revolt." *Archiv* 60(1969), 145–60.
Hillerbrand, H. "Anabaptism and the Reformation: Another Look." *Church History* 29(1960), 404–23.
————. "Andreas Bodenstein of Carlstadt, Prodigal Reformer." *Church History* 35(1966), 379–98.
Hopf, C., ed. "Bishop Hooper's 'Notes' to the King's Council." *Journal of Theological Studies* 44(1943), 194–99.
Horn, E.T. "Adiaphorism." *Encyclopedia of Religion and Ethics*. Vol. 1.
Janelle, P. "La Controverse entre Etienne Gardiner et Martin Bucer sur la

discipline ecclésiastique, (1541–1548)." *Revue des Sciences Religieuses* VII (1927), 452–66.

Joyce, G.H. "Fundamental Articles." *The Catholic Encyclopedia*. Vol. VI.

Knappen, M.M. "William Tindale—First English Puritan." *Church History* 5(1937), 201–15.

Lau, F. "Adiaphora." *Die Religion in Geschichte und Gegenwart*. Vol. I.

Mallard, W. "John Wyclif and the Tradition of Biblical Authority." *Church History* 30(1961), 50–60.

Manschreck, C.L. "The Role of Melanchthon in the Adiaphora Controversy." *Archiv* 49(1957), 165–81.

McNeill, J.T. "Alexander Alesius, Scottish Lutheran, 1500–1565." *Archiv* 55(1964), 161–91.

Melody, J.W. "Acts, Indifferent." *CE* Vol. I.

Meyland, E.F. "The Stoic Doctrine of Indifferent Things and Conception of Christian Liberty in Calvin's *Institutio Religionis Christianae*." *Romantic Review* 28(1937), 135–45.

New, J.F. "The Whitgift-Cartwright Controversy." *Archiv* 59(1968), 203–11.

Opie, J. "The Anglicizing of John Hooper." *Archiv* 59(1968), 150–77.

Reesor, M.E. "Indifferents in Old and Middle Stoa." *Transactions and Proceedings of the American Philological Association* LXXXII(1951), 102–10.

Ross, D.S. "Hooper's Alleged Authorship of *A Brief and Clear Confession of the Christian Faith*." *Church History* 39(1970), 18–29.

Rupp, G. "Word and Spirit in the First Years of the Reformation." *Archiv* 49(1958), 13–26.

Schaff, D. "Fundamental Doctrines." *The New Schaff-Herzog Religious Encyclopedia*. Vol. IV.

Schneider, J. "Die Verphlichtung des menschlichen Gesetzes nach J. Gerson." *ZKTh* 75(1953), 1–54.

Tatnall, E.C. "John Wyclif and *Ecclesia Anglicana*." *Journal of Ecclesiastical History* 29(1969), 19–43.

Tavard, G. "'Hierarchia Veritatum': A Preliminary Investigation." *TS* 32(1971), 278–89.

Teichtweier, G. "Adiaphora." *LTK* Vol. I.

Thompson, W.D.J.C. "The 'Two Kingdoms' and the 'Two Regiments': Some problems of Luther's *Zwei-Reiche-Lehre*." *Journal of Theological Studies* 20(1969), 164–85.

Trillhaas, W. "Adiaphoron, Erneute Erwägungen eines alten Begriffs." *Theologisches Literaturzeitung* 79(1954), 457–62.

Trinterud, L.J. "The Origins of Puritanism." *Church History* 20(1951), 37–57.

Verkamp, B.J. "Clerical Marriages, Reformation Style." *America*, March 3, 1973, pp. 185–88; *Intellectual Digest*, June, 1973, pp. 58–60.

———. "Cultic Purity and the Law of Celibacy." *Review for Religious* 30(1971), 199–217.

———. "The Limits upon Adiaphoristic Freedom: Martin Luther and Philip Melanchthon." *TS* 36(March, 1975), 52–76.

————. "The Zwinglians and Adiaphorism." *Church History* 42(Dec., 1973), 486–504.

Yost, J.K. "Hugh Latimer's Reform Program, 1529–1536, and the Intellectual Origins of the Anglican *via media*." *Anglican Theological Review* LIII(1971), 103–14.

Zacherl, M. "Die *Vita Communis* als Lebensform des Klerus in der Zeit zwischen Augustinus und Karl dem Grossen." *ZKTh* 92(1970), 385–424.

IV. UNPUBLISHED DISSERTATIONS

Manschreck, C.L. "A Critical examination and appraisal of the adiaphoristic controversy in the life of Philip Melanchthon." Unpublished Ph.D. dissertation, Yale University, 1948.

Street, T.W. "John Calvin on Adiaphora, An Exposition." Unpublished Ph.D. dissertation, Union Theological Seminary (N.Y.C.), 1954.

INDEX

Abelard, Peter, 23, 24, 160
Abstinence, and Fasting, 3, 10, 44, 45, 116, 120, 134, 137, 55n.31, 113n.73
Accolti (canonist), 57n.64
Act(s) of Uniformity, 146, 148, 168. *See also* Uniformity
Actions, good, bad, & indifferent, 21-24. *See also* Adiaphora
Adiaphora: absolute, 21, 23, 160, 30n.16; in the concrete, 117-18, 166, 31n.35; definition of, 15, 20-21, 23, 24, 24-25, 28, 29, 36-37, 40-41, 46-47, 70-74, 75, 76-77, 99, 117-18, 159-60, 160-61, 164, 170, 30nn.3 & 16, 31n.38, 32n.42; "doing" and "election" of, 117, 119, 125, 166, 167; and edification, 117-18, 170 (*see also* Edification); legislation of, 40-42, 47, 48, 50, 52, 126, 132-34, 140, 141, 142, 145, 150-51, 167, 168, 171; liberty in (*see* Liberty, adiaphoristic); preferred and rejected, 21, 22-23, 160; and Scripture, 25-26, 29, 61-79, 162, 163; and things permitted, 25-26, 28, 29, 32n.52, 35n.80 (*see also* Permitted things); true and false, 71, 103; and tyranny, 93-94, 165, 166, 114n.84 (*see also* Tyranny); use of, 70-71, 73-77, 79, 81, 82, 125, 135, 163, 165; usefulness of, 74
Adiaphorism: Peter Abelard and, 23, 24, 160; Thomas Aquinas and, 23, 24, 25; Augustine of Hippo and, 22, 23-24, 25, 132, 138, 32n.49; Robert Barnes and, xv, 41, 42; Bernard of Clairvaux and, 22-23; Martin Bucer and, 66, 74-75, 100, 142, 87n.50; Heinrich Bullinger

and, 65, 85-86, 91; John Calvin and, xv, 107, 133, 142-43, 34n.72, 112n.58; John Cassian and, 22; John Chrysostom and, 22; Clement of Alexandria and, 22-23, 25; John Colet and, 101; Council of Trent on, 34n.72; Cynics and, 20, 21, 22, 22-23, 159-60; and differentiation of reform parties, xvii, 69-77, 162-63; doctrinal, xv, 94-99, 102-3, 164-65, 109nn.16 & 17, 110n.31, 111n.33; John Eck and, 34n.72; John Epinus and, 20; Erasmus and, xv, 11, 24, 25, 36-38, 74, 82-83, 96-97, 100, 132-33, 160-61, 32n.45, 109n.16; John Frith and, xv, 97-99; Wesel Gansfort and, 24; Stephen Gardiner and, 93-94, 116, 173, 108n.6; Jean Gerson and, 45-46; historical studies of, xiv-xv; historical development of, 173-74; Hooper and, 72-73, 75-76, 149-51; Jan Hus and, 23-24, 56n.52; Flacius Illyricus and, 71, 104; John Knox and, 84-5n.15; and late medieval reformers, 14-15; John à Lasco and, 73-74, 75-76; Hugh Latimer and, xv, 36, 100, 161, 89n.78; Martin Luther and, 26-29, 78, 94, 96, 107, 142; in Marian reign, 173; William Marshall and, 143; Peter Martyr and, 66, 78-79, 117-18; Melanchthon and, 24, 26-29; John Milton and, 132; negative connotations of, 36-54; Origen and, 22-23, 25, 134-35; philosophical, 20-25, 159-61, 32n.42; positive connotations of, 61-83; preaching and discussion of, 99-101; "puritans" and, 20, 71, 76, 163; C. C. E. Schmid's study of, xv,

Bradwardine, Thomas (theologian), 14, 48
Brethren of Common Life, 14
Brief Declaration of the Sacraments, A
(Tyndale), 97
Bucer, Martin: and adiaphorism, 87n.50;
on celebration of Eucharist, 69–70; on
diversity, 138–39; on freedom of conscience, 58n.79; on legislation of
adiaphora, 142; rejects biblical reductionism, 65–66; on vestments, 74, 75,
100, 89n.78
Bullinger, Heinrich, 65, 70, 150, 58n.71,
85n.21, 91n.96, 154n.64

Cajetan, Cardinal (Tommaso da Vio), 49,
57n.64
Calvin, John: on celebration of Eucharist,
69–70; on ceremonies, 11, 121–22,
142–43, 91n.102, 128n.27; on Christian
liberty, 93–94, 124–26; on Christian
maturity, 121–22; on externals,
91n.102; *Institutes*, 50; on instruction
of weak, 130n.45; Letter to Somerset,
100; on obligation of civil law, 50, 142–
43; rejects biblical reductionism, 65–66.
See also Adiaphorism, John Calvin and
Canon law. *See* Church law
Carpocrates (Gnostic), 21–22
Cartwright, Thomas (Puritan), 67–68, 69,
76, 90n.81
Cassander, George (theologian), 96,
109n.17
Cassian, John (theologian), adiaphorism
of, 22
Castro, Alfonso de (theologian), 49
Catechism (Nuremberg), 89n.78
Celibacy, clerical, 2–5, 41, 101–2, 104–5,
119–20, 122, 113n.78. *See also* Marriage
Ceolfrith, 152n.27
Ceremonies, 1, 1–2, 6, 12, 13, 36–38, 62,
65–66, 69, 70, 71, 77–82, 116, 120–21,
126, 136, 137–38, 142–43, 157–58,
160–61, 56n.41, 58n.79, 86n.27,
92n.110; definition of, 15n.2; determination of by Christ, 16n.7; diversity in,
4, 133–40, 141–42; excessive estimation
of, 2–3, 6–7, 10, 11–13, 36, 37, 115, 158,
159; excessive proliferation of, 1–3,
9–12, 158, 15n.1, 19n.76; in Foreigners'
Church, 146–48; indifference of, 3, 13,

14–15, 29–30, 36–38, 40–41, 72–73, 82,
83, 162–64, 90n.92, 106n.6; Jewish,
12–13, 25, 28, 68, 77–79, 102, 105–6,
169–70, 90n.92; legislation of, 1–3, 6,
142–43; necessity to salvation, 7; pagan,
79, 136; preferred to divine commandments, 9–10, 11, 12–13, 115, 158; protest against, 1, 12–13, 79–81, 136;
quantitative reduction of, 36, 54, 158,
159; retention/rejection of, 36–37, 53,
74, 83, 120, 121–23, 145, 148–49, 164,
166–67, 169, 170–71, 173; "special" and
"universal," 137–38; sacralization and,
3; spiritual significance of, 24, 82, 158,
129n.40; usefulness of, 120–21, 122,
128n.27
Cerularius, Michael (patriarch), 136,
17n.45
Charity, 12, 26–28, 37, 169; and exercise
of adiaphoristic liberty, 116–26, 166–68;
and indifferent mean, 171–73; primacy
of, 36–37, 39–40, 115, 160–61
Charlemagne, 4–5, 7–8, 136, 17n.45,
18n.48
Charles V (emperor), 105, 106, 107, 123,
142–43, 146–47, 173, 87n.52
Cheke, Sir John, 113n.81; *Treatise on
Superstition,* 36
Chrysostom, Saint John, 22, 25
Church law: binding force of, 6–9, 38–41,
42–50, 52, 53–54, 95, 124–25, 162,
59n.91, 60n.100; confused state of in
middle ages, 5–6; devotion of Saint
Boniface to, 5–6; divine foundation of, 8,
9–10; proliferation of, 2–3, 6, 10; medieval collections of, 6; and monastic
idealism, 2–3; need of, 8, 68, 126, 133;
obedience of, 6, 7–11, 139–40; "puritans" on, 68; revision of, 8
Church, local, 14, 53, 133–34, 136–37,
138–39, 167
Circumcision, 10–11, 77, 78, 119, 90n.92,
128n.22
Civil law: binding force of, 38–41, 42–47,
49, 50, 51, 52; and conscience, 49–50,
52, 58nn.71 & 75 & 76 & 77; divine
content of, 39–40; obedience of, 41,
126, 135. *See also* Authority, civil
Clement of Alexandria, 22, 23, 25
Clement V (pope), 6
Clichtove, Josse (theologian), 57n.66

Precepts, New Testament, 27–28. *See also* Divine law
Prohibitions, biblical, 27, 28. *See also* Divine law
Protestation (1536), 63
Providence, divine, 169–70
Pupper, John. *See* Goch, John Pupper of
Purgatory, doctrine of, 98, 99, 102, 110nn.31 & 33
"Puritans," 30n.2; and adiaphorism, xvii, 20, 50, 70–71, 76, 77, 117–18, 162, 163, 167; and biblical reductionism, 63–64, 67–68, 69, 76, 163, 168–69; and Bucer, 87n.50; and mainline reformers, 69, 70; and obligation of civil law, 50; on rejection of ceremonies, 164

Quartodecimans, 7, 77
Quietism, 170

Rationale of Ceremonial, 82
Ratio verae Theologiae (Erasmus), 39–40
Reason, 1, 21, 23–24, 25, 26, 44, 47, 170, 171, 172
Reductionism, biblical, 14, 62, 159, 163, 172; Anabaptists and, 62–63, 67, 84n.9; John Knox and, 63–64, 84n.15; Lollards and, 46, 62, 66–67; "puritans" and, 63–64, 66–67, 68, 69, 70, 76; rejected by mainline reformers, 64–70
Reformation, English: complexity of, xiv; early stage of, xvi–xvii, 169; geared to the weak, 121–22; general direction of, xiii, xvii; hiddenness of, 172–73
Religion, 122, 137; essence of, 36, 37–38, 39, 94–95, 125–26
Reuchlin, John (humanist), 14
Rheinhart, Anna (wife of H. Zwingli), 106
Ridley, Nicholas, 63, 123, 149–50; on diversity and unity, 139–40; and freedom of conscience, 156n.112; on Jewish ceremonies, 78–79; on images, 75, 89n.78; on obligation of church laws, 53–54; opposition to Foreigners' Church, 147; rejects biblical reductionism, 66–67; on vestments, 72, 78–79, 150, 151
Rites. *See* Ceremonies
Roman Church, 3–4, 5–6, 124, 133, 134, 135, 138, 139, 146–47

Ruchrat, John (late medieval reformer), 14, 161
Ruysbroeck, John (mystic), 14

Sacralization, 2, 3, 6–7, 14
Sacramentals, 7
Sacraments, 7, 10, 15n.5, 91n.102. *See also* Baptism; Eucharist; Penance
Sampson, Thomas (priest), 149
Scandal: and adiaphora, 71, 74, 103; and clandestine marriages, 105; and consciences of the "weak," 118, 119, 120, 122–23, 166–67, 128n.21; giving and taking of, 105–6, 112, 166; and observance of laws, 40, 53, 54, 148
Schatzgeyer, Kaspar (theologian), 49, 57n.63
Schism, 4–5, 96–97
Schmalkald League, 141
Schmid, C. C. E., xvii, 161
Schwenkfeld, Casper (Radical Reformer), 91n.102
Scripture: and adiaphorism, 29, 61–62, 64, 70, 71, 73, 75–76, 99, 162 (*see also* Adiaphorism, Scripture and; Permitted things); and Anabaptists, 76; Thomas Cartwright on, 76; and celibacy, 104; and content of faith, 94–95, 96; and doctrine, 96, 98; and Law, 46, 68, 134; Lollards and, 62, 76; Martyr on, 87n.47; and necessary articles of faith, 96; nonrepugnance to, 69, 70; permits what is not forbidden, 61–62, 70, 82; positive accord with, 69, 70, 71, 75, 76, 163; and "puritans," 68, 70–71, 76; respect for, 171–72; silence of, 61–62, 76, 77, 163; *sola Scriptura,* 14, 46, 62, 158, 163; and Spiritualists, 79, 80, 81; study of, 10; sufficiency of, 46, 47, 49, 52, 53, 69, 162, 57n.69; Zwingli and, 64, 85n.18, 91n.102; and Tradition, 14, 45–46, 49, 162, 57n.69; Zwingli and, 64, 85n.18, 87n.50
Scrupulosity, 52–53, 158
Secrecy, in exercise of liberty, 51, 52, 106, 119, 166, 128n.24
Sedition, 151, 167–69
Seneca, 12
Sextus, *Sentences,* 31n.21
Shaxton, Nicholas (bishop), 61
Siricius (pope), 4

BERNARD J. VERKAMP

received his bachelor's degree in systematic theology from the University of Innsbruck, Austria (1964) and his Ph.D. in historical theology from St. Louis University (1972). He has taught courses in the history of religion and medieval Christianity at Vincennes University and at Notre Dame.

The book was designed by Vladimir Reichl. The typeface for the text is Primer, designed by Rudolph Ruzicka for Mergenthaler Linotype in 1951. The display face is Athenaeum, designed by A. Butti in 1945.

The text is printed on Lakewood text paper, and the book is bound in Joanna Mills' Arrestox A cloth over binder's boards. Manufactured in the United States of America.